DESIRE & ICE

DESIRE & ICE

Searching for Perspective atop Denali

David Brill

NATIONAL GEOGRAPHIC
ADVENTURE PRESS

WASHINGTON, D.C.

Published by the National Geographic Society
1145 17th Street N.W., Washington, D.C. 20036-4688

Library of Congress Cataloging-in-Publication Data

Brill, David, 1955-
 Desire & ice : searching for perspective atop Denali / David Brill.
    p. cm.
Includes bibliographical references and index.
 ISBN 0-7922-6935-7
 1. Brill, David, 1955- 2. Mountaineers--United States--Biography. I.
Title: Desire and ice. II. Title: Searching for perspective atop Denali.
III. Title.
 GV199.92.B755 A3 2002
 796.52'2'092--dc21

                        2002009481

One of the world's largest nonprofit scientific and educational organizations, the National Geographic Society was founded in 1888 "for the increase and diffusion of geographic knowledge." Fulfilling this mission, the Society educates and inspires millions every day through its magazines, books, television programs, videos, maps and atlases, research grants, the National Geographic Bee, teacher workshops, and innovative classroom materials. The Society is supported through membership dues, charitable gifts, and income from the sale of its educational products. This support is vital to National Geographic's mission to increase global understanding and promote conservation of our planet through exploration, research, and education. For more information, please call 1-800-NGS LINE (647-5463), write to the Society at the above address, or visit the Society's Web site at www.nationalgeographic.com.

Interior Design by Melissa Farris
Printed in the U.S.A

*For Mom, who over a lifetime has proven that the
richest rewards belong to those who dare, and who passed along
the genes of my hero, Walter A. Laufer—
Olympic champion, adventurer, and loving grandfather.*

CONTENTS

"Climb if you will, but remember that courage and strength are naught without prudence, and that a momentary negligence may destroy the happiness of a lifetime. Do nothing in haste, look well to each step, and from the beginning think what may be the end."

—Quote posted on the door of a climbing hut at 10,000 feet on Mount Rainier. The words are those of Edward Whymper (*Scrambles Amongst the Alps*), a British artist and climber who summited the 14,690-foot Matterhorn in 1865.

Members of the Rainier Mountaineering Inc. (RMI) Denali Expedition, May 28–June 18, 2001

Charles Richard (Dick) Bowers: 61, former U.S. ambassador to Bolivia; now resides in Louisville, Tennessee. Thru-hiked the Appalachian Trail in 1998.

Nat Brace: 41, former Microsoft group manager who lives in Seattle with his wife and infant son.

David Brill: 45, writer, father of two preteen daughters; now lives in Lancing, Tennessee.

Ken Coffee: 39, engineer and company owner from Tulsa, Oklahoma; one teenage daughter.

Bill Hatcher: 42, expedition photographer from Dolores, Colorado.

Joe Horiskey: 50, guide and part owner of RMI; has summited Denali 13 times since he began climbing in Alaska in the mid-1970s.

Clay Howard: 53, railroad executive from Keller, Texas; stricken by altitude sickness just above 14,200 feet.

Matt McDonough: 42, commercial real-estate broker and father of three from Mendham, New Jersey,

Brad Skidmore: 40, neurosurgeon from Fort Thomas, Kentucky.

Gary Talcott: 47, Denali veteran and lead RMI guide; resides in Ashford, Washington.

Kent Wagner: 38, RMI guide on Denali and during winter mountaineering seminar on Mount Rainier.

Doug Yearly: 41, home builder from Huntington Valley, Pennsylvania; left expedition at Talkeetna.

SUPPORTING PLAYERS

Dan Cosgro: physician's assistant from Bend, Oregon; staffed the medical tent at 14,200-foot camp on Denali.

Dave Johnston: veteran of first winter ascent of Denali (1967). In 2001 Johnston climbed the mountain with his his wife, Cari, and 11-year-old son, Galen.

Mike Gajda: ski patroller from Whistler, British Columbia; dubbed the Crazy Canadian for his ski-borne derring-do above the 14,200-foot camp.

Katy and Rachel Garton: sisters and experienced climbers from Utah, first encountered at the 11,000-foot camp.

Paul Maier: lead RMI guide during winter mountaineering seminar on Mount Rainier.

Keith McPheeters: member of Farmington, New Mexico, Police Department and leader of the Cops-on-Top Denali Expedition, which placed on the summit personal effects of James Saunders, a police officer killed in the line of duty.

Yeling Lee, 27; **Yihua Lin,** 27; and **Mei Liang Lee,** 30: Taiwanese women climbers first encountered by the RMI expedition at the 11,000-foot camp.

Daryl Miller: South District Ranger for Denali National Park and Preserve and Denali veteran.

Brent Okita: Everest veteran and leader of an RMI Denali expedition that the author's team encountered at 14,200 feet.

COURAGE IN A BEER STEIN

MY ATTEMPT TO SCALE 20,320-FOOT-HIGH DENALI* began in a pub not far above sea level. I was standing at the bar with two friends, Feldman and Duncan, when suddenly the conversation veered from college football to more extreme pursuits. With a little weight training and the proper footwear, the three of us had convinced ourselves, you can accomplish *anything*—provided you can get the time off work, of course.

We started thinking big.

Just after we had planned our reenactment of the Lewis and Clark Expedition and just before we discussed the prospects of being the first men to play beach volleyball on the surface of the Moon, Duncan took a long pull on his brown ale and uttered a single word: "Denali."

"Yeah, Denali," echoed Feldman, enthusiasm rising in his voice. "Weather, altitude, avalanches, corpses. That mountain has it all."

I'd been there numerous times before, envisioning myself kicking steps to the top of North America's highest peak. In fact, I'd wrestled with the mountain for nearly 15 years without once setting a cramponed boot

---

* Though the mountain is officially called Mount McKinley, most mountaineers refer to it by the Athapaskan Indian name of Denali, meaning the High One.

on its icy flanks. The assault began just before I turned 30 and regarded the mountain as a fitting challenge for someone who had arrived at the chronological threshold that, from the perspective of 29, seemed to form the portal to senescence.

But then my first daughter, Challen, was born. Two years later, her sister, Logan, came along. The ensuing years led me down the adventuresome path of parenthood while my lug-soled boots and backpack hung idle in the basement.

Just before my 44th birthday, the mountain returned, encroaching on dreams in which I was roped up and peering through swirling snow toward a distant summit. Though I had no basis in fact—or experience—for conjuring such a scene, I knew it was Denali. Leave it to the subconscious mind to transfigure the emotional mountains looming in one's path into such a tidy metaphor.

At that point in my life, my tolerance for physical discomfort was unremarkable, but I had begun to gain the benefit of some intense training in emotional resiliency that culminated in an unexpected return to bachelorhood and the end of an 18-year marriage. Nineteen ninety-nine was a wretched year, no matter which angle I view it from. I left my home, surrendered daily contact with my daughters, took a long leave from work, and retreated to a three-room cabin at the back edge of 68 acres of woods.

I had built the cabin the year before, hoping it would become a decompression chamber for a stressed-out suburban family. I pictured the four of us swinging in hammocks, singing "Kumbaya" by the campfire, and idling away the hours reading good books by the woodstove. I had anticipated that the time away from the city would incline my now ex-wife to experience an epiphany and realize that, though our relationship was less than perfect, it really wasn't all that bad—and, quite possibly, even worth saving.

Things didn't work out that way. I spent the better part of the following year as inert as the lichen-covered rocks dotting the cabin's landscape. I spent the first few months in a daze, muttering "This can't be happening," and the next few trying to stanch the bleeding. The remaining half-year involved a costly and frustrating foray into the world of lawyers and tense mediation sessions during which the most inconsequential points took on epic proportions.

It was a year of holing up, holding fast, and surrendering to the realization that my marriage was dead. Eventually, I grew tired of living the life of a despondent Henry David Thoreau wannabe, and even my trusty sidekick, Benton—a golden retriever with a gentle demeanor and a brain the size of a walnut—seemed to grasp the notion that if I didn't reengage soon with the world, my self-imposed exile threatened to turn me into a disciple of Howard Hughes or Ted Kaczynski. Benton began pacing, gnawing at his fur, and sprinting off into the woods whenever I opened the cabin door.

If he had been Lassie and I had been Timmy, I would have asked, "What is it, boy? Are you trying to tell me something?"

Despite Benton's efforts to reach me, it was a human friend who jarred me from my dismal reveries.

"Why don't you stop regarding your life as the story line from a tragic Flaubert novel," he asked, "and start viewing it as an adventure?"

I considered his suggestion for several weeks and eventually grasped what he meant. Through the lenses of rose-colored Oakleys, the world suddenly seemed trembling with possibility.

As the fog began to lift, I started to view my circumstances as less crisis than opportunity; in many ways I stood at the threshold of a new life. My emotional paralysis gave way to a yen to gain my feet and start moving again—to follow Benton as he tore through the woods, reacquainting myself with the world that lay beyond them.

The very thing that I had feared most had happened. The divorce may have reconfigured my definition of family and left me financially strapped, but my legs and lungs were still functioning. And that's when the dreams began. In the arms of Morpheus, I became a mountaineer angling for a barren, windswept summit. I began ascending toward deliverance.

I had just started searching for a place to stage my midlife resurrection when Duncan mentioned Denali. Over the following months, I devoured book after book about the mountain. Somewhere along the way, I fell victim to the delusional thinking that besets most folks who read harrowing tales of survival while seated in a comfortable chair, sipping single-malt scotch in a climate-controlled room.

I read with detached fascination about the seven climbers of the Wilcox party who died high on the mountain in a brutal storm in 1967. I read about Ray Ganet, Art Davidson, and Dave Johnston getting pinned down for nearly a week at 18,200 feet while making the first successful winter ascent of the mountain in the same year. During the trio's emergency bivouac, the windchill drove temperatures to 148°F below zero.

From the perspective of my easy chair, -148°F did not seem all that cold because it was a complete abstraction. Outfit me with a beefy parka, a stout pair of gloves, and some warm boots and I'd be fine— or so I thought.

As I read, I experienced an arrogant and inflated sense of personal safety and prowess. I've discerned it in other people before, but never in myself. I recall, for instance, watching rescue workers pull a dead boater from Tennessee's Ocoee River. When I asked the kayaker standing next to me—a woman still wearing her spray skirt and clutching her paddle— if the specter of entrapment drowning frightened her, she replied, "Not at all. He made a mistake; I don't make mistakes."

An Everest veteran I interviewed for a freelance story had a similar attitude: "You pretty much have to fuck up to die; I don't fuck up."

World War II historians cite this sort of thinking as the reason the U.S. Army decided to throw raw recruits rather than battle-hardened troops against the beaches of Normandy. The neophytes possessed a strong sense of invulnerability that convinced them the worst might well happen to their comrades—but never to them. The veteran soldiers, by contrast, had seen enough of war to know that catastrophes could (indeed, very likely would) befall them.

The newcomer's sense of inviolability is apparently fairly prevalent. How else to explain the fact that one year after the appearance of Jon Krakauer's book on the 1996 Everest disaster, more paying clients than ever—many of them relative tyros—sharpened their crampons and booked flights to Nepal?

So I pursued my Denali dreams with the cavalier attitude that three weeks of misery wouldn't amount to much over a lifetime of relative comfort. Ultimately, I figured, if weather, fitness, and other key factors all converged in the most serendipitous way, I just might make it.

Beyond that, I had a pretty good motivation for pushing my limits. Though George Mallory may have attempted to scale Everest "because it's there," I set my sights on Denali because I was "here," trying to adjust to this unique juncture in my life.

With regret I recognized that I would never reach the summit of the Himalayan behemoths. That didn't mean I was prepared to go gentle into midlife, nor to quietly accept that I had topped out careerwise as a middle manager at a state university. On the contrary, my instinct was to rage against both career and chronology—at least for a circumscribed period of time. The Denali summit, I hoped, would be the end goal of a grueling but survivable month-long pilgrimage over glaciers and up steeply pitched ice slopes.

I suspected I wasn't alone in this quest to get my ya-yas out. If I had been, there would be no commercial white-water outfitters, mountain guides, or sky-diving instructors, no boot prints on the snowy flanks of Denali or Everest or the Earth's other imposing peaks.

SUMMITS SUCH AS EVEREST ARE (or should be, in my opinion) off limits to all but the elite of the mountaineering world. Peaks such as Denali, by contrast, are accessible even to climbers with limited alpine experience—provided the aspirants are in top physical shape and willing to contend with the worst weather in the world.

Consider a few particulars: Denali presents the greatest vertical gain of any mountain on Earth—from just above sea level to 20,320 feet. Situated just below the Arctic Circle and 35 degrees, or 2,400 miles, north of Everest, it's known for storms that pack 100-mile-an-hour winds and temperatures that plunge to 100 degrees below zero. Because of its extreme northern latitude and its proximity to the polar ice cap, where the air is notoriously thin, Denali "feels" like a 23,000-foot peak.

Oh, and then there's the specter of death on the mountain. Since 1910, when a group of miners known as the Sourdough Expedition defied all odds and dragged a 14-foot spruce flagpole to the top of Denali's North Peak (850 feet below the South Peak, the true summit), the mountain has claimed 91 lives.

That's not to say I had any sort of death wish myself. What I sought most was affirmation of life. In that sense, I represented a man determined to confront mortality by tackling a major challenge that would require months of intense physical training and subject him to some emotional and physical extremes. Consider me "everyman"—one of about 1,100 climbers who attempt Denali each year.

Had I been a betting man, I would have considered it even odds to reach the summit (about half of Denali aspirants make it to the top), despite the fact that Gail, a respected and normally eloquent university colleague, branded my plans those of an "idiot." My own father challenged my competence as a parent: "Who's going to raise those daughters of yours while your frozen corpse molders on the mountain?"

I responded by paraphrasing a mountaineering maxim: "The ascent is optional; the descent is mandatory. I have every intention of coming home." Which was all true enough. "It's the experience I seek," I added, "not necessarily the summit."

The fact of the matter is, I found myself in the grips of a vague but powerful urge to confront my fears, to tap my reserves of strength and courage, to push myself further into the realm of the unknown than I'd ever been before.

My deep love for my daughters—and my commitment to parenting them into adulthood and beyond—moderated but did not quell my drive to achieve something grand in the middle years of my life. Through some transparent rationalizing, I convinced myself that bagging the Denali summit would bestow abiding peace and contentment, tame my wanderlust, and transform me into a better father. But I also realized that if I ever had to choose between the summit and my own survival, my devotion to my girls would incline me to do the right thing.

I HAD KEPT MYSELF IN PASSABLE SHAPE over the years through daily runs, long weekend bike rides, and the occasional climb of various peaks in the Appalachian Mountains and the Cascade Range. My adventuring résumé, if not particularly extreme, was at least respectable. In 1979, for example, I had completed a thru-hike of the 2,167-mile-long Appalachian Trail. Those six months of living in the gentle and forgiving embrace of the Eastern forest had imparted a deep love of wilderness and a lifelong aversion to suburban neighborhoods so cramped that a man could pee out his window and hit his neighbor's vinyl siding.

Though transforming, the AT experience didn't teach me much in terms of mental toughness—an essential attribute for anyone attempting Denali. That would come two years later, when I joined a four-man team making one of the first attempts on the proposed Pacific Northwest Trail.

Shouldering 60-pound packs and clutching a dozen photocopied pages of sketchy directions for the next 1,200 miles—many of them devoid of maintained trails—we set out from the east side of the Continental Divide in Glacier National Park, bound for the Pacific coast of Washington. The directions, obviously written by someone who had never visited that sprawling wilderness, might just as well have read like this: "Enter woods somewhere between mile markers 10 and 60 on Nameless Montana Logging Road, immediately reach stream, remove boots, wade up to your now-shrunken testicles through churning water so cold that if it weren't moving it would be ice. Shred feet on razor-sharp rocks, emerge from water, wedge numb feet back into boots, and crawl on hands and knees through impenetrable, junglelike growth. Gain 6,000 feet in altitude, emerge above treeline, and swivel head about in bemused wonderment like an errant gopher. Scale sheer cliff leading to summit of Greater Mount Crumpet; draw compass bearing on Lesser Mount Crumpet 15 miles to the west, and proceed apace."

That expedition instilled some useful skills. Chief among them was the ability to endure protracted periods of discomfort and to abide long stretches of time without making much linear progress—perfect preparation for Denali. By the time we reached the Salmo-Priest Wilderness in northeastern Washington nearly a month after setting out, we had come to associate cross-country wilderness travel with pain and suffering, and we greeted the network of well-maintained trails with paranoid apprehension that if the going was easy, we must be lost.

OVER THE INTERVENING YEARS, I had twice been to the summit of 14,410-foot Mount Rainier, where I got my first taste of real mountaineering and experienced the gravity- and sanity-defying ailment know as summit fever.

For me, as for most American climbers on Denali, Rainier represented a gateway to higher-elevation mountaineering. Nearly all American Everest veterans have crunched ice on Rainier, including Phil Ershler, the first American to reach the summit of Everest by a northern route. It was Ershler who led my rope team on my first Rainier climb in 1989, and he offered his perspective on why Rainier is the premier training ground for America's elite climbers: "Rainier basically has everything the Himalaya have, but on a smaller scale. The glacial terrain, the configuration of crevasses, the ice-fall problems, and the weather are similar to what you encounter in the Himalaya. Rainier also helps you get used to humping loads and developing that mental and physical toughness you need to climb bigger mountains."

Before the Rainier climb, I had been curious about the mountain—about the vast glaciers draping its sharp-angled slopes, and about how features such as "Disappointment Cleaver" and "Cadaver Gap" had earned their gruesome names. But I was even more intrigued by how a low-key hiker like me would do on a heavily glaciated mountain.

Preparing for that trip, I regarded Rainier as an end point, not a stepping stone to higher, more celebrated peaks. I figured I would nail the summit, check off that particular box on my list of lifetime goals, and then take up a less expensive and far less hazardous hobby such as gardening or classical guitar.

The reality was different: I returned to Rainier in 1998, when I climbed it again with my brother, Steve. Most men and women, I suspect, likewise fail to content themselves with a single excursion to the snow-cloaked summit of any challenging mountain. The fact is, if you tough it out on Rainier, gain the summit, and derive some meaning and reward from the experience, chances are good that you'll eventually start shopping around for a follow-up challenge—one that ratchets up the risk along with the altitude.

In that sense, mountaineering seems to encourage the sort of escalation described by the Peter Principle, whereby one rises to one's level of incompetence—or runs headlong into a wall of suffering so profound that it confers lifelong immunity to the lure of adventure. I regarded Denali as an opportunity to apply that principle to myself, though I realized I had a long way to go—physically and mentally—before I booked my flight to Anchorage. Even under ideal conditions, the risk and hardship on Denali would be an order of magnitude greater than any I had faced.

On my previous adventures, in fact, the most life-threatening hazards I had encountered were sunburn, insect bites, poison ivy, and jock itch.

When Duncan mentioned Denali, I could see, even through my beer goggles, that an important door was closing. In the waning years of my life as an adventurer, the time to bag a big peak was now or never—unless, of course, I was destined for reincarnation as Reinhold Messner or a snow leopard.

Think of me then as 1 part Walter Mitty and 2 parts George Plimpton. While the former's adventures were purely fanciful, the latter's exploits involved real-time and real-life immersion into, among other realms, professional football. In *Paper Lion*, Plimpton chronicled his evolution from mild-mannered writer to stand-in field marshal for the Detroit Lions, where a few steroid-dosed defensive tackles helped him redefine the meaning of pain and humility.

NOW IT'S NOVEMBER 2000, a temperate month in east Tennessee, and my transformation from couch sloucher to hard-bodied mountaineer has begun. I've reserved a slot on a Denali expedition that begins May 28 and will be led by three guides from Rainier Mountaineering Incorporated.

RMI, based in the shadow of Mount Rainier in the Paradise Valley of Washington, leads climbers to the top of some of America's most challenging summits. It is one of only six outfitters that the National Park Service has licensed to guide clients on Denali.

Eight other clients—most of them fellow middle-aged fathers and nine-to-fivers—will join me on the expedition.

If our odds hold, half of us will reach the summit.

But which half?

Chapter One

TRAINING DAYS

I LEARNED DURING MY FIRST FEW DIFFICULT WEEKS on the Appalachian Trail that there is only one sure way to prepare for an extended backpacking trip: It is, of course, to undertake an extended backpacking trip. If that notion applies to training for Denali, I may be in trouble.

The RMI expedition pamphlet for Denali urges us to train in a way that "simulates, as nearly as possible, the type of climbing you will do on the trip." That's fine if you live in Seattle or Anchorage or Kathmandu. I don't. My cabin in east Tennessee lies within 20 minutes of the Cumberland Mountains, which run parallel to the Appalachian Mountains, about two hours to the east. Whereas the Appalachians top out just under 6,700 feet, the Cumberlands attain the lofty height of 3,300.

If you discount the 17,000-foot discrepancy in height between Denali and Frozen Head (the highest point of ground in the Cumberlands); if you ignore the 90-degree variance in daytime summit temperature (60-plus on Frozen Head in early May versus 30-below on Denali) and the average snowfall (a light dusting versus a gazillion feet), Frozen Head is Denali in microcosm.

But at least I've got mountains. Two of my Denali teammates, Clay Howard and Ken Coffee, hail from the flats of Texas and Oklahoma. They will have to content themselves with climbing stadium steps, working out on Stairmasters, or traveling vast distances for the benefit of training on vertical terrain.

Frozen Head, by default, becomes the centerpiece of my workout regimen. I approach my six months of training with three primary goals: to build cardiovascular endurance for long days of climbing in thin air; to strengthen my legs for carrying large loads; and to inure myself to the cold. The first two are easy enough to achieve in my familiar environs. The third proves to be a bit more troublesome.

I've heard stories of Denali aspirants subjecting themselves to cold showers and ice baths to toughen their constitutions. I opt instead for a February trip to New Hampshire and an ascent of 6,288-foot Mount Washington, a peak that's known for some of the worst—and coldest—weather in America. As it turns out, the mountain won't disappoint me.

My routine is simple: I will combine a weekly ascent to the top of Frozen Head with almost daily aerobic workouts. I've been a lunch-time runner for the past 10 years, covering anywhere from three to five miles a day, and that has given me a suitable fitness base on which to build. I continue my daily runs but boost the distance to seven miles, seeking out hillier routes and stepping up my pace from nine- to eight-minute miles. I grant myself a rest day after each trek to the top of Frozen Head.

Heeding the instructions in the RMI guide, I also make an honest effort to train with weights at the university gym. Doing multiple repetitions indoors on a machine Jules Verne might have invented, however, seems antithetical to the notion of training that "simulates, as close as possible, the type of climbing you will do on Denali." I forsake the gym in favor of the great outdoors.

Beginning in November, I arrive at Frozen Head once a week wearing the red plastic mountaineering boots I purchased before my second ascent of Mount Rainier in 1998. (Later on, I'll switch to the warmer but heavier bright-yellow Koflachs I'll wear on Denali.) I load my pack with some combination of birdseed, dog food, river rocks, canned peas or green beans, and gallon jugs of water. I begin with 50 pounds and gradually increase the load to 80—nearly half my body weight, and close to what I'll be hauling up Denali.

Bearing these extreme loads, I experience some troubling twinges in my lower back and hips. My body emits alarming pops and creaks, particularly in the knees, and I'm forced to ratchet down my expectations right from the start. On the Appalachian Trail, I could cover a mile in 20 minutes or less, even on steep terrain; during my early training hikes on Frozen Head, while hauling a relatively light 50-pound load, it takes me two hours to cover the 3.5 miles (and 2,000 vertical feet) to the top; my jackrabbit starts force frequent rest breaks that leave me bowed over my ski poles, gasping for breath.

Gaining strength while avoiding injury becomes my mission. Counter to my former habit of barreling down trails bewitched by visions of beer and food, I creep rather than dash on my descents. My Denali dreams could easily end in a twisted ankle or stress fracture.

As I settle into a slower pace, I establish a comfortable rhythm measured out by the tapping of my ski poles, the crunch of boots on rock, the rise and fall of my breath. On later trips I manage to gain the summit without stopping. By my last training hike at the end of March, I've shaved the ascent to an hour and a half, and my body is adjusting nicely to the burgeoning load.

Rarely do I encounter others on the trail. The exception is this final trek, when the woods are crawling with gaunt, exhausted men and women whose gait is a spirited stagger. Attempts to engage them in conversation prove futile until I come across a man in his mid-20s, prone and propped on his elbows by the side of the trail. His contorted posture suggests he's been dumped into the brush from a great height. He's wearing a fanny pack and a 2,000-yard stare.

"Wha time izzit?" he mumbles.

"It's 1:30," I answer. "Hey, you look kinda beat."

"I've been running since yesterday morning," he says. "Popped my last caffeine pill an hour ago, I'm starting to bonk, and I still have 40 miles to cover. I feel like shit."

"Why are you doing this?"

"I'll be goddamned if I know," he says. "Got any food?"

Figuring that an industrial-strength can of green beans might weigh him down, I hand him a granola bar instead.

"Thanks," he says, struggling to his feet. He stumbles toward the summit muttering, "I *am* an aerobic monster. I *can* take the pain!"

The frazzled runner and all the other dazed athletes on the trail are competing in the Barkley 100-mile run. According to widely circulated accounts, the event has a somewhat ignominious origin: The route it follows was pioneered during a 1977 jailbreak by Martin Luther King's convicted assassin, James Earl Ray. After escaping from Brushy Mountain State Penitentiary, a maximum-security fortress plainly visible from the fire tower atop Frozen Head, Ray spent 50 hours scrambling around the Cumberland Mountains near Frozen Head before being caught. By then Ray was so dog-tired, bug-bitten, bramble-torn, and snake-spooked by numerous run-ins with rattlesnakes and copperheads that he offered little resistance to recapture. In fact, he seemed grateful to return to his cell.

Since 1986, when the Barkley 100-mile race was inaugurated to roughly retrace Ray's flight path, only one man—Mark Williams of England—has completed the 100-mile course. It took Williams nearly 60 hours to slog through all five undulating 20-mile loops, each of which involves a cumulative elevation gain of 10,000 feet.

Although the trail runners provide an amusing diversion, they also impart some valuable perspective: Suffering is relative. Unless something goes horribly wrong on Denali, I doubt I'll ever look as gaunt and hollow-eyed as these runners do, nor suffer the fatigue that has reduced them all to wobbling zombies.

Over the next week, as I pack my gear for an RMI-sponsored winter mountaineering seminar on Mount Rainier, I discover that I've taken in a couple of notches on my belt. I've dropped 10 pounds and now weigh 165—leaner than I've been in a decade. My joints may still ache, but the soreness in my calves and thighs is gone. Maybe I'm ready to tackle an Arctic peak or two after all?

Chapter Two

"DECIDING TO LIVE
IS ALWAYS THE RIGHT CALL"

WHILE SCALING THE CUMBERLANDS, I encountered temperatures that climbed into the 50s and 60s, even in winter. Anxious to toughen my body to the cold, I'd peel down to a T-shirt or bare skin. But even during Frozen Head's most frigid days, when the temperature dropped into the teens, I realized I was basking in temperatures that might be considered tropical compared with Denali's brutal and relentless cold.

While some of my Denali climbing mates were forced to travel to find mountainous terrain, I headed north in search of biting winds and subzero temperatures. In February, I traveled to New Hampshire to spend a few days with some old friends. My girlfriend, Dee, joined me for the remainder of the week. In my quest to pit my constitution—and equipment—against raw-visaged winter, my timing could not have been better.

The White Mountains of New Hampshire are almost universally regarded among AT thru-hikers as the most majestic and challenging mountains on the entire 2,167-mile route. That reputation stems in part from the mountains' high alpine cirques and bowls and their open, rocky ridgelines that lope above treeline and stay there for miles and miles—unique in the densely forested East. The other part of the Whites' mystique arises from the extreme weather and high winds that pummel the range throughout the year.

The crown jewel of the Whites is 6,288-foot-high Mount Washington, which has claimed more lives than Denali—many of them in summer. In fact, a rough wooden cross wedged among granite boulders near the top marks the spot where two hikers died of exposure in a whiteout in the middle of July 1958. They were less than 200 yards from the safety of the summit house.

Washington is also renowned for a notable superlative: On April 12, 1934, the weather station on the summit clocked winds of 231 miles an hour, the strongest ever recorded on Earth. The reading might have gone even higher had the next gale not broken the anemometer.

Hikers who follow trails to the high ridges of the Whites encounter a bright yellow but sobering sign: "Stop: The area ahead has the worst weather in America. Many have died from exposure even in the summer. Turn back now if the weather is bad."

I had read that warning on six earlier ascents of the mountain, always in summer, and never really took it to heart. The Whites had always been kind to me. I had even led each of my daughters up Mount Washington when they reached the age of seven. On both trips, we basked up top in warm, windless sunshine.

Throughout my week in New Hampshire, whether skiing or driving, I continually confronted the looming profile of Washington and struggled to resist its lure. While Denali is the coveted continental high, a winter ascent of Mount Washington remains among the East's most fabled mountaineering plums. The peak's brutal—and notoriously fickle—weather, rather than its altitude or difficult terrain, drastically thins the ranks of those who reach the summit.

At 6 a.m. on February 10, 2001, Mount Washington registered a maximum temperature record for the day of 37°F. By 11 a.m., as a powerful cold front pushed through, winds were gusting to 145 miles an hour. Temperatures plunged, and by next morning 100-mile-an-hour winds drove the windchill index to 91°F below zero. Even discounting the windchill, the temperature hovered around -23°F.

By early that afternoon, a group of friends and I had snowshoed almost all the way to the top of 2,758-foot Black Mountain. From just below the crest, I could see Mount Washington's summit, about eight miles away. It wore a UFO-shaped lenticular cloud cap, indicating a deadly combination of cold and wind.

Leaving my friends huddled around a woodstove inside a cabin below the summit, I pushed about a quarter-mile higher, post-holing up to my knees in pristine powder. (A storm the previous week had blanketed the region in almost two feet of fresh snow.) In about 20 minutes I reached the unremarkable summit knob. I sat down in the snow with my back to the wind, trying to convince myself that feeling the cold penetrate the seams and zippers of my shell layer to my sweat-soaked fleece was good training for Denali.

As I gazed on Mount Washington, it occurred to me that a dash to the top of that notoriously frigid mountain might do me some good. In particular, it might expose me to conditions equal in severity to those on Denali, compensating for three months of training in the comparatively balmy South.

I realized that no sane mountain guide was going to ascend into the teeth of a 100-mile-an-hour wind, but I had five more days in the Granite State to await a break in the weather. As it turned out, by 6 a.m. on Friday morning summit temperatures had climbed to 9 above, and though the moderate 18 mile-an-hour wind drove the windchill index down to -23°F, the guides at Eastern Mountain Sports (EMS), an outdoor specialty shop in North Conway, were back in business.

The closest Dee had ever come to winter mountaineering was the mile-long trek she once had to make through the snow to reach her Vermont high school. I had mentioned the Mount Washington climb during one of our many stops at EMS earlier in the week, and her response had been unequivocal: "What, are you nuts?" By week's end, however, after several days of downhill skiing with Mount Washington as the enticing backdrop, she began to reconsider.

On Thursday afternoon, while we wandered the aisles at EMS, Dee disappeared into the back room, which houses the EMS climbing school. By the time I caught up to her, she had booked us slots on a guided climb that was leaving the next morning.

"Are you sure you want to do this?" I asked.

"Not at all," she said. "But I really do want to understand what you're going through on Denali. Besides, I've been looking at the Mount Washington summit all week, and I'm kind of curious."

Having dated her for nearly a year, I had learned that when Dee—a goal-oriented, first-born, Type-A personality—decides she wants to do something, you step in line to follow or get the hell out of her way. On Washington, that drive would amply offset whatever she may have lacked in fitness or skill.

We spent the remainder of the afternoon buying clothing and equipment for the summit as prescribed by the EMS brochure. All of it would prove useful on Denali. I purchased a pair of Moonstone Gore-Tex bibs— replete with chest pouch, shoulder straps, full-length side zippers, and a trapdoor back—and a pair of heavy fleece mittens and nylon shells. At the L. L. Bean outlet down the road, we found ski goggles, neoprene face masks, chemical heat packs for mittens and boots, and Mini Mag lights (to illuminate a descent through darkness, should that become necessary).

THE NEXT MORNING AT 7, we meet guide Paul Cail at the EMS store. A tall, sandy-haired man in his late-30s with a pronounced New England accent, Paul outfits us with rental plastic double boots, gaiters, crampons, and ice axes.

He then explains the particulars of the climb. We will ascend nearly 4,300 feet in just over four miles to the 6,288-foot summit of Mount Washington along the Lion Head Trail—a steeper but safer alternative to the more moderate (but avalanche-prone) Tuckerman Ravine Trail.

Throughout the day, Paul, like most mountain guides, continually offers instruction, much of it via the instrument of stories about climbers doing precisely the wrong thing and suffering the consequences. The latter include ice axes piercing livers, lungs, or other key organs; deadly interment in avalanches; compound fractures caused by unarrested falls, with jagged femurs jutting through nylon climbing pants; and loss of fingers, toes, noses, and even ears to frostbite.

According to Paul, every such calamity had occurred when climbers: a) failed to execute proper technique, b) kept ascending after weather conditions had deteriorated, c) ignored the guide's expert instruction, or d) failed to designate—and honor—a drop-dead turnaround time. Paul establishes a turnaround time of 2 p.m. for our three-person group. If we have not reached the summit by then, we will begin our descent— or risk getting stranded on top in the dark.

Though Paul insists that the turnaround time is inviolate—and goes on to relate a story about a hapless climber who died because he failed to monitor his time—he will prove more flexible in practice.

By 8 a.m. we've left the parking lot at the Pinkham Notch visitor center and begun walking through shin-deep snow along a Jeep road. Within half a mile, the road angles steeply upward. Paul uses the slope to demonstrate how to kick steps into the soft snow on the ascent. He also paces us through some important techniques for arresting a fall higher on the mountain. A short time later, we reach the junction with the Lion Head Trail, don our crampons (steel spikes that attach to the sole of each boot), and began climbing in earnest.

The trail is impossibly steep in places—it's more of a vertical chute, really—and we are forced to front-point with our crampons while pulling ourselves up with our ice axes or by clinging to the trunks of evergreens lining the path (bad form because of its dendritic destructiveness, but even Paul occasionally resorts to this method of ascent). After about two hours of tough climbing, we rise above treeline and pause for a break in the lee of a rock below the relative flats of the Alpine Garden, where a 40-mile-an-hour wind awaits us.

Five months from now, this expanse of tundra will be carpeted in pincushion thickets of sedge, evergreen moss, bunchberry, mayflower, and alpine heath. For now, however, it sports a dense cloak of ice and snow, and the frigid temperature makes it difficult to imagine that anything could survive a New Hampshire winter.

Across the deep cut of Pinkham Notch to the east, we can make out the groomed ski trails of Wild Cat Mountain, where we had spent a day on the slopes earlier in the week. To our immediate left, we peer down into the snow-choked bowl of Tuckerman Ravine. Skiing the near-vertical headwall of "Tucks," as this cirque is locally known, ranks as one of New England's most daring feats; for most skiers, it blurs the line between skiing and falling. Above us we can see the lower flanks of Mount Washington's summit cone, but Paul cautions us not to get ahead of ourselves.

"It may look close," he says, rising to his feet and shouldering his pack, "but it's actually a few hours away. It's about 11 now; we're really going to have to push to nail the summit by 2."

"How you doing?" I ask Dee.

"Fine," she insists, but the brevity and neutrality of her response suggest otherwise.

Back on the trail, we reach the ridge of the Alpine Garden and lurch about drunkenly in the powerful gusts of wind. Paul instructs us to put on our goggles and face masks, and to insert the heat packs in our gloves. He also delivers a brief lecture on frostbite.

"Cover as much skin as you can," he instructs us. "If you notice any flesh turning white, let me know right away. That usually indicates frostbite."

By 2 p.m. (our supposed turnaround time), Dee is beginning to drag. While she pauses often to lean on her ice ax, Paul urges us to pick up the pace. Not yet having reached the base of the summit cone, we are still well over an hour from the top.

I tell Dee it's no big deal if we have to turn around; the trip will have been worth it even if we don't make it to the mountaintop.

"I am *not* stopping," is her reply. I turn to Paul to see if he's willing to fudge the turnaround time—bad mountaineering etiquette on the part of this beginner. He peels back his parka sleeve to check the time—something he's been doing more and more frequently.

"Okay, let's keep moving," he says. "But if we're not on top by 3, we really do have to turn back."

By 3 p.m., we intersect the Tuckerman Ravine Trail, still 600 vertical feet and half a mile from the summit. In a bid to motivate us, Paul pulls farther and farther away. I can see that Dee is just about cooked. Each time I stop to check on her, she conveys her resolve in a simple imperative: "Go!"

The top of the mountain is not yet in view. Above the rounded arc of the slope, though, I can see the tip of a steel communications tower piercing the clouds. The tower is just one of several man-made fixtures that mar Mount Washington's summit. The Mount Washington Observatory, for example, housed in the visitor center, is staffed by meteorologists throughout the year. As the guidebooks make clear, however, winter climbers are discouraged from dropping in for a cup of hot cocoa and a chat before they begin their descent.

Though locked in ice and inaccessible at least four months of the year, this mountaintop is a testament to humankind's unforgivable urge to tame wild places. In summer the site becomes a tourist mecca, with throngs of paunchy vacationers "trekking" to the top in sedans and minivans along an eight-mile access road. Vehicles that complete the ascent earn a bumper sticker reading, "This car climbed Mount Washington."

The longest hike most visitors make leads from their autos to the aggressively ugly visitor center that straddles the summit, purveying cafeteria food, souvenirs, and books on the mountain's history. Since the mid-1800s, the summit has hosted restaurants, hotels, observation towers, and even a daily newspaper. Hundreds more visitors are ferried to the top by a cog railway, built in the 1860s and known among local hikers as the "Iron Pig" for the dense black column of coal smoke that issues from its stack.

For those who gain the summit under their own steam, the carnival atmosphere can be jarring. When I reached the top of Mount Washington during my AT hike, my disappointment at the commercial scene was driven home by a chance encounter with a plump young boy wearing an Indiana Hoosiers T-shirt. After studying my pack, he accosted me and asked, "You mean you can *walk* to the top of this mountain?!"

FOR DEE AND ME, the sight of the steel tower elicits a drastically differ-ent response. The fat kid and his ilk have gone. Today the summit belongs to us.

If Paul doesn't turn us back, that is. "I shouldn't be doing this," he advises us. "But the weather seems stable and the snow is solid, so let's keep going. We just won't be able to spend much time on top."

At that moment, summit fever grips me for the first time. We can see the summit; it's right *there*, a few hundred yards away. Even to think about turning around when we are this close is inconceivable. "So what if it gets dark?" I tell myself. "So what if a wicked storm blows in? So what if we have to bivouac high on the mountain without shelter or sleeping bags? At least we'll have conquered the summit."

That line of reasoning doesn't alarm me while we are on the moun-tain and under the watchful eye of a seasoned guide such as Paul Cail; during the ascent, the associated risks seem almost inconsequential compared with the triumph of standing on top. Once we return, how-ever, the reckless vacuity of my first bout of summit fever terrifies me. Recalling the many summit bids that Denali rebuffed in the early days of mountaineering, I begin to fathom the force of will that must be required to turn back when the summit beckons just ahead.

On the morning of June 28, 1910, three climbers—Belmore Browne, Herschel Parker, and Merl La Voy—left high camp at 17,200 feet on Denali, poised to be the first men to stand atop that peak. When they reached about 19,000 feet, they got their first clear glimpse of the summit.

"It rose as innocently as a tilted snow-covered tennis court," Browne remembered in *The Conquest of Mount McKinley*, "and as we looked it over we grinned with relief—we *knew* the peak was ours!"

Then the wind picked up, and it began to snow. When the trio reached

19,800 feet, Browne realized that they "were fighting a blizzard," but they continued on.

According to Browne's estimate, the climbers advanced within 100 feet of the crown before he turned them around. "The game is up!" he yelled to his climbing mates. "We've got to get down!"

Browne, who recalled the final stage of the climb as "the memory of an evil dream," clearly made the correct decision, even though it deprived him of being the first to reach that long-sought continental high. I'm not at all sure I would have done the same.

On Mount Washington, fortunately, the decision isn't mine. Forty-five minutes after we spy the tower, the entire complex of summit buildings heaves into view. Soon our crampons are clattering across the parking lot—I can make out painted lines on pavement beneath the ice—and up a flight of wooden steps.

The transformation from the warm, sunny peak I had visited so many times in the past to this austere, ice-caked realm is staggering. The spectacle erases any doubt about the utter dominance of nature over the ephemeral ornamentations of civilization.

Rendering this stark tableau even more severe is the wind-etched coating of ice—several feet thick—that layers everything, muting the hard angles of human-made structures. Like microbes devouring the hull of a sunken wooden ship, the ubiquitous white coating suggests some voracious organism is slowly consuming the buildings.

Long feathers of rime ice—more than a yard long in places—jut from the windward side of every upright object, including antennas and the wires that guy the buildings to the ground, keeping them from being snatched up by the wind and hurled off the mountain. I try—and fail—to imagine the summit a few days before, scoured by 100-mile-an-hour winds and seized by temperatures that neared -100°F; it's impossible to envision an environment more visually disquieting than the one surrounding us.

After snapping a few obligatory photos by the summit sign—which itself wears a fringe of rime—we retreat to a protected corner of the visitor center and crouch out of the wind. If the surrounding structures don't suffice to remind us that we've scaled a "developed" peak, the plywood sheet protecting the entrance to the visitor center does the trick. It reads: "Please don't piss in our doorway."

Who would dare do that in this indescribable cold? The windchill has driven the temperature to -20°F. The water in my bottle has frozen nearly solid, and when I remove my gloves to pull a granola bar from my pack, my hands go numb in seconds.

"I'm not sure I can make it back down," says Dee. Paul hands her a package of GU—essentially calorie-dense cake icing dosed with caffeine—with the promise that it will pick her up. It works. Just shy of 4 p.m. we begin our descent, and Paul, intent on leading us off the mountain before nightfall, instantly becomes a distant speck moving downslope.

By now Dee's legs have been rendered "stupid" by fatigue, and she stumbles repeatedly on the steep slope of the summit cone. The descent down the vertical chute on the lower Lion Head Trail proves even more challenging: One of us negotiates much of it sitting on her butt.

Darkness has descended by the time we return to Pinkham Notch, where Dee collapses in a bank of snow.

"I'm so tired I can't move," she says, "but damn I'm proud of myself! Let's go have a beer."

A WINTER ASCENT of Mount Washington doesn't count for much among elite mountaineers, but for complete beginners such as Dee it rivals Maurice Herzog's epic ascent of Annapurna—with the happy exception that we have retained all our fingers and toes.

An hour later, still clad in our climbing clothes, we are seated in a bar drinking a hand-crafted New Hampshire microbrew and basking in our success. The two guys next to us, both sporting Marine Corps haircuts, overhear us talking.

"Washington's a cold-ass mountain," one of them says. "But let me tell you, Denali is a hell of a lot colder."

The serendipity is striking; I had just been thinking about Denali. It turns out the man once belonged to a special forces unit that trained in alpine environments. The year before, he and some fellow members of his unit had attempted to climb Denali.

I let him know I'm heading to Alaska in May.

"That mountain is brutal," he informs me.

"How'd you do?"

I might just as well be interviewing a modern-day Belmore Browne; the story is essentially the same.

"We got caught in a storm just a few hundred feet from the summit," he says. "It's amazing how the smallest things can screw you on that mountain. One of the zippers on my bibs wouldn't close all the way, and that cold wind blowing into my clothes just frosted me. We were a few minutes from the summit, but I could feel myself freezing, and I knew I had to get down."

"Do you regret the decision?" I ask.

"Hell, at first, yeah," he replies. "But deciding to live is always the right call."

Chapter Three

A MOUNTAIN OF GEAR

I WILL ARRIVE at the RMI winter mountaineering seminar possessed of only rudimentary mountaineering skills, but thanks to a marathon shopping spree in Seattle I will be togged to the nines.

For gearheads armed with credit cards, Seattle is a city fraught with risk. Within a few miles of one another are Marmot, North Face, Recreational Equipment, Inc. (REI), Mountain Safety Research (MSR), Outdoor Research (OR), and Feathered Friends. What Antwerp is to the diamond trade, Seattle is to outdoor gear.

I begin the acquisition process at REI. Clutching my three-page, single-spaced equipment checklist, I humbly enter the sprawling, two-story shrine to rustic chic. I've foolishly set aside only two hours in which to acquire nearly $4,000 in gear that the guide service deems essential. Half of it will allegedly prevent me from fouling up; the remainder will save me if I do. Before I'm done, the process will consume the better part of two days and drain nearly all of my savings.

Nothing is simple, so I rely heavily on the advice of my new personal assistant, a fit young clerk named Toby or Tyler or some similar appellation in vogue among child-bearing couples of the early 1980s. Although he proves to be a fount of knowledge on specs and tolerances, he insists on citing the relative merits of *all* makes and models of *every* gear item without betraying the slightest allegiance to any single one of them. For a tyro like me, this makes the selection process exponentially difficult.

I approach him and surrender my list.

"I'm climbing Denali this summer, and I need to pick up a few items."

The clerk glances at the list and lets go a patient sigh. Apparently he's seen *the list* before.

"Where do you want to start?" he asks.

"Let's start at the bottom; I need boots."

We wander into the boot department, where I join a cadre of other aspiring but shoeless mountaineers. Together we clomp around on the padded carpet, sporting various models of gigantic plastic double boots that would mimic the sort of footwear favored by Herman Munster if they weren't these electric hues of red, green, and blue.

I eventually opt for the lemon-yellow Koflach "Arctis," the hands-down front runner for Denali expeditions. The boots' silver "arctic" liners will keep my feet from freezing in the subzero temperatures at altitude. As I clean and jerk the ponderous box into the shopping cart, I realize that each boot must weigh at least 10 pounds.

My internal cash register begins a rough tally. Boots, $350. *Ka-ching.*

From there, we move to gaiters—fabric sleeves that cover and protect the lower legs, preventing snow, rocks, and dirt from working their way into a climber's boots. I select the Outdoor Research (OR) Gore-Tex pro series model. The Velcro closure down the front will be easy to manipulate with frozen fingers, and the girth is sufficient to fit over the cuffs of my new boots. Cost: $75.

To keep my fingers warm, I go for the OR Ed Viesturs 8,000-meter gloves. If they're good enough for a guy who's scaled Everest numerous times without oxygen, I try to reassure myself, surely they'll be good enough for me. The gloves resemble the sort of heavy mitts a welder might wear, or those of a knight outfitted for a joust. The gauntlets reach nearly past my elbows, while the articulated fingers convey the creepy impression that the gloves come complete with severed human hands. Cost: $100.

I had already purchased a North Face Inferno down sleeping bag through the mail for $600—and that was the sale price. The bag, rated to -40°F, features a Gore Dry-Loft shell that will prevent moisture from penetrating the down insulation and rendering it useless. I have no doubt the bag will keep me warm through cold Arctic nights, but its sheer mass troubles me. The sleeping bag comes with a stuff sack the size of a G.I. duffel—meaning it will consume almost the entire main compartment of my pack—so I buy a nifty molecule-scrunching compression stuff sack. After I cinch a series of straps, the voluminous sleeping bag is reduced down to a tidy package the size and heft of a cannon ball.

My Mountain Hard Wear Gore-Tex jacket is still serviceable, and in New Hampshire I had picked up the Moonstone Gore-Tex bibs. The remarkably small crotch zipper on the bibs barely provides access for an *ungloved* hand. On Denali I will amuse my teammates with my patented "potty dance," which involves hopping frantically from one leg to the other while digging around inside my multiple layers in search of a cold-shrunken nub the size of a Tater-Tot.

I spend at least an hour studying a wall covered with crampons. You've got your 10-point and your 12-point models. Some are hinged in the middle, while others are rigid. Some you strap on; others you step into like ski bindings. Of the strap-on type, there are four-strap, two-strap, and Scottish models, all with long belts that pass through a series of metal loops before being wrapped and buckled. (Just thinking about the buckles—roughly the same size as those on the Mary Janes my daughters wore when they were two years old—makes my fingertips go numb.) And finally there are hybrid crampons, which combine features of both the strap-on and step-in varieties.

Befuddled by the range of options, I appeal to the clerk for help in picking the crampon best suited to conditions on Denali. He recommends a new Charlet Moser hybrid model.

"Best crampons out there," the clerk assures me. "They're easy to put on with cold fingers, they won't pop off, and they're a snap to adjust."

"Good," I say. "I'll take a pair of those."

"That could be a problem."

"Why is that?"

"We haven't gotten them in yet."

"Oh."

We move on to the climbing hardware section, where I find myself repeatedly posing two persistent questions: "Okay, tell me again how I attach this device to my body? And once I've got it attached, what exactly does it do?"

I buy a rescue pulley (to help extract the victim of a crevasse fall); a Petzel mechanical ascender (for use on the fixed lines at 16,000 feet on Denali); a Petzel seat harness (to tie me into the 165-foot kernmantle team ropes); 24 feet of 7mm rope (for making prusik slings and climbing from a crevasse); 20 yards of one-inch webbing (for tethering the gear sled to my pack on Denali); seven regular carabiners; and two pear-shaped locking carabiners.

A quick word of explanation about some of these potentially unfamiliar equipment terms: Kernmantle rope—considered the strongest available—consists of braided nylon filaments encased in a nylon sheath. Prusik slings are looped around the kernmantle rope and connected to the seat harness. The prusiks slide freely upward, but grab the rope whenever the climber applies his weight. By using two prusiks, a climber should be able to extricate herself from a crevasse.

I also pick up the following luxury items:

- a Lexan bowl and spoon and a 3-foot length of light cord (later on, I will drill holes in the bowl and spoon handle and connect them with the cord; white spoons apparently have a way of disappearing in the snow)
- a full-length inflatable Therm-a-Rest and a full-length Ridge Rest (layered together, these two sleeping pads will provide adequate insulation from the ice underlying the tent floor)
- four pairs of Wigwam wool socks

- four pairs of polypropylene sock liners
- three blue Lexan liter-size Nalgene bottles for water
- one yellow Lexan liter-size Nalgene bottle for pee. Never in all my years as an outdoorsman have I stooped to urinating inside a bottle inside a tent. Then again, never have I climbed from a warm sleeping bag to answer nature's call when it's -25°F outside. From my very first night on Rainier, I will become an avid convert to this arrangement.

My two shopping carts are now full, and the clerk looks eager to hand me over to the checkout staff. Total cost: $900. *Ka-ching, ka-ching!*

Across the street at North Face, I drop an additional $125 on a pair of fleece pants with full side zips, which makes them easier to pull on or slip off without first removing my boots. The lack of a front zipper on the fleece pants compounds my anxiety about how I'll reconcile my overactive bladder with the bibs, which will form yet another layer over the pants.

I buy a Wind-Bloc fleece balaclava, a head covering with a mesh square over the mouth to facilitate breathing. In the notoriously thin air high on Denali, the mesh will ice over, turning my high-priced headgear into a black garbage bag that threatens to asphyxiate me. Cost: $40.

At Marmot, across Lake Washington in Redmond, a clerk expounds on the virtues of various ice axes.

"Short is good on the steep-pitched slopes of Rainier," he says. "Longer is better on the relatively flat stretches lower on Denali."

"I'm not sure I can use that advice," I say. "I'm going to climb both."

He recommends a compromise: a 70mm Grivel Mount Blanc, significantly lighter than the generic axes available at REI. Cost: $80.

Angling toward a rack of down summit parkas, I pull on a blue model with a breathable but waterproof shell and interior pockets large enough to accommodate water bottles. Suddenly I'm the Michelin Man, and beads of sweat are popping out all over my forehead.

"This one seems adequate," I say, straining to imagine conditions that would necessitate wearing such an item.

The clerk looks disappointed.

"Is that the last size Large?" he asks.

It is.

"I've had my eye on that parka."

He selfishly tries to steer me to a beefier model, but I hold fast. Cost: $300.

The front door opens and a man in his mid-30s enters the store. Clad from head to toe in tight-fitting black Lycra adventure togs that accentuate a trim but muscular physique, he's a dead ringer for the cover model of a Mountain Hard Wear catalog. He removes his glacier glasses with rehearsed efficiency and begins to cruise the aisles with a swagger that suggests one too many self-esteem workshops.

The clerk is rolling his eyes.

"Don't take this guy too seriously," he whispers. "He's climbed a few peaks and now he thinks he's a mountaineering icon. Try not to get him talking. He'll never shut up."

That proves impossible. I'm the only other customer in the store.

Cover Boy saunters over to me and checks out the parka.

"You must be going someplace *cold*," he ventures.

"Yeah, I'm attempting Denali this summer."

"Which route?"

"West Buttress."

"Good, safe route, but *bo-ring*."

"I'm sure it'll be challenging enough for me."

"I'm doing the West Rib. It's rated a 4 out of 5 for danger and difficulty. We're heading there in early May. I'm hoping the cold early-season weather will amp up the difficulty a bit."

"Good luck," I say, hoping to end the conversation. The effort fails.

"How's the training going?"

"Okay, I guess. I've been hauling 80 pounds to the top of a mountain near my home in Tennessee."

"Tennessee?" he snorts. "Those aren't mountains, man, those are *bumps*. Won't do you a bit of good. What you need is altitude, man, *altitude!* You need to train in *lean* mountain air. I've been humping loads on Rainier, working out on the climbing wall, pumping weights, the whole nine yards."

He strikes a body-builder pose. "Who you climbing with?"

"RMI."

"Oh, you're doing a *guided* climb. Personally, I'd hate that. Those guides have to cater to the lowest common denominator. That slow a pace would drive me *nuts!* I'm climbing with a few buds, all solid mountaineers. We're hoping to nail the summit in less than two weeks."

"I'm just hoping to nail the summit, no matter how long it takes."

"After Denali, we're off to Nepal for some *really* big mountains."

"After Denali, I'm off to my couch."

"We'll, good luck to us both," says Cover Boy, crushing my hand in his bionic grip. "To the top!"

If every climber I meet on Denali is as intense, fit, and self-inflated as the man in black, I'll be hard-pressed to muster the confidence required to make it to the top. I catch myself hoping he'll be roundly defeated—no, make that abjectly humbled—on Denali. Not that I wish Cover Boy any *serious* harm, of course—maybe just an extreme case of upper-elevation *flatus expulsion,* described by *High-Altitude Medicine* as "the unwelcome spontaneous passage of colonic gas at altitudes above 3,000 meters." That should knock him down a peg or two, I reason, while testing the bonds of friendship with his tentmates.

As it turns out, "Big Mac" (McKinley) will inspire humility and respect in every climber I meet, no matter what route of ascent they've chosen.

According to the equipment list, even my water bottles need parkas, so I buy three OR insulating covers to keep my water from freezing.

Like his counterpart at REI, the clerk at Marmot extols the virtues of the new Charlet Moser crampons—with the crucial difference that he has them in stock. The crampons feature molded plastic cups that fit over the boot heel and toe, as well as a single strap that passes through only one loop at the toe before cinching tight at the ankle. Cost: $125.

Apparently, my $350 Arctic mountaineering boots won't be warm enough for the summit of Denali; I need to buy neoprene overboots—

essentially a scuba diving suit for each foot. I opt for the Minus Forty Below models with the stout zipper up the front rather than snaps. I pick them partly because I know they'll be easier to put on and take off while I'm wearing gloves and partly because I love purple. My Denali tentmate Nat Brace will sport the same overboots, earning us both the nickname "Brother Smurf." Cost: $125.

Totting up the damage, I'm both amazed and abashed to discover that my shopping spree for gear so highly specialized I'll likely never use it again—including the countless accessories and add-ons—totals nearly $4,000.

I LOAD THE GEAR IN THE CAR and drive due south through a pattering rain for two hours to reach Ashford. Every bit of this hamlet—its modest houses scattered over huge lots, its general stores, its handful of rustic eateries—lies in the shadow of Mount Rainier National Park. I need four trips to haul my gear into the hotel room. Then I crack open my first beer, nibble on some jerky, and experience the swell of joy familiar to gearheads everywhere as I begin to tear open packages and organize a mountain of stuff.

First, however, I yield to the urge to behold my newfound sartorial glory in the full-length mirror. I felt a similar impulse at six years old, when I opened the package containing my first Little League baseball uniform. I stood before the mirror, listening to my metal spikes bite into the hardwood floor (sorry about that, Mom and Dad) and feverishly punching the pocket of my new mitt. "Koster's Auto Service"—our team's sponsor—materialized in the looking glass in backward type. I had arrived as a baseballer.

Back in the here and now, I pull on midweight long underwear tops and bottoms, fleece pants and jacket, liner and outer socks. On go the Gore-Tex bibs, summit parka, and glacier glasses, the fleece cap, Viesturs gloves, and outsize yellow boots. (Out of deference to the management, I leave the crampons in their box.) I step into my seat harness, cinch it tight, and attach the full complement of mountaineering hardware. Then I step in front of the mirror.

Gazing back at me is a middle-aged kid bundled up for school by an overzealous mom. Everything looks brand new and squeaky clean.

Still arrayed in my finery, I start to deposit gear items in my pack. There is no method to my mania; positioning the most frequently used items at the easiest access points will come later—much later.

My Lowe Contour IV backpack, which has proven perfectly adequate for a decade of backpacking excursions, is overwhelmed by the load. The sleeping bag—even in its compression sack—gobbles up nearly half the main compartment. Six thousand cubic inches may suffice for a three-day winter camping trip in the Great Smoky Mountains, but it's woefully inadequate for a six-day trek on Mount Rainier. I wonder how this thing will stand three weeks on Denali.

After hauling this scale model of the Leaning Tower of Pisa up and down Mount Rainier—suspended gear items jangling on the outside, seams straining to pop—I will purchase a Gregory Denali Pro. With a cargo capacity of more than 7,000 cubic inches, the Denali Pro is one of the largest packs on the planet. If your thighs could take the weight, you could use it to lug a Volkswagen Beetle to the summit.

Forced for the time being to rely on my Lowe, I wedge as much gear as I can into the pack, then lash the excess items to the top, the bottom, the back and sides. I hoist the pack onto my shoulders, strut around the room, and strike one last heroic stance in front of the mirror.

For reasons I can't quite explain, I then conclude that the underlying organizational structure is all wrong. This precipitates an endless process of packing and repacking—a procedure familiar to anyone who has done much hiking. I've met hikers who keep an organizational chart of their backpacks, designating each specific gear item by its appropriate location: main compartment, top pouch, side pockets, and so on.

Tonight, it appears, such harmony will elude me. At 2 a.m. I mutter, "Fuck it," load the pack one last time, and collapse into bed.

The futility of this compulsive ritual will not manifest itself until the next morning. Before the climbing group leaves for Mount Rainier, the guides take pains to establish that the clients have everything we need— and not one ounce extra—by conducting an inspection: It requires us to pull every last item of gear from our packs and scatter it over the floor.

Chapter Four

RAINIER WARM-UP

MOUNTAIN GUIDES HAVE AN IRRITATING TENDENCY to frame activities involving extreme risk in terms of entertainment.

"Okay, guys, it's blowing like a mother, the snow is falling *sideways,* visibility is zero, the air temp will freeze exposed flesh in seconds, and avalanche risk is off the scale. Let's go have some fun!"

Those conditions, only slightly mitigated, characterize my six days on Mount Rainier in April 2001, when I take part in a winter mountaineering seminar conducted by RMI. The seminar, a prerequisite for anyone hoping to complete an RMI-led Denali trip, focuses on expedition-style climbing: Climbers work as a team, schlepping extraordinarily large loads of both personal and group gear.

The seminar gives the guides a chance to teach critical mountaineering skills while evaluating the competence of their clients. Better to wash out on Rainier than to be airlifted off Denali.

Though mild compared with what I'll face on Denali, the six days on Rainier expose me to the most extreme conditions I've ever encountered. Rainier in winter, I discover, is vastly different from the balmy peak I had scaled twice before—both times in August.

Prior to April 8, the longest I had spent at altitude with "steel points on ice," as one mountaineering friend put it, had been two days—far from the nearly month-long immersion awaiting me on Denali. Now I'm counting on this crash course in basic mountaineering technique to boost my proficiency in the skills essential for an Alaskan expedition. My six days on Rainier will also be an opportunity to test—and even temper— my mental and physical toughness, which are perhaps even more essential than technique.

I WAKE AT 6 A.M. ON APRIL 8 to heavy skies and a steady drizzle, realizing that what's falling as rain here is snow at 5,000 feet. I spend the next half-hour enjoying my last hot shower for nearly a week, then resist the temptation to once again tinker with my gear.

At 7 a.m., just before reaching the pretrip orientation at Summit Haus, a no-frills B&B for mountaineers, I pass a Camaro engulfed in flames by the side of the road. Is this how they dispose of clunkers in backwoods Washington? No one seems to have noticed the column of dense black smoke; all of Ashford looks to be asleep. I slow to a crawl, feeling the heat from the burning vehicle through the window, then remember the gas tank. I gain speed to the Summit Haus parking lot a short distance down the road.

Locking my rental car, I hear a fire truck pull up. Along with two seminar colleagues, John Turner and Mike Heckel, I watch the small-town volunteer fire squad turn a meager trickle of water on the conflagration.

John, a sturdy man in his early 30s, began climbing in the Alps when he lived in France as a kid. Mike is a commercial pilot from Cincinnati.

"Might be our last chance to warm our hands by a fire," I say, peering down the road at the smoldering car. Just when it appears the fire fighters have the blaze under control, the gas tank blows. The guy with the hose drops it and runs.

"Think someone's looking to collect on an insurance policy?" John asks.

"Let's see," says Mike. "An abandoned car on an abandoned road spontaneously combusts at 7 a.m.—nothing suspicious about that."

We gather with the bulk of the group in a heated room at the Summit Haus for our pretrip orientation. The 17 clients are tricked out in mountaineering finery; the seven guides arrive looking surprisingly unremarkable in their street clothes. Before we depart, they will slip into the back room and emerge, as if from a phone booth, clad in dirt-smudged parkas, scuffed plastic double boots, and threadbare gloves, transformed into bronze-skinned alpine superheroes.

Just before the orientation begins, I glance up and see a familiar face at the end of the row of folding chairs. I had met Dick Bowers, 61, when I gave a talk on my Appalachian Trail book to a Great Smoky Mountains hiking club in December. Dick, the former U.S. ambassador to Bolivia and a fellow AT thru-hiker, had seemed particularly attentive when I mentioned my plans to take part in the winter mountaineering seminar and the Denali climb. Apparently he liked the sound of the challenge, because he has signed on for both. Dick's drive, unassailable optimism, and conversance in many—if not most—of the world's languages will come in handy on Denali, an international climbing destination.

Paul Maier, a tall, lean redhead who sports a goatee, will serve as lead guide. He introduces himself and the six other guides. All have extensive experience on Rainier, and most have climbed on Denali.

George Dunn, the senior guide in the group, is in his late 40s; he summited Everest in 1991. If there is a central message to the pretrip orientation and the activities of the coming week, says George, it is this: "You need to constantly ask yourself, 'Do I want to continue on and die or go home and try again?'" George's credibility is rock-solid on this point. He turned back three times before reaching the summit of Everest on his fourth attempt.

My prayer over the past few weeks leading up to the seminar has been a simple one: "Please, Lord, don't let me be the fattest, slowest, or least capable member of this team."

I'd rather dine on shards of broken glass than be the one guy on the trip who can't hack it and becomes the target of patronizing sympathy. ("Check out Brill. He just tossed his breakfast all over his Gore-Tex jacket, and now it looks like he's going to cough up a lung. Poor guy. And he thought he was going to climb Denali!")

I've witnessed similar scenes on my two previous Rainier climbs. The guides gently pull a struggling climber aside, letting him know what a valiant effort he has put forth and how proud he should be of himself. Then they tell him he's benched.

On my 1989 Rainier climb, the first washout occurred at about 11,000 feet at 3:30 a.m. The guides led the climber—a marathon runner—to a flat patch of glacier, gave him a sleeping bag, some food, and a bottle of water, and left him alone there in the dark. His solitary bivouac lasted nearly eight hours, until we picked him up on our return from the summit.

This client offered no protest. In fact, he seemed relieved that his suffering had come to an end. Apparently, not everyone surrenders so peaceably. In some cases, I've heard, a foundering client who seems determined to press on despite his condition may be required by the guides to surrender one of his boots. The result is a hobbled climber who poses no risk of making a foolhardy solo push for the summit.

A quick scan of the room assuages some of my concerns. A few of the clients appear to be in their 50s and 60s. Many sport pristine gear that, like mine, was hanging on a hook at REI a scant 24 hours earlier. (New equipment is the surest mark of an amateur.)

My misgivings are disspelled once and for all by a person I'll call Roger. Never has a less-skilled mountaineer clipped onto a rope, gripped an ice ax, or abused equipment with such naive alacrity. For those tied onto his rope, Roger's gaffes will be utterly terrifying; to those fortunate enough to be roped to sturdier mountaineers, they will provide a lifetime of belly laughs. As long as the guides are forced to coddle Roger, I reason, I can comfortably blend into the crowd.

We go around the room, introducing ourselves, explaining our motivation for taking the seminar, and articulating our short- and long-term mountaineering goals. Most of the 17 clients are preparing for Denali.

We disgorge the contents of our packs for the guides' inspection before repacking. Everything fits into my pack, but just barely, and I begin to relax. Just then the guides emerge from the back room carrying large bundles of group gear—stoves, cook pots, shovels, tent pieces, climbing hardware, ropes, and food—and begin doling it out. I experience a moment of panic as I glimpse my fully loaded pack, which George has informed me is already "way too heavy." So I'm supposed to put all this stuff *where?*

Alex Van Steen, who has been guiding on Rainier since 1989 and is waging a one-man moratorium on tact and grace, intervenes. "You've done a shitty job of packing," he says. "Look at all those lumps and bulges. You've got to fill *every cubic inch* with gear."

The man has a point. The pack's tubular main compartment looks lumpy, like the colon of someone who's binged on steak and potatoes without bothering to chew before swallowing.

As I look on in shock, Alex rips everything out of my pack and throws it on the floor, where it mingles with gear from other clients' packs, likewise rifled by the guides. Eventually, with Alex's gentle assistance, my pack accepts the load.

Rainier, with its steep slopes and heavy snowfall, poses significant avalanche risks to climbers. The guides therefore equip each of us with an avalanche rescue beacon, a battery-powered device about the size of a Walkman that we strap to our bodies beneath our parkas. During our travel on snow and ice, we set the devices in "Send" mode. The beacons remain on throughout our days on the mountain, increasing our chances of being rescued after an avalanche.

If that were to occur, any team members not buried in the snowslide would become searchers, switching their beacons from "Send" to "Receive." A series of pulsating beeps grows progressively louder as searchers approach a buried victim.

All 24 of us climb into a bus and leave the parking lot in a light drizzle. Soon we turn onto the access road leading into Mount Rainier National Park. Within a few miles, the road becomes a sheet of snow and ice, and the driver stops to put on chains. As we pass the remainder of the climb to the parking lot at Paradise Inn (elevation 5,000 feet) jouncing and vibrating on the chains and uneven road surface, I begin to regret my efforts to hydrate by drinking a liter and a half of spring water.

Within an hour, we emerge from the bus into blowing snow and biting wind; the air temperature up here is about 20°F—at least 20° colder than it was at the base. Though it's early April—and officially spring—Mount Rainier is still very much in the grips of winter.

Set amid pastures abloom with wildflowers in high summer, the sprawling and rustic Paradise Inn is now a four-story mound of ice. The abundant evergreen trees are bowed down beneath their weighty mantles of snow. Footprints indicate various paths up the mountain toward our base of operations at 10,000-foot-high Camp Muir, 5,000 feet above us.

By midafternoon we've strapped on snowshoes, shouldered our packs, and fallen into formation. Then begins the slow, rhythmic march up the mountain. En route, the guides frequently remind us of the benefits of two techniques designed to enhance efficiency and conserve energy on steep climbs.

Pressure breathing—the process of forcing air out through pursed lips—increases pressure in the lungs and helps offset the effects of thin air. It's also an audible signal to the guides that we're breathing. Pressure breathing will prove essential higher on this mountain; we will gain Camp Muir puffing like a bunch of trainees in Lamaze natural childbirth.

The second technique is the rest step. It involves lifting one leg and letting it swing forward into the slope and bite into the snow. While this forward, bent leg rests, the rear leg remains stiff, with knee locked, placing the climber's weight on the skeletal system and sparing the muscles. After a brief rest, the climber straightens the front leg, unlocks the back leg, swings it forward, kicks in a step, and shifts the weight to the downhill leg, which is now locked.

That's the way it works in theory, and 16 clients are doing a pretty fair job of approximating proper technique. Roger, however, is reeling and staggering like a drunken sailor on shore leave. Having neglected to try on his spanking new Denali Pro pack before he bought it, he failed to realize that the waist-belt of a size Large could wrap twice around his narrow hips and still permit the pack to slide down to his knees. Thus his bony shoulders are bearing his entire load.

Roger's snowshoes seem to be giving him trouble as well. Because he is not spreading his feet far enough apart with every step, he constantly pins one snowshoe beneath the other, causing him to totter and crash into the snow.

We climb for about an hour, gaining 600 feet before stopping to make camp. This leaves about 4,400 feet of tough climbing tomorrow before we reach Camp Muir.

THOUGH I HAVE DONE A FAIR AMOUNT of studying and reading up for this climb, I have grossly underestimated the time involved in hewing a camp from a wintry mountain slope. While the snow swirls around us, we spend an hour and a half wielding shovels and swinging ice axes to carve out platforms before erecting our tents. We dig a foot-deep pit in front of the tent doors inside the vestibules—sort of a stoop—to make it easier to put our boots on in the morning. Then we trench out a pit toilet, flagged with bamboo wands, about 20 yards from the tents.

We are instructed to pee into the snow beside a wand and to shit into the pit nearby, packing up our deposit after we're done. We enjoy a graphic 10-minute presentation on how best to excrete on a mountain. Like Denali, Rainier had become a veritable heap of frozen human dung before the Park Service introduced strict regulations in the early 1990s to clean up the mountain. Among them is the demand that all human waste be packed out in small blue plastic bags (furnished by the Park Service) closed with twist-ties.

Standing beside me as we listen intently to the guides' instructions is Anita Lundstrom, a buff, attractive Norwegian massage therapist who is the only woman on the trip. Her sexy, sultry looks emphasize the horrible incongruity of the topic under discussion.

I've kept my bathroom habits a closely guarded secret from all the women of my life, including my wife of 18 years. Rainier and Denali will rid me of my last measure of modesty.

Kent Wagner, one of the guides who will join me on Denali, explains the options.

"I personally prefer the 'direct deposit' method," he says. "You hold the bag directly under your butt and..." He looks at Anita and struggles for the most delicate word to convey his meaning. "And you *defecate* right into it. But you obviously have to have good aim."

Alex steps forward and demonstrates another method. He places the bag over his hand like a mitten, then mimes picking up a semifrozen mound of shit. Alex rolls the bag off his hand and over the ersatz lump of waste.

"It's just like cleaning up after a poodle in Seattle," he says.

From there, we move on to the proper use of the pee bottle.

"Some people kneel; others are able to lie on their sides and pee into the bottle without leaving their sleeping bags," Kent says. "Again, aim is *very* important."

Anita, born without an exterior drain hose, queries Kent about the feasibility of a woman using a pee bottle.

"Yes, women can use these, too. You just press it against yourself," he says, demonstrating with an empty bottle, "and let it go."

"Oh, and remember to keep your pee bottle in your sleeping bag with you," he adds. "Otherwise it'll freeze in your tent. No sense in hauling a liter of frozen piss up the mountain."

Just before dark, the guides emerge from the sunken kitchen with the large pots containing our dinner: red beans and rice, crackers, and canned fruit cocktail.

As part of some purification ritual, Roger has become a vegan—a person who eats no dairy products, eggs, or meat. The vegan's diet, restrictive enough at sea level, becomes an exercise in madness on the mountain, where guides are cooking one-pot meals for two dozen people.

Apparently tonight's chef, Alex, hasn't been brought up to speed on Roger's dietary restrictions.

"I'm a vegan," Roger announces as Alex drops a big dollop of camp glop into his empty bowl. "I put on the registration form that I eat a very restricted diet. Does this have any eggs, milk products, or meat?" He studies his steaming bowl intently.

"Um, well, I have to be honest," says Alex. "It has tiny little shrimp. I mean *tiny*. Barely visible to the human eye. You won't even taste them."

"Shrimp would technically be considered meat, wouldn't they?"

"Only if they're regular-size shrimp."

I can see Alex's ruddy face turning a deep shade of purple. Moments like these tempt mountain guides to pursue other careers.

"And there's a *minute* amount of powdered milk," he adds.

Roger evaluates his options: ingesting forbidden food items or starving. He turns to me. "Is powdered milk real milk?"

"Heck no," I say. "Bunch of chemical dyes, fillers, and binders. You've got nothing to worry about." Alex throws me an appreciative glance.

Roger digs in with his spoon. "Hey, this is pretty *good!*"

An hour after dark, now wearing our headlamps, we scamper to our tents. I room with Rusty and Ted Barber, two financially secure brothers from Massachusetts who have climbed extensively in Europe, the White Mountains, and Colorado's San Juans.

I drift off to sleep clutching my pee bottle to my chest like a stuffed teddy bear. Once again I've taken to the extreme the guides' admonishments to stay well hydrated. I urinate once at 12:30 and again at 2:30, when I max out my bottle in midstream. Few things in life—not even the bluster of a 30-mile-an-hour wind and an ambient air temperature in the low teens—are as uncomfortable as pinching off a stream of urine *in medias res*.

So I twist tight the cap, quickly slide from my bag into the chill air, and pull on my liner boots—which, I will soon discover, offer absolutely no traction whatsoever. I zip open the tent and the vestibule; then, gripping my pee bottle, I emerge into the night.

The reward is immediate—and impressive. The clouds have blown off, and a full moon lights the flanks of Mount Rainier. I can trace the cracked blue glaciers and knobby rock outcroppings all the way to the domed top.

Overwhelmed by the sight, I blurt out the well-turned phrase that reflexively comes to my lips whenever I view something so dramatically beautiful that it verges on the ineffable.

"Holy Shit!" I shout, forgetting that 23 fatigued mountaineers are sleeping all around me. Roused from slumber, they mutter and turn in their bags. Ted yells from our tent, "What's wrong?"

"You should *see* this," I answer, just as the slick bottoms of my liner boots lose their purchase and I slide 10 feet downslope before falling on my ass.

"Shit!"

"Now what's wrong?"

"Gravity."

I rise to my feet and climb carefully to the bamboo-wanded "urinal." I empty bladder and bottle, then stand shivering, remembering the warmth of my sleeping bag but reluctant to abandon this miraculous sight. By morning the clouds will have returned; this predawn jaunt to the pisser will be my one and only clear view of the summit.

Next morning we're back in formation by 11 a.m. (breaking camp takes even longer than establishing it), climbing steadily through clouds and snow. On either side the vague outlines of evergreen trees—the last vestiges of plant life below treeline—materialize from a swirling wall of white, then vanish just as quickly into the maw of the storm.

By noon, at about 7,000 feet, we emerge into full sunlight. Below us sprawls a sea of white clouds—Rainier's famed undercast. Suddenly our concerns shift from keeping warm to preventing sunburn. Shedding gloves, hats, and Gore-Tex shells, we slather on sunscreen and continue the push to Camp Muir.

Late in the afternoon we arrive at the compound of stone huts built under the guidance of the National Park Service in 1916. RMI added a more modern—though hellish—wooden bunkhouse in 1970.

The guides use ice axes to pry loose the board covering the door to the shelter—a dismal, 12-by-20-foot plywood structure with two small serving tables for food, four tight-packed tiers of bunks for sleeping, and two tiny windows. We enter with our sleeping bags and pads, and the place quickly acquires the charm of a football locker room, with bodies wedged shoulder to shoulder and sweat-soaked clothes hanging from nails driven into the walls. For the next five days, Camp Muir will serve as bedroom, dining room, classroom, and home.

While most of the other clients sort gear inside, I flee the chaos and step outside. It's a familiar view: The stratus of silver clouds hovering below at 7,000 feet. Cobalt blue sky above. Far off to the south, the snow-capped volcanic cones of Mounts Adams, Hood, Jefferson, and St. Helens poke above the clouds. Beyond the hut to the east lies the crevasse-laced Cowlitz Glacier, the arched spine of Cathedral Rocks—and, somewhere above, the 14,410-foot-high summit of Mount Rainier, presiding over the Pacific Northwest.

In 1998, on my second ascent of Rainier, I stood in this very spot at 2 a.m., ready to rope up for our climb to the summit. I was cold, sleepy, and inclined to question my sanity—until I began to absorb the surroundings. Above, meteors streaked across a moonless, star-studded sky. Below, the volcanic cones rose above the clouds and glowed white in the ambient starlight. Had I gone no farther, I would have felt amply rewarded for the trek to Muir.

Later, back in the hut, we crowd around a steaming pot of spaghetti and sauce, a meal even a vegan could love. Despite the guides' best efforts, animal products find their way into Roger's mess kit once more. An errant bird, a junco—one of the few creatures that can survive these harsh conditions—has gotten trapped in the hut. In its frantic effort to escape, it drops an organic projectile directly into Roger's drinking cup.

OUR INSTRUCTION ON RAINIER is divided into two essential themes—technique and safety—with frequent reminders that the two are inexorably linked. Every tip, trick, revelation, and warning will come in handy during my weeks on Denali.

The guides conduct the morning and afternoon sessions outside, regardless of weather. After-dinner lectures take place nightly in the hut. Though most of us arrived hoping for a shot at the summit, the guides make it fairly clear that, barring a miracle, conditions on the mountain— primarily avalanche risk—will limit our ascent to about 11,000 feet. According to the guides, only one party has reached the summit all winter. It took the climbers 18 hours to get up and partway back down, at which point they had to be helicoptered off the mountain.

The next morning, we awaken to 40-mile-an-hour winds and blinding snow. Most of us leave the hut wearing our summit parkas, goggles, and crampons, and gripping our ice axes. The guides march us to a steep wall of snow that tapers to a gentle slope where it joins the snowfield below the hut. Here, we practice self-arrest using our ice axes, the most valuable tool in a climber's arsenal.

A properly executed self-arrest ends with the climber face down, butt in the air, crampons kicked in, with the serrated ax pick buried deep in the snow at the shoulder and the ax shaft running diagonally across the chest.

When a climber starts to slide on an icy slope, she has only a few seconds to execute self-arrest before momentum makes stopping improbable, if not impossible. As she gains speed, an out-of-control climber will begin to bounce and tumble until one of several things happens: The power of impact against the hard ice breaks limbs or knocks her unconscious; she tumbles into a crevasse, which then breaks limbs or knocks her unconscious; or she slams into some fixed object, most likely a rock, which breaks limbs, knocks her unconscious, or kills her outright. The problem is compounded if the climber is wearing a heavy pack or is roped to other tumbling climbers.

In theory, though, one solidly anchored climber possessed of unimaginable composure and herculean strength can stop the slide of an entire rope team.

The instructors tell us the story of two RMI guides and a Park Service ranger who started to slide on surface ice just below this hut. They finally came to a halt on the snowfield 800 feet below. All three of the climbers survived, but two of them sustained broken backs in the fall.

For the drill, we practice falling in every conceivable position: On our backs, legs downhill. On our backs, legs uphill. On our stomachs, legs downhill. On our stomachs, legs uphill. We alternate holding the axes in our right and left hands.

Our slick nylon parkas and rain pants turn us into human toboggans, and the adrenal rush of falling makes it difficult to coordinate the requisite motions. The exercise is carefully staged, the slope flattens out a mere 40 feet below us, and we're not burdened by loaded packs, but the visceral experience of tumbling out of control before I can maneuver into proper self-arrest position and set my ice ax imparts an instant devotion to careful foot placement.

On Denali, a slip can turn into a fall, and a fall can turn into a chaotic plunge of as much as 9,000 feet. Although the moves become almost instinctive after an hour or so of practice, I pray I will never have to use them.

I experience the same feelings later in the day as we practice locating buried avalanche beacons. In a real rescue situation, these would pinpoint the location of a buried climber. My greatest fear is being buried and immobilized under tons of ice, gasping my last breath through nostrils and mouth packed with snow. So I'm particularly attentive during this drill. (My second greatest fear is being forced to sleep in a tomblike snow cave—a possibility on Denali if wind shreds our tents or unimaginably cold temperatures force us underground.)

Again we hear stories, this time about avalanche victims who survived and those who did not. We learn the sobering distinction between a "rescue" and a "recovery."

"A person located in the first 15 minutes has about a 90 percent chance of survival," Kent tells us. "After that, survival probability drops off rapidly."

One at a time, we turn our backs, and Kent tracks up the snow to disguise his path and buries a beacon—housed in a plastic container— three or four feet down. Then he nods, starts his stopwatch, and we begin the search. Skimming the surface of the snow with our own beacons, we try to find the intersection of the lateral and vertical signal lines where the audible beep is strongest. When we think we've located the "victim," we begin probing in the snow with a ski pole until we strike the plastic container. Then we dig with a shovel like rabid bloodhounds on the scent of a buried T-bone steak.

Meanwhile, Kent plays the role of drill instructor, giving everyone a glimpse of the intensity and perfectionism that will emerge full-blown on Denali.

"Dave," he yells at me, "your victim is *suffocating* right now! He's going to *die* if you don't find him!! There's *no* time for mistakes!!!"

The more-skilled among us execute "rescues," while others settle for more leisurely "recoveries" and suffer Kent's reproving lectures.

The next day, we come at avalanches from a preventive perspective, learning to study snow layers—each one denotes an individual "storm event"—in order to pinpoint poorly consolidated strata. These lamina can trigger a dreaded slab avalanche: An entire sheet of snow, sometimes many feet thick, breaks loose from the bed layer and becomes a deadly surfboard.

Paul demonstrates the shovel-shear test, which involves digging out a three-foot-square column of snow that's loose in the front and on the sides but still anchored to the slope in the back. The tester then cuts through the back edge of the column with a shovel and pulls forward slightly. As he does, the weak layers break free and slide, indicating potential avalanche risk.

Yet the shovel-shear test is of limited use, Paul explains.

"This test tells you what conditions are like right here," he says. "It doesn't tell you much about what's happening 100 yards from here. But if you see shearing happen here, you need to realize that it could happen anyplace."

"The best mountaineers are concerned, bordering on paranoid," Kent adds. "I assume things are dangerous and look for proof that they're not. And what we just saw does not offer me the proof I need to climb higher on this mountain."

The next day the sun returns—that should help fuse dangerous snow layers—and Paul and fellow guide Ned Randolph reconnoiter a route up the mountain, checking snow conditions and evaluating our chances for climbing higher. Through the morning, we watch their lone forms move toward the upper reaches of the Cowlitz Glacier at Cathedral Gap, nearly a mile—and about 1,000 vertical feet—above us.

Near the top, they stop, turn, and beat a hasty retreat. When they get back to camp, they describe hearing an eerie, resounding thud underfoot as a snow layer collapsed. Had they pressed on, they might have triggered a slide.

Rainier has had more than its share of avalanche disasters. In 1981, a huge icefall buried an 11-person climbing party under thousands of tons of debris, killing every one of them. Two years earlier, in March of 1979, Willi Unsoeld, an American climbing legend who had been part of the first successful U.S. Everest climb in 1963, was swept 500 feet downslope and buried in an avalanche not 20 minutes from Camp Muir. A plaque mounted on a rock nearby memorializes the climber.

WE GATHER IN THE HUT AFTER DINNER to discuss the physiological effects of altitude. Paul gives clinical names to many of the minor but bothersome symptoms we've been experiencing. Because most of us hope to climb Denali, the bulk of his commentary addresses that peak. The amount of oxygen available at 17,200 feet on Denali is about half the amount available at sea level.

"You can—and you will—suffer a great deal on Denali and still be okay," says Paul. "The key is distinguishing between normal misery and problems that indicate something serious."

Okay, he has my attention.

He lays out the symptoms of acute mountain sickness (AMS)— headache, insomnia, fatigue, nausea, water retention, shortness of breath, loss of coordination—and paints them as the price of admission to the lofty alpine world. They are nothing to be too concerned about, he assures us—provided the symptoms resolve within a day or so.

"Most of you are probably experiencing some of the symptoms of AMS right now," Paul says.

AMS is no big deal compared with high-altitude pulmonary edema (HAPE) and high-altitude cerebral edema (HACE), twin killers that cause the lungs (in the case of HAPE) or the cranium (in the case of HACE) to fill with fluids. Either one can kill a climber in less than 48 hours. AMS, if it doesn't resolve, can progress to HACE.

There are only two sure cures for HACE and HAPE. The first is a rapid descent of 3,000 feet. The second is placement in a portable hyperbaric chamber, known as a Gamov bag. Once the victim is in the bag, another climber (presumably a healthy one) stomps on a foot pump that increases the barometric pressure inside the bag to replicate atmospheric conditions at lower altitude. On Denali we will find Gamov bags stored at the 14,200-foot and 17,200-foot camps.

"When you ascend to a new altitude on Denali," Paul says, "you'll feel like crap. You can count on it. Once you've acclimatized, you'll start to feel better. Slow ascent is the key."

When Paul describes the ailment known as Cheyne-Stokes breathing, I resist the impulse to raise my hand and confess to an intimate familiarity with it. This condition occurs when a climber's respiration slows as he drifts off to sleep. He awakens repeatedly through the night, gasping for breath and tearing at his clothes or the zipper of his sleeping bag. During the first few days here at 10,000 feet, I had difficulty sleeping and awoke frequently, struggling to breathe.

Though there's no certain prevention or cure other than descent for any of these illnesses, Paul mentions the drug Diamox (acetazolamide); it's a powerful diuretic, which seems suicidal in a setting where hydration is so important. Diamox turns the blood alkaline, stimulating respiration— the body's way of restoring chemical balance. Increased respiration (hyperventilation, essentially) charges the red blood cells with oxygen.

I will depart for Denali with a veritable medicine chest in my pack, including Diamox, heavy-duty painkillers, antibiotics, antinausea and antidiarrheal drugs, and Dexedrine—the last an emergency remedy should I find myself sprawled on the summit with no energy left to descend.

THE ONLY TIME DURING THE SEMINAR when the guides actually make good on their invitation to "have fun" involves a short hike to a nearby playground. It's a huge block of ice—a serac, in mountaineering terms— jutting about 40 feet above the floor of the Cowlitz Glacier.

Shortly after we arrive on top, for the purposes of training, I become a crevasse-fall victim. Kent has rigged an impressive network of redundant safety ropes and anchored them in the ice with three-foot-long aluminum shafts known as pickets. He checks the security of my seat harness, a webbing device that encircles my waist and upper thighs. A loop on the front of the harness attaches to the climbing rope; carabiners and other climbing hardware attach to additional loops. Kent then lowers me 20 feet down into a crevasse. Never having rappelled, I find the act of walking backward over a sheer drop a bit unsettling.

Soon I've got more pressing concerns, chief among them extracting myself. The crevasse is damp and exceedingly cold, and my gloved fingers respond only marginally as I unclip the three-foot-long loops— known as prusik slings—from my harness and twist them around the rope from which I'm suspended.

The prusik slings, once tied off, create a slip knot that slides freely up the rope but grabs when I apply my weight. I will use two prusiks, one running from the main rope to my right boot and the other attached to the front loop of my harness.

"All right, Dave," says Kent, poised above me, "let's see you get yourself out of the mess you're in."

Prusiking out of a crack is, in theory, a simple matter of slipping your boot into the loop, rising up until your leg is fully extended, sliding the sling that's attached to your belt up three feet or so, leaning back to let the harness take your weight, then sliding the now-slack boot loop up and repeating the process. In short order, you should be back on the surface, basking in sunlight and the congratulatory backslaps of your buddies, who had given you up for dead.

In practice—under genuine crisis circumstances—it's a different matter altogether. Keep in mind that you're suspended from a rope, twisting and turning accordingly, while trying to slip the sling over your boot, which has two-inch-long spikes attached to the bottom. Then imagine that, dangling down there with you, is a 60-pound pack. Add in the blunt trauma to your head and the compound fracture of your left arm, both of which occurred when you slammed into the crevasse wall as you fell, and you've got the ingredients of a significant challenge.

After 10 minutes of intense exertion—not to mention frustration— I clear the crevasse lip, clip off the safety line, and settle onto the ground to watch my colleagues take their turns. I try to conceal the quaking of my hands.

Two hours later, as we're packing up to leave, we come uncomfortably close to real-time disaster. We're all tired, and with three groups simultaneously practicing the technique, there are so many ropes crisscrossing the top of the serac—which slants downward at a 20-degree angle—that it looks like the phone exchange for a major U.S. city. At this point, we're unroped and maneuvering to gather our packs and reform into our rope teams. I slip into my pack and begin to move toward the low end of the serac. As I step over two ropes and try to climb under a third, it catches my pack and sends me tottering.

Guide Phil Arnold lurches toward me and grabs my arm.

"Damn, man, be careful," he says. "This is no place to end your climbing career."

Just then, client John Turner crosses the same path, catches a crampon on the same rope, sprawls face down on the ice, and starts to slide toward the edge of the serac.

Again, Phil jumps to his rescue.

"Hey, you guys are freaking me out."

THE NEXT DAY, we make our "summit bid," rising early and forming into rope teams by 8 a.m. As we climb to the upper reaches of the Cowlitz Glacier, I'm particularly attuned to any noticeable shifts in the snow below me, recalling Phil and Paul's description of the sick sound of collapsing snow layers. We've had more than two feet of snowfall this week, and the slopes look loaded and ready to slide.

We reach Cathedral Ridge, a spine of alternating patches of ice and loose rock, and each step releases rivulets of scree onto the helmeted heads of the climbers below us. By now we're used to ascending in heavy snow, but as we clear the ridge and climb onto the Ingraham Glacier, a 50-mile-an-hour wind belts us in the face. We gain the last few hundred yards to Ingraham Flats in a whiteout.

We stand huddled on the flats, nearly lifted off our feet by the wind. To the guides, the storm is a teaching tool.

"This is very much like a Denali blow," says Paul. "Storms like this can last five days or more up there."

"Is it safe to climb in conditions like this on Denali?" I shout over the wind.

"If you encounter a storm like this on Denali, you'll never leave your tents," he says, which I find hugely reassuring.

Two hours later, we're back at Camp Muir, and the ambient temperature has dropped to near zero, without the windchill. My beard is layered with rime ice, as is the windward side of my goggles, hat, parka, and pants.

Kent approaches, drops a rope, and grabs his camera.

"Hey, you look like a real mountain man," he says. "Got to get a picture of this for your kids."

The day's final bit of instruction involves digging snow caves. Kent halfheartedly paces us through the process of trenching out an entrance and excavating walls and ceiling, but he obviously does not expect any of us to sleep there. The wind is up, we're all cold, and the hut—despite the stench and the congestion—looks downright inviting.

But this is something I've got to do. In the weeks leading up to the seminar, the only times I've awakened in the middle of the night, drenched in sweat, were prompted by thoughts of being buried alive beneath the snow. If you see a thread linking my fears of avalanches and snow caves, you're right on target: I'm so claustrophobic that I get the heebie-jeebies from tight clothes.

I've done enough reading to know that snow caves represent the final stage in many survival scenarios on Denali. Odds are I'll never have to sleep in one, Kent insists, but I don't want my first experience with a snow cave to involve a life-or-death struggle. If I have a panic attack in the snow cave on Rainier, I can always claw my way out and dash 30 yards to the hut, losing nothing but my dignity in the process. On Denali, the stakes will be a whole lot higher.

Rusty, Ted, John, and Andre Girard, whom I met while shopping for boots at REI, take turns with the shovel; in two hours we create a cave that measures about two and a half feet from floor to ceiling. After layering the bottom with sleeping pads, we slither in. I grow edgy as my cavemates pile up snow blocks, sealing off the entrance. They leave a tiny, two-foot-square hole at the bottom for emergency evacuation. We are effectively entombed.

"For reasons I'd prefer not to explain," I announce, "I AM SLEEPING CLOSEST TO THE DOOR!"

I awaken frequently throughout the cold, dank night, caught in the throes of horrid nightmares in which I'm *sleeping in a snow cave*. I jerk upright, bash my head on the low ceiling, and realize it's no dream.

THE NEXT MORNING, though I've come to hate conditions in the hut, I plow a shoulder into the snow blocking the door to the cave, struggle to my feet, and eagerly duck back inside the hut. The interior strikes me as positively spacious.

As I peel off layers in the relative warmth, I glance around at the others in the room. After five days on this mountain, we're beginning to look like real mountaineers.

We all stink, and our once-pristine clothes are grimy. Even Roger is starting to look like he belongs here. He's just as grody as everyone else, but unlike the others, his crampons have thoroughly shredded his new black gaiters. They are now a mass of gray duct tape, which he has used to make repairs. Under no circumstances, I've learned this week, should you rope yourself to a guy with shredded gaiters; every tear represents a fall-in-the-making from a snagged crampon spike.

The shafts of our ice axes are nicked and scraped. Our faces are wind-lashed to a deep red, and we have white raccoon eyes where our skin has been sheltered by goggles or glacier glasses. My own nose and cheeks have suffered frost nip. Upon my return home I will peel slabs of dead skin from my face, inviting comparisons to a shedding snake.

So much for the external changes. Each of us will also leave this mountain with the ability to communicate in the parlance of initiates—indeed, we will henceforth stop referring to various pieces of mountaineering hardware as "thingies" and "gadgets" in favor of their rightful names. And most of us will have learned sufficient technique—and respect—to tackle peaks far less forgiving than Rainier.

Before I head to bed on our last night at Camp Muir, I focus the beam of my headlamp on a quote tacked to the front door of the hut. It's by Edward Whymper, a 19th-century British climber: "Climb if you will, but remember that courage and strength are naught without prudence, and that a momentary negligence may destroy the happiness of a lifetime. Do nothing in haste, look well to each step, and from the beginning think what may be the end."

As I drift off to sleep on our final full day on Rainier, that last phrase— "from the beginning think what may be the end"—plays over and over in my head. Climbing a mountain, like any other climactic pursuit in life, demands synthesizing a seemingly limitless number of disparate factors—personal skill and strength, the fitness of the other members of your rope team, the hours of remaining daylight, reserves of food and fuel, snow conditions, equipment tolerances, weather—and determining your upper limits. You dare to push yourself to the brink, then turn back the instant before you reach it.

WE ARRIVE BACK AT THE SUMMIT HAUS in late afternoon, and I seek out Kent with an urgent question.

"Kent, don't bullshit me now; do I have what it takes to climb Denali?"

"I've been watching you all week, Dave. You're gonna do just fine."

"When we're up there, promise you'll keep an eye on me; I've got two kids counting on me to come back home."

"I'll cover your back," he says.

That he will. Just over a month from now, Kent will distinguish himself as one of the most skilled and competent climbers on Denali. And though we will all fall short of his expectations, I'll clip onto his rope every chance I get.

Chapter Five

A DRINKING TOWN
WITH A CLIMBING PROBLEM

THE FOUR DAYS BEFORE OUR ARRIVAL on the glacier—two spent in Anchorage, two in Talkeetna—are eerily reminiscent of my brief stay in Atlanta before I set out on the Appalachian Trail. Now as then, I stand at the brink of a great unknown, consumed with worry about gear and logistics and the struggle and hardship that await me. These last days in civilization are the most emotionally difficult I will experience in Alaska, largely because my imagination has transformed Denali into the world's premier arena for pain, suffering, and loss.

Though I endeavor to remain upbeat and force myself to keep active by sorting gear and checking and rechecking supply lists—which has, by this point, evolved into a compulsive ritual—I succumb to a pestering preoccupation with the seemingly endless cascade of what-ifs and worst-case scenarios.

I know myself well enough to realize that at the moment I step out of the plane and onto the ice of the Kahiltna Glacier—beholding the enormous peak from *within* the mountainscape for the first time, feeling the cold work its way into my joints—the reality of the mountain will supplant these grim imaginings. I will then engage in doing, rather than thinking about doing, and become an active agent of my own fate.

Such was the case with my 1,200-mile trek across the Pacific Northwest in 1981. In preparation for that trip, I had digested a library of books that detailed grizzly maulings, drownings in rain-swollen rivers, rattlesnake attacks, death by hypothermia, violent thunderstorms, freak late-season blizzards, and crippling backcountry injuries hundreds of miles from the nearest medical aid. All fueled anxieties that began to wane only after my partners and I had arrived at the trailhead in Glacier National Park and shouldered our packs.

From then on, although I did experience some—if not many—of the things I feared most in the weeks before setting out, I found myself to be more steady and competent than I had imagined. In fact, when I finally encountered a grizzly a few weeks into the trip, rather than run away or climb a tree, I stalked him cautiously with my camera. Of course, he *was* moving rapidly away from me at the time....

But here in Alaska, from the perspective of D-day minus 4, I am consumed by a free-floating sense of dread. This is an all-volunteer climb, I constantly remind myself; I can back out at any time. Even after I'm on the mountain, I can cry "Uncle!" and the guides will lead me back to terra firma in a day or two. On a typical guided trip, in fact, as many as half the clients leave Denali of their own free will once the mountain proves too much for them.

Dee has told me repeatedly—and perhaps somewhat selfishly—that she could fully respect my decision not to go. Her uneasiness grew exponentially after the December night when she and I watched a *Dateline* news report about the helicopter rescue of two British climbers stranded high on some formidable mountain. Because we had caught the report in the middle, we had no name to attach to the ice-locked peak whose hulk filled the screen.

The announcer was describing the climbers' four harrowing days in a snow cave at 19,000 feet in subzero temperatures with no food. The climbers had taken a 300-foot fall in which one of them broke a leg, and both were suffering from extreme frostbite. Severe weather had delayed their rescue for several days.

"Oh my God," said Dee. "That better not be Denali."

"Hell, that's not Denali," I said, certain I was right. "It's too big to be Denali. That's got to be a Himalayan peak."

After a few minutes of footage of the still-unnamed mountain in the grips of a violent winter storm, Stone Phillips appeared on the screen and confirmed Dee's fears: It *was* Denali. The report was describing the 1998 helicopter rescue of British soldiers Martin Spooner and Carl Bourgard.

"*Please* change the channel," Dee begged. But I couldn't. I would have been transfixed by the report under any circumstances; the fact that this was "my" mountain made the segment even more perversely irresistible. She had maintained a similar head-in-the-sand position about the movie *Vertical Limit.* She would not watch it, she announced, until my safe return from Denali. I had avoided the movie myself after a friend suggested that viewing it prior to my trip would be roughly equivalent to watching *The Perfect Storm* before setting out on an open-water voyage in a sailboat.

On my arrival in Anchorage, all my fears—so conveniently compartmentalized during the long months of preparation and training—emerge fully blown. There's no premonition of my own death on the peak; considering that our three RMI guides will protect me from the mountain as well as from my own ineptitude, such an outcome is highly unlikely. Still, I devote my first morning in Alaska to writing last letters home. Though my motivation is to articulate things I've meant to say but haven't managed to, I'm sure the letters carry the tone of battlefront missives. I resist the urge to print on each envelope the words "To be opened in the event of my demise."

I write to my parents, letting them know how much I value their love and the stable home they provided for my brother, Steve, and me. I write to my two preteen daughters, Challen and Logan, urging them not to worry and reminding them that they are—and always will be—the center of my universe. Dad will be home soon with some nifty souvenirs from Alaska, I promise them.

I write a much more candid letter to Dee, revealing to her how fearful I am.

After I've sealed the envelopes and sent the letters, I return to my room and sort through the personal effects I'll take on the mountain: a four-leaf clover I found in the meadow near my cabin and preserved between strips of packing tape; pictures of the girls; personal notes from both of them.

I visited the girls at their schools on my way to the airport. They laughed at my buzzcut hair, cried when I hugged them, and each handed me a note. Ten-year-old Logan had folded hers into a dense nugget the size of a lima bean—hoping, she explained, to conserve space in my pack. Not a day will pass on Denali that I don't study the pictures, read the notes, and experience a swell of longing for home.

"Daddy, don't let your nostrils freeze," reads the note from 12-year-old Challen.

"No mercy!" writes Logan, who seems to favor brute force over finesse in negotiating her way through life.

Dee presented her letter to me on our last night together. It reads, in part:

> Dave:
> Tomorrow has seemed really far away for the past year. It wasn't very real to me; it's not even real now. I have one voice saying, "It's okay; no worries," and another saying, "Tell him how much he means to you, just in case...." It's very hard to put into words what I do not go near: the thought of losing you. But despite my fears for you, I think this expedition will reveal much and make you stronger. My heart is with you. Come home to me soon; we have so much to live for.

A few days earlier, my friends had hosted a going-away party for me at the pub where, two years before, I had dreamed up my Denali adventure. John Craig gave me a copy of *The Worst-Case Scenario Survival Handbook*, which includes useful instructions on how to contend with an avalanche.

J. J. Rochelle and Jon Jefferson presented me with a box containing a tube sock connected to a voltage tester. The enclosed product description explained the purpose of the device:

> Penile Frostbite Prevention System—Model XL-4400: For the man with a lot to protect.
>
> Congratulations on your choice of the PFPS XL-4400, the finest dickwarmer ever engineered. You'll bask in the warmth of its nine custom settings, from a tingling 1.5 volts all the way up to the wiener-siz-zlin' 22.5 volts! Traditional steady-state, hands-free operation, or new Jolt-o'-Joy push-button feature. One test, and you come in from the cold forever!
>
> **Caution:** Ejaculation or urination while wearing the XL-4400 may cause serious injury or death by electrocution. Heart patients, bed wetters, and compulsive masturbators should not use this device.

I opened a second box from J. J., which contained a stainless-steel flask inscribed "David Brill—Mt. McKinley 2001" and a bottle of 12-year-old single-malt scotch. Both have accompanied me to Alaska.

JUST WHEN MY HOMESICK REVERIES are tempting me to ditch the entire enterprise, the phone rings. It's photographer Bill Hatcher, a veteran of several high-elevation climbs in the Himalaya, and he wants me to perform a seemingly simple errand. Instead, the task winds up consuming most of the afternoon—a hidden blessing in my current mental state.

Just as Mr. Robinson offers "one word: *plastics*" to Benjamin Braddock in *The Graduate*, Bill whispers four simple syllables in my ear: "Sal-mon jerk-y."

"What?"

"When you lose your appetite for everything else up high—and trust me, you will—salmon jerky will become your main dietary staple. Beyond that, you can use it to barter for things you want and need. The stuff is like gold on the mountain."

I had heard that toilet paper—often in short supply after extended storms or bouts with "the mung" (mountaineering parlance for diarrhea)—is commonly called "mountain money," but I had never heard salmon jerky described as the coin of the realm.

Because I arrived in Anchorage a day ahead of Bill, he feels justified in asking me to procure enough for both of us.

"How much will we need?"

"I'll want about two pounds."

"Okay, I'll get four. This stuff tastes good, right?"

"Delicious."

Finding salmon jerky in Anchorage should be no problem, Hatcher assures me. "It's like buying pineapples in Hawaii."

Regrettably, he has overestimated the supply chain. For two hours, I scan the Yellow Pages for packing houses that process game meats—a "You kill it, we clean it" arrangement with the state's hunting population. No one seems to have the quantity I need.

Finally, I reach the manager of Trapper's Creek, an Anchorage-based meat packer. He's got some jerky. He might be able to get some more.

More than a quarter of a century has passed since I purchased a substance measured in ounces from a person I didn't know, but the acquisition process is amazingly similar. The more I buy, the cheaper it is. For a few seconds, I consider offsetting the cost of my trip by becoming the head of Denali's salmon cartel.

"I need four pounds, and I need it by tomorrow," I tell him.

"Let me see what I can do," he says. "Give me your phone number, and I'll call you right back."

He calls back in five minutes.

"We can probably get you a few ounces by the end of the day and the balance before noon tomorrow, but scoring that amount right now is tough; the supply is way down," he says. "Have you contacted other dealers?"

"Yeah, most of them, and their supply is short, too."

"What we can get will be divided into 1.5-ounce packages," he says.

"Can't you deal in bulk?" I'm imagining the challenge of peeling plastic wrappers with numb fingers.

"No. Our supplier packages it that way." Apparently, the machine that moves salmon jerky in Anchorage is as hierarchical as a classic drug syndicate.

Late in the day, just before closing time, I find my way to Trapper's Creek. The manager plops a brown paper bag on the counter.

"Do I get to sample the stuff?"

"Cost you $3.50."

"You're kidding, right? I'm buying *four pounds,* and you're going to charge me for a 1.5-ounce sample? I don't even know if I'll like it."

"You'll like it."

"We'll see."

I count $3.50 onto the counter and try to tear open a 1.5-ounce package of peppered salmon jerky. If the meat is as tough as the wrapper, I'm screwed.

"Got scissors?"

"Try your teeth."

I use my incisors to rip into the package. In a flash, my eyes tear up and the room fills with the aroma of a Seattle fish market, drowning out such weaker competing smells as those of elk sausage, venison steaks, and ground caribou.

I hazard a bite. The red, peppery flesh tastes like an anchovy smoked over a woodfire—flavorful, intense, not bad. When I next address the manager, he instinctively takes a step backward. Evidently he's been exposed to salmon-jerky breath before.

"Let's do the deal," I say. "I'll be back tomorrow for the rest."

LATE THE NEXT MORNING I pick up the balance and toss it into my duffel bag in the back seat of the rental car, which contains the rest of my food for the next few weeks. RMI will provide breakfasts and dinners, but we climbers are responsible for our own lunches and snacks.

In amassing these stores, I've made a fundamental mistake. Under normal circumstances, it's unwise to shop for groceries when you're famished; when you're heading off for a month on the world's coldest mountain, however, you should precede your shopping trip with three or four days of fasting. Instead, I went the previous evening, after gobbling a New York strip steak, a loaded baked potato, three pints of beer, and 1.5 ounces of salmon jerky. As a result, I wandered the aisles of the grocery store thinking "healthy" rather than "tasty and calorie-dense," yielding a food supply better suited to an ashram than an expedition.

I bought one pound each of raisins, granola, almonds, pumpkin seeds, banana chips, and sunflower seeds; two pounds of CytoMax carbohydrate powder; two cases of "Orange Burst" GU (the sugary substance that fueled Dee's descent from the summit of Mount Washington); 40 coffee bags; and 20 fruit roll-ups. Almost as an afterthought, I purchased four one-pound blocks of Hershey's chocolate. My food bag now weighs about 14 pounds.

AT 3 P.M., after dividing the jerky into halves for Bill and me, I load all my gear into the rental car, alarmed by both the heft and the bulk of my combined equipment. My exquisitely heavy pack and duffel are ready for the mountain, but apparently I am not. As I strain to lift the pack into the car, the load gets away from me, and the crampons tethered to the outside rake the rear panel of the Ford Taurus. I try to buff out the scratches with my shirt tail, spooked that this is some kind of omen.

I'm supposed to meet the rest of the team in front of the Alaskan Airways baggage claim at 4 p.m. I begin to worry that somehow I'll fail to spot them, missing the shuttle to Talkeetna. It doesn't occur to me that 11 men—each toting a backpack and a duffel the size of a body bag—will be difficult to overlook. At 3:50, I drive past the rendezvous spot and glimpse a Mont Blanc of baggage piled at the curb. I dump my gear, say a few quick hellos, and drop off the car. I'm back in 10 minutes, meeting the men whose lives will be roped to mine—literally and figuratively—over the next several weeks.

Gary Talcott, 47, leader of our trio of RMI guides, is a sturdy, compact man of about 5-feet-8 and the first to greet me. I'm immediately taken by his large blue eyes and gentle smile. A dead ringer for the actor William H. Macy, his mien is hardly consistent with the gruff, impatient prototype of a mountain guide. Gary has stood on Denali's summit three times. He was planted at 14,200 feet during the Arctic blast of 1992, which dumped 60 inches of snow in 24 hours and contributed to the deaths of seven climbers. His appearance matches the soft voice I've come to know on the phone during our frequent chats over the previous months.

Next I greet Kent Wagner, 38, one of the guides on the Rainier seminar. Standing about 5-foot-7 and sporting a neatly trimmed goatee, Kent, the youngest member of the team, can't possibly weigh a pound over 145. As I've learned on Rainier, however, body type is no measure of a mountaineer's strength and will; Kent's intensity more than counterbalances his small frame. During his first and only attempt on Denali in 1998, Kent advanced to within a few hundred feet of the summit before being forced to turn back because of a struggling client. As a result, Kent is as hungry for the summit as the rest of us.

Our third RMI guide, 50-year-old Joe Horiskey, is something of a Denali guru; he has reached the top 13 times since he began climbing in Alaska in the early 1970s. He stands about 5-10 and sports a gut suggesting that his training took place at the local pub. Here again, looks can be deceiving: Joe's nearly 30 years of climbing on Denali have imparted essential skills and a kinship with the mountain and its moods that will see him through just about anything.

Upon meeting my fellow expedition clients, I'm relieved to note that most of them, like me, are unremarkable physical specimens. In the aggregate, they look like the kind of fathers who spend Saturday mornings on the margins of soccer fields or Little League baseball diamonds.

Nat Brace, 41, a computer systems specialist from Seattle, stands 6-foot-1. Plastered on his freckled face is a wide, inviting grin. A transplanted Easterner who recently became a father, Nat has been training for the climb in the 10,000-foot mountains around Seattle. He will distinguish himself as the strongest climber among the clients.

Nat will share a tent with me and Ken Coffee, 39, the owner of a Tulsa-based engineering company that designs ultrasound equipment. Ken stands 5-9. His hair and eyes are dark, and he has the long, lean lines of a distance runner. Thoughtful, quiet, and accommodating, Ken will sleep each night with his head two feet from my fetid socks and only once bitch about it. He and I will find we have much in common as divorced fathers.

Brad Skidmore, a 40-year-old neurosurgeon from northern Kentucky and a contented bachelor, sports a Marine Corps haircut. You'd expect his intense focus and precision from someone confident enough to slice into a human brain. Though Brad looks barely old enough to hold a driver's license, his experience on Argentina's 22,834-foot-high Aconcagua—the highest peak in the Western Hemisphere—has conditioned him to expedition life. At 5-foot-8, the strikingly lean Skidmore will serve as a determined driver, and his assertive bent and steady mood will form the emotional keel of the group.

Dick Bowers, 61, the senior member of our team, is the former U.S. ambassador to Bolivia. He's 5-foot-11 with graying brown hair, soft brown eyes, and the stocky build of a former AT thru-hiker (he completed the trail in 1998). Dick immediately emerges as the group's consummate extrovert and toastmaster. He will be loath to hole up in his tent on Denali when there are people to meet and stories to share. Having become conversant in many of the world's languages during a career's worth of state cocktail parties, Dick will startle members of the international climbing community by greeting them in their native Chinese, Russian, Spanish, Portuguese, French, German, or Polish.

Matt McDonough, 42, is a commercial real-estate executive from New Jersey. Matt is the father of three young children but has managed to squeeze in a few winter training trips to the White Mountains of New Hampshire. Matt has also honed his mountaineering technique on several of the snow-capped volcanoes of the Pacific Northwest, including Mounts Rainier (14,410 feet), Baker (10,778 feet), Hood (11,235 feet), and Adams (12,307 feet).

Matt was talked into climbing Denali by a man who will not make it to base camp. His friend and climbing partner, Doug Yearly, is a 41-year-old home builder from Huntington Valley, Pennsylvania, with the brawny shoulders and burly arms of a body builder. Doug's shaved head and altimeter watch seem to signal that he will be the one among us to constantly push the pace, short-roping the rest of the team to the summit. His apparent fitness and physical strength will make the events of the following days even more mystifying.

Clay Howard, in his early 50s, is a lanky Texan and railroad executive with the slim build of a former college athlete. Clay had no choice but to train for the climb in the searing, sun-baked flats of Keller, Texas—a decided disadvantage in a sport that rewards climbers who train at altitude.

The most experienced mountaineer among the clients is Bill Hatcher, 42, a professional photographer from Dolores, Colorado. He grew up climbing in Europe and has since pursued highly technical routes on peaks in Chile, Argentina, Turkey, and Pakistan. Bill, a rail-thin 5-foot-8, has forged a life of travel and adventure. His boundless stores of energy will keep him awake through many a frigid Arctic night, waiting for the light to give him a chance at capturing that perfect image.

WE LOAD GEAR ONTO THE TOP OF A VAN and its attached plywood trailer, then we all pile in. (The cramped quarters are excellent practice for the small three-person tents we will occupy on the mountain.) I grab a seat in the back with Nat and Ken, and we pass the miles to Talkeetna talking of careers, family, children, gear, and the mountain. The quick friendship persuades us to share a tent. The fact that we're all non-snorers simplifies the decision.

Two hours north of Anchorage on Alaska 3, the van turns onto the 15-mile spur road to Talkeetna (permanent population 772), the staging area for all but a few Denali expeditions. We arrive at the hangar for Hudson Air Service, which has been shuttling adventurers around these parts ever since Cliff Hudson founded the company in 1946.

After wheeling a Cessna out of the hangar and onto the tarmac, we deposit our gear on the cement floor amid a jumble of propellers, gear casings, pistons, and the carcass of a plane that's been stripped of its engine. From the airstrip in Talkeetna, the Alaska Range is just a 45-minute hop northwest.

Our gear stowed, we climb back into the van and continue half a mile to the village of Talkeetna, which commands the junction of the Talkeetna, Chulitna, and Susitna Rivers. No surprise, then, that Talkeetna means "where the rivers join" in the language of the native Tanaina Indians. They occupied the site until whites arrived in 1896, establishing a trading post and mining town that predate both Anchorage and Wasilla. Within a few short years, a gold strike on the Susitna River was drawing prospectors to the town, and by 1910 Talkeetna had become a bustling riverboat station. In 1915, the Alaska Engineering Commission chose Talkeetna as its base of operations for the Alaska Railroad, an ambitious undertaking that ultimately connected Seward (on the Gulf of Alaska) with Fairbanks (deep in the state's interior) by laying more than 450 miles of track through the wilderness.

In Talkeetna we will enjoy the last of the amenities conspicuously absent on the mountain: hot showers, soft beds, pay phones, good food, and cold beer—or any beer at all, come to think of it. These indulgences will occur amid the most eclectic assortment of cranks, eccentrics, and colorful characters I've ever met.

A rough, hand-painted sign at the edge of town reads: "Welcome to Beautiful Downtown Talkeetna." It may as well read: "Give me your sports fishermen, your leather-clad disciples of Harley-Davidson, your late-middle-aged tourists in Rockport walking shoes, your bearded homesteaders, your summit-crazed mountaineers, your aging hippies and their barefoot offspring yearning to be free spirits."

IF MARTIANS WERE TO SET DOWN IN TALKEETNA, they would behold a variety of human culture unrivaled anywhere in the mainstream United States. So dominant is the notion of diversity and tolerance here that the off-worlders would blend right in. Trappers sporting fur hats (and beards to their belt buckles) commingle and converse with well-groomed yuppies in the town's numerous watering holes. Shortly after we arrive, a man in his early 20s, wearing ragged shorts, a filthy yellow sport coat, and a bright red top hat, pedals his bicycle down the center of Main Street. He attracts not a glance.

A thriving population of mongrel dogs—their uniform coloring and body type betraying their origins in a very shallow gene pool—roams the streets through the 24 hours of functional daylight, littering the road with droppings.

And then there are the mountaineers. They hail from 39 countries around the globe, and during the April-to-July climbing season they outnumber the local population 2 to 1.

The climbers in Talkeetna can be divided into two distinct castes: those who have been on the mountain and those who are about to depart for the mountain. Bronze-skinned and hollow-cheeked, the former totter about on unsteady legs. The latter, us included, skitter energetically along Main Street, fortifying fat stores at the local eateries or laying in last-minute supplies.

Like its inhabitants, Talkeetna's dwellings bracket the spectrum. Rough-hewn cabins, Quonset huts, and canvas yurts squat beside dilapidated (and now residential) school buses that have been lent an air of permanence through the removal of their wheels. Single-wide trailers share narrow side streets with cabin tents faded to a dull white by the relentless summer sun.

A few early buildings survive. The Roadhouse—a two-story, steep-roofed frame structure built in 1917 as a supply point and flophouse for gold miners—now harbors a bakery, a restaurant, seven guest rooms, and a bunkroom. It will be my home for the next two nights.

Lining Main Street are gift shops offering stuffed bears and moose, native Alaskan crafts, and gold-nugget jewelry. The main drag also hosts Talkeetna's entertainment center—the dank, malodorous Fairview Inn. Built in 1923 as a boardinghouse for passengers traveling north and south on the Alaska Railroad, the inn—a simple two-story clapboard structure—appears to have endured more than its share of harsh Alaskan weather (not to mention the rowdy eruptions of drunken patrons crazed by cold, dark winters).

Late in the day, Dick, Ken, and I step from blazing daylight into the cavelike recesses of the Fairview. As soon as our eyes adjust to the darkness, we realize we'll be drinking in a morgue. Stuffed and mounted on the walls is a representative of every mammalian species indigenous to the region, including a moose with six-foot antlers.

The bartender, a woman sporting a ball cap and the shoulders of a Russian shot-putter, uncaps our beers and slides them down the bar with an air of indifference. Enough mountaineers have passed through this taproom that we don't even try to impress her with our daring.

"Enjoy these beers, boys," says Dick, raising his bottle. "They're the last ones you'll see for quite a few days."

"Have you made your last call home?" I ask him.

"Yeah, and I picked up a little anxiety on the other end of the line."

"Me too. Dee started crying as soon as she picked up the phone. We had a great night together just before I left—nice dinner, good bottle of wine—but somehow it doesn't seem like enough. While I'm busy on the mountain, she'll have a month to fret and stress with no news of our progress."

"I figured a frequent reminder of me would help my girlfriend get through the next few weeks," Ken Coffee says. "I arranged to have flowers sent to her every Friday I'm gone."

"No shit!" I say, feeling romantically challenged. "I didn't know you could do that."

"Sure. You just call in the order and give them the dates. With a credit-card number, you can get people to do just about anything."

I drain my beer and run across the street to the pay phone. Within 10 minutes I've arranged to have fresh flowers delivered to Dee's door over the next three weeks.

I return to the Fairview to find Dick and Ken working diligently on their second beers.

"You know," says Dick, "for all the money I've spent on this trip, I could be tooling around Key West on a Harley. Lying on the beach, sipping a cerveza. So tell me, David, what the hell are we doing here?"

"You could lie on the beach in Key West long enough to get skin cancer," I tell Dick, "and it wouldn't amount to shit compared with our time on Denali. Just think how great that beach is going to feel after dealing with the temperature extremes up here. I don't know about you, but this waiting game is driving me nuts. I want to get on that mountain and start moving—or freezing, or falling, or whatever is going to happen to us."

"I'm with you on that," says Ken. "We've spent the last six months planning and training, and now we're down to the last few hours before the real adventure starts. It's hard not to get ahead of ourselves."

Dick's baritone bursts into a spiritual that will become his theme song on the mountain: "One day at a time, sweet Jesus. One day at a time.... Boys, it's all up to the mountain now—whether we live or die, whether we summit or get skunked. Let's just enjoy ourselves and not worry about how things turn out. Think about it: We're drinking a cold beer in a genuine backwoods Alaskan watering hole, surrounded by the cast from Northern Exposure, and tonight we'll be sleeping in soft, warm beds. Life is good!"

As Dick, Ken, and I speculate on what the coming days will bring, a fisherman enters the bar gripping a 15-pound salmon by the gills. After ordering a beer, he spreads a newspaper on the bar and cleans and guts his catch right then and there. He deposits the bright red flesh in the bar's ice reservoir. Familiar with this ritual, the bartender carefully scoops ice for mixed drinks from the opposite end of the ice chest.

We finish our beers and walk a quarter-mile to the east bank of the Susitna River, a lazy waterway coursing down a gravel channel 300 yards wide. In a month's time, this languid creek will be a raging torrent of meltwater, tinged milky-gray by glacial silt and choked with uprooted trees. Beyond the river, 75 miles away, Denali and the Alaska Range shimmer in the late-afternoon sun. This is my first unfettered view of the mountain. Even from this distance, it's more massive and imposing than I had imagined. I aim my camera at the faraway hills and examine them through the frame of my telephoto lens. As I do, my heart begins to pound. In less than 48 hours—and for the next several weeks—that mountain-scape will represent the entirety of my world.

Chapter Six

"DENALI IS ALL ABOUT TIMING"

THE FOLLOWING MORNING we gather in the airplane hangar to sort gear. When I left Anchorage, I had foolishly convinced myself that I'd packed for the last time.

"Okay, guys, I want you to empty your packs," says Kent. "We need to do a final gear check."

In a repeat of the pretrip procedure on Rainier, I gut my pack and scatter its contents on the cement floor. I also dump the contents of a ditty sack. Guide Joe Horiskey sifts through the accoutrements, eager to ferret out inadequate or unnecessary gear. He spots a tiny LCD flashlight.

"Dead weight," he says. "It'll be light enough up there to read in your tents at 3 a.m. if you want to. Ditch it."

I've also packed a ballcap and four insulating hats. "Pick the warmest," Joe instructs me. "We'll leave the others here."

Kent is concerned about our hands, a particularly vulnerable part of the body.

"Show me your warmest combination of mittens," he commands.

I hold up my fleece mitts and shells from New Hampshire.

"No, Dave, I said your *warmest* combination."

"This *is* my warmest combination."

"If it gets to 20 below or colder on the summit—and it very likely will—you're going to be in trouble with those."

Ken Coffee comes to my rescue, handing me a beefy pair of OR double-fleece liner mitts.

"Most people don't know this about me," he says, "but I have a glove fetish. I brought about a dozen pairs, and I won't be needing these."

Ken has just become my best friend, gaining unlimited access to my salmon jerky.

Once the guides have assessed our gear, we move onto the landing strip and erect our new three-person Mountain Hard Wear dome tents. The exercise has two aims: First, it allows us to attach the guy lines, which are essential in keeping the tents from blowing off the mountain in high winds. Second, it familiarizes us with the setup procedure in an environment where the risk of screwing up is minimal. Or so we think.

As we begin to raise the tents, a stiff breeze kicks up. Soon we're sprinting down the runway, chasing stuff sacks and tent flies and tent bodies borne by the wind.

"If this had happened on the mountain," Kent explains after we've collected the scattered parts, "you'd be *fucked.* One of you should have hold of the tent at all times while the other two insert the poles. If you lose a tent up there, your trip—and possibly your life—is over."

It takes us 20 minutes to figure out the proper configuration of hooks, loops, grommets, sleeves, and poles. As we do, I try to imagine performing this task in subzero temperatures and a 50-mile-an-hour wind.

Later in the afternoon, we tackle our final bit of official business. All 12 of us troop over to the Talkeetna Ranger Station for the pretrip orientation session that is required of all Denali expeditions. At the front desk, we each pay a climbing fee of $150; the money will finance Park Service efforts to keep the mountain clean. More important, it will help defray the cost of Park Service rescue missions on the mountain. Each climber then registers his climbing résumé and a set of medical approval forms signed by his doctors.

Lying on the countertop is a faxed "Summit Status Report" for the mountain. As of Friday, May 25, the summit success rate stood at a measly 32 percent—far below the typical 50 percent average. At this very moment, Matt Cantrell, who climbed on Rainier with me earlier in the spring, is making his way back down to base camp after spending seven days pinned in his tent at 17,200 feet. Hammered by brutal cold and high winds, his team never got a shot at the summit.

South District Ranger and Denali veteran Daryl Miller, who greets Joe Horiskey like an old friend, leads us into a conference room. He runs through a list of Park Service regulations—the gist of which seems to be "Leave no trace"—then briefs us on what to expect on the mountain. His PowerPoint presentation includes images of frozen, contorted bodies and frost-blackened faces, hands, and feet.

"Denali is all about timing," Miller informs us. "It all depends on what wind and weather window you draw." (Miller should know; he made eight attempts before finally nailing the summit in 1992.) He segues to a list of favorite statistics:

- The Park Service executes 8 to 12 rescues each year.
- In a typical year, 1 in 10 climbers suffers frostbite.
- Though the route from base camp to the summit along the West Buttress Route is only 16 miles long, most climbers need two weeks or more to reach the summit.
- Those who move more slowly acclimatize better; they are thus less susceptible to altitude-induced illnesses.

Miller then covers the perils of ascending to high camp at 17,200 feet. This elevation is considered the threshold of the "death zone," where the life-sustaining systems of the human body begin a gradual and inevitable decline that culminates in descent or death.

"You can stay at 14,200 feet indefinitely and get stronger," says Miller, "but once you go up to 17,200 feet you've bet the farm. Nothing heals up there, and little things just drag you down. Because of the debilitating effects of altitude, cold, and dwindling supplies, most climbers get only one summit attempt once they reach high camp."

Paul Maier, the lead guide on Rainier, had dwelled on the topic of judgment: Disasters result not from one big cataclysm, but from a concatenation of small missteps and mistakes.

Miller echoes that sentiment. "Judgment is what kills mountaineers," he tells us. "Weather and altitude just compound problems with judgment. Keep in mind that at 18,000 feet you have only 50 percent of the oxygen saturation at sea level, so you're only half as smart.

"When people push for the summit at all costs and go beyond the point of no return, they lose control. It could start with a problem with cold hands and feet or altitude sickness that gets worse, but from there it progresses to the point where they become nonambulatory and can't get down. Ultimately, they wind up getting snuffed."

FUZZY LOGIC PLAYED A ROLE in the deaths of most of the climbers who perished on Denali between March and July of 1992, the mountain's deadliest year, when 11 climbers lost their lives.

The trouble began shortly after May 11, when meteorologists predicted the worst storm to hammer Denali in more than a decade. Though weather reports for Denali are notoriously inaccurate, this time the weather guys nailed it. In just over two days, five feet of snow fell at base camp at 7,200 feet; higher on the mountain, winds topped 110 miles an hour.

It was a wild couple of weeks. At the height of the storm, two Italian climbers died in a fall on the technically demanding Cassin Ridge. Giovanni Calcagno's body swung from a rope at 15,400 feet, visible to dozens of climbers camped in the basin at 14,200 feet.

Three Korean climbers became stranded in a snow cave at nearly 18,000 feet and had to be airlifted out.

Another three Koreans unknowingly camped on a snow bridge spanning a crevasse at about 15,000 feet. The bridge fractured, and two of the climbers tumbled into the crevasse. The third ran for help. He got it: Two American mountaineering legends—John Roskelley and Jim Wickwire—

rushed to the rescue along with five other climbers. They pulled one of the climbers from the crevasse and began searching for the second.

Rescuer Matt Culberson had descended into the crevasse when he felt a hand grab his ankle. Looking down, he beheld a troubling sight: One of the Koreans—buried up to his chest and immobilized in the ice, and assuming he was going to die—had tried to hasten his demise by chewing on his tongue. The rescuers freed him and found his only injury to be self-inflicted lingual lacerations. His climbing partner was not so lucky. Completely buried under the debris, he had sustained a broken pelvis and was hypothermic. The climbers were eventually airlifted to safety, and both survived.

In another storm three days later, yet a third Korean trio fell to their deaths while attempting a desperate descent of the Orient Express, a steep couloir on Denali's west face. The incline earned its macabre nickname in 1972, when three Japanese women took a fatal fall there; they, too, were descending. The Orient Express has claimed the lives of more climbers than any other spot on the mountain.

A few days later, a Canadian climber descending the 40- to 50-degree Messner Couloir—named for Reinhold Messner, who pioneered the route with Oswald Olz in 1976—took a fall, pulling his three ropemates off their feet. The quartet plunged 2,500 feet, plowing into rocks and spiraling through thin air before coming to rest at 16,800 feet. All four were killed. The gruesome scene was witnessed by a number of climbers camped at 14,200 feet. They were powerless to intervene.

THE QUIETLY INSISTENT VOICE of park ranger Daryl Miller returns me to the conference room at the Talkeetna Ranger Station.

"Another important factor to consider," he is saying, "is that group dynamics change a lot in the stressful environment up there. Commit yourself to giving more than you take. Practice patience. Don't let yourself succumb to frustration or anger—both are compounded by altitude. Don't let your team morale break down."

As we leave the ranger station an hour later, a thoughtful silence has replaced the easy banter among my teammates. I can't speak for the others, but I'm having a hard time shaking my mental images of dead bodies and frozen appendages.

Late in the evening, just before I head to bed, Bill Hatcher and I meet for a beer at a small table in front of the Roadhouse. Bill translates Miller's final admonition about a breakdown in morale into much starker terms: "One thing you should know, David, is that these expeditions get really stressful—especially if we're forced to deal with long stretches of bad weather. Nerves get frayed and people snap; they say things they don't mean. There are guys on this climb who will never speak to each other again once the trip's over. I've seen it happen many times."

"Not this group," I say. "The macho factor is way down the scale, and everyone seems so easygoing."

"Maybe it won't happen," Bill concedes, "but it's best to be prepared. If you let the building friction among team members get to you, it can really grind you down."

For some reason, this eventuality troubles me more deeply than the prospect of high winds, harsh weather, or even a thwarted summit attempt. I've never been very good at handling strained human relationships—particularly in the tightly packed environment of a mountain camp with notably few escape routes.

THIS LAST NIGHT before our departure is a sleepless one for me—and, I suspect, for most of my teammates. My mind churns with doubts about gear (have I remembered everything?), fitness (did I train hard enough?), altitude (will the shortness of breath I experienced on Rainier buy me an early ticket home?), and closure (did I say goodbye to all my friends and loved ones?). And now, thanks to Bill Hatcher and his doomsday scenarios of dysfunctional dynamics, I get to fret about the fragmentation of our 12-man team.

These heavy-duty existential ruminations would make it difficult to sleep under the best of circumstances. In Talkeetna—a party mecca in the land of the midnight sun—they're enough to make a heavily sedated narcoleptic toss and turn the livelong night. The late hour notwithstanding—it's now 10:30 p.m.—sunlight floods in through the window beside my bed. I steal a towel from the community bathroom and hang it over a barren curtain rod.

In the now-darkened room, I settle into my pillow and begin to drift off. Just as Morpheus wraps me in his arms, I realize I'm front and center in the theater of the absurd. A three-act play by Samuel Beckett is about to begin.

Act I: I've become accustomed to the constant drone of single-engine airplanes shuttling climbers to and from base camp, but now a new and far more horrid noise issues from the common room directly below.

A woman possessed of the most piercing voice I've ever heard—imagine *Laugh-In*'s Joanne Worley on an especially stentorian night—shrieks and chortles on the telephone. Despite a voyeuristic urge to learn what's inspiring such unbridled excitement, I can't make out her words.

After about an hour, Ms. Worley's doppelganger hangs up and departs. I twist open the inscribed flask containing the 12 ounces of Scotch I had planned to haul up Denali (before Joe convinced me it weighed too much) and take a hearty swig; had there been a rubber mallet in the room, I would have used that instead.

Act II: Ms. Worley is replaced by a sparring couple. They stand outside, directly below my window, which is open a crack. This time the words are crystal clear.

"You know I've been way too trusting of you," she says.

"I haven't done anything wrong!" he says.

"Then why didn't you tell her you were living with someone?" she says.

"Well, it never came up."

"I want you out of here!"

"Okay, I'm leaving!"

"If you leave, don't you dare come back!"

"Fine with me!"

I take a second swig from the bottle, bigger than the first.

The man departs, and Act III begins: The heavily amplified house band a block down the street at the Fairview kicks off its opening set. Supplying in volume what they lack in skill, they start by butchering a Rolling Stones standard (it bears a vague resemblance to "Brown Sugar"). The cacophony will continue until well past midnight.

By the end of the first set an hour or so later, I've consumed half of the flask, yet still I'm edgy and wide awake. Surrendering to the inevitability of flying onto the glacier at 9 a.m. tomorrow and starting up Denali in a state of sleep deprivation, I flick on the light and dip into my stash of books. It's heavy on graphically detailed accounts of mountaineering disasters: *Into Thin Air* by Jon Krakauer, *Facing the Extreme* by Ruth Anne Kocour, *White Winds* by Joe Wilcox. The only thing less soporific than reading these books, I realize, would be reading them to the accompaniment of machine-gun fire and an earthquake. Plus I've already committed all three texts—and their death tolls—to memory.

As it turns out, the innkeepers have provided the antidote for just such preclimb insomnia. The row of books on the nightstand includes the blessedly anodyne *Outhouses of Alaska* by Harry M. Walker.

Two hours later, with images of cozy backwoods crappers crowding my consciousness, I drift off to sleep.

Chapter Seven

THE HAUL OF THE MOUNTAIN KING

MAKING THE HUMP FROM BASE CAMP

THE APPROACH TO DENALI, unlike that of most of the world's great mountains, begins not with a trek through the lowlands but on the paved runway of the Talkeetna airport. The constant drone of the single-engine ski planes is as familiar in these parts as the buzz of Alaska's ubiquitous mosquitoes, and the process of plucking climbers from base camp continues through much of the 24 hours of functional daylight.

At 9 a.m. on May 28, Bill Hatcher, Clay Howard, and I—clad in full glacier gear—head from downtown Talkeetna toward Hudson Air Service, one of a handful of operators whose fleets of Cessna 185s and vintage DeHavilland Beavers fly tourists, climbers, and sportsmen into the Alaskan backcountry. As we approach the hangar, we see half a dozen climbing teams, surrounded by massive loads of gear, getting ready to depart with other air services.

At the Hudson hangar, I struggle to make conversation with a group of Asian climbers who have spread their gear on the grass behind the building to dry in the sun. They've just returned from the mountain, but the language barrier makes it impossible to determine how they fared. My rudimentary hand signals for "mountain summit" elicit enthusiastic head nodding, and the man who seems to be the leader keeps repeating, "Denali, yes!" which I take to mean their summit bid was successful. I only wish that Dick Bowers, the team's extroverted polyglot, were here to interpret, but he's still abed, scheduled on a later flight onto the mountain.

The three of us will be the first of our team to plant our boots on the ice of the Kahiltna Glacier. Though I could have used a few extra hours of sleep, I'm eager to end a year of anticipation and begin the climb in earnest, whatever that entails. After running through the gear checklist one last time—fully aware that if we forget an essential item now, we'll be forced to do without it for the next several weeks—we stow our packs and duffel bags behind the seats of the plane, strap into our safety harnesses, and put on headphones and mikes so we can converse over the noise of the engine during the 45-minute flight to base camp at 7,200 feet.

Jay Hudson—whose father, Cliff, started shuttling sportsmen and women around these parts back in the 1940s—peers through aviator sunglasses at a panel of dials and gauges. He tweaks knobs, yanks levers, and turns the crank on our Cessna. Never having flown in a small plane, I find the instrumentation remarkably low-tech. In fact, the most sophisticated gadget on board seems to be my $35 Timex watch.

My outsize Arctic mountaineering boots are immobilized between the front and back seats. Clad in multiple layers of polypropylene, fleece, and Gore-Tex, I feel like a mummy swaddled for burial. I begin to suffer twinges of claustrophobia, then panic—embarrassing, given that the plane hasn't started to move.

Soon we're bumping down the paved airstrip. Once airborne, we bank left and bounce on thermals over the marshy delta marking the confluence of the Sustina and Chulitna Rivers, which await the spring melt-off. Jay grips the stick with one hand and works a hydraulic crank with the other; this pulls skis forward beneath the wheels in preparation for our snow landing.

The sun glints off pockets of still water—"mosquito farms," Jay calls them—dotting the landscape below. Evergreen trees fringe the rivers' margins, forming perfect habitat for bear and moose. Both are populous in wild Alaska. Some 75 miles ahead, the greening Alaska tundra abruptly surrenders to a world of ragged peaks locked in snow and ice, and I glimpse a narrow notch that looks like a gunsight.

The plane sounds reluctant and tired—and rightfully so. For the past two months, or ever since the start of Denali's short climbing season (April to July), it's been flying this route up to 10 times a day. A feeble whine has replaced the groaning from the engine, and I measure the distance to the notch against our sluggish ascent.

Over his years of flying, Jay has developed a remarkable knack for scaring the shit out of his passengers, largely through harrowing (and carefully rehearsed) stories about engine failure and fatal plane crashes. I'm too focused on our flight path to register the particulars of his stories, but the central message is that a lifetime of narrowly averted disasters makes bush piloting at least as hazardous as mountaineering.

Jay's narrative builds to a crescendo as he explains the sobering particulars of "One-Shot Pass": You have a single chance to clear it. If not, you, your gear, and the aluminum body of the plane become colorful adornments on an otherwise monochromatic mountain landscape.

"I think we may be a little heavy," he says with remarkable calm. "But with a little luck, we just might get the lift we need to clear the notch. Then again, you never know...."

My toes curl involuntarily inside my boots, and it occurs to me that if anxiety could be measured in pounds, we'd splatter like a paint ball against the snow-draped granite walls that loom ahead.

Aptly named, the pass serves as the gateway to the Alaska Range and some of the most unforgiving mountains on Earth. At the apogee of our flight, we've gained sufficient altitude only to confront a gap so narrow that a miscalculation of 30 yards to either side would snap off a wing.

Safely through the notch, I shift my focus forward and glimpse Denali—the Great One—presiding over a complex network of fractured glaciers and a court of lesser peaks, including 17,400-foot Mount Foraker and 14,850-foot Mount Hunter.

There are few moments in life—and this is one of them—when the concept of "grand scale" becomes fully articulated right before your eyes.

In an instant you surrender any delusions you may have held about your own significance, your physical prowess, or the benevolent character of nature. Every cirque, snowfield, avalanche chute, shaft of blue ice, granite crag, and glacier of the Alaska Range reminds you that you are entering a realm that defies life and that you will earn Denali's upper slopes only through hardship and struggle—not to mention luck.

I recall but one other event in my life that exposed me to such an overwhelming spectacle of enormity. In 1964, when I was eight years old, my family traveled from the Midwest to visit the New York World's Fair. As we crossed the bridge from New Jersey in the predawn twilight, the towering skyline of New York filled the windshield, setting my adrenaline pumping in a mixture of arousal and dread. Then as now, I was entering *terra incognita* and a world that operated by very different rules from the ones to which I was accustomed.

After parking the car and following a labyrinthine route through the city, we arrived at the fair site and merged with a throng of hundreds of thousands of people, many of them speaking foreign tongues. I clung to Dad's hand, fearful that if I let go, I'd be swept away and disappear forever into the crush of the crowd.

But as I began to grasp the lay of the land, fix on notable landmarks, and surrender to the orderliness of Dad's strategy for gaining the most from our 15 hours at the fair, I started to relax and revel in the sense of adventure. By day's end, I returned to the car as an exhausted initiate to the nation's largest city; the perception of danger and risk only enhanced the experience.

I hope the same will occur here in the Alaska Range, but for now I'm unnerved by the prospect of being deposited in a hostile setting so far removed from the comfortable context of my life.

"More than 90 people have died here," I think. "And *everyone* who's entered this palace of the ice gods has endured hardship." I recall the words of Paul Maier from the Rainier seminar: "You can, and will, suffer a great deal on Denali. But you'll still be okay."

The unanticipated bouts of suffering that life subjects us to are bad, but the ones you know are coming—the dentist's drill, the surgeon's scalpel, the vice-principal's paddle—are the worst: Through the minutes or hours of anticipation, your mind turns and tumbles these events, fashioning them into elaborate stage sets on which you envision yourself undergoing the dreaded incident. Once it's past, of course, you tell yourself it wasn't all that bad—largely because nothing could ever be as bad as the fanciful experience fabricated by your own mutinous imagination.

Here in the Alaska Range, I wonder what it will be: Crevasse fall? Frozen digits? An out-of-control tumble down an icy slope? Psychic and physical paralysis induced by a foot-wide ridge poised above a 2,000-foot drop? Or perhaps ignoble defeat on the mountain's upper reaches, where each gulp of air provides only half the oxygen available at sea level? In my mind I've experienced all of them, both simultaneously and in turn.

As the plane descends from the pass and angles toward the glacier, my once-green world goes white. Shielded by dark lenses, my eyes begin to pick out features on the Arctic expanse below. I see the tiny forms of climbers, spaced evenly along their 165-foot ropes, navigating between and around gaping crevasses and beginning the long slog to the summit. Then I see a sprawling village of tents marking base camp at 7,200 feet— and, just beyond, the tracks of ski planes slicing the Kahiltna Glacier and marking the landing strip.

Jay eases the plane down, navigating skillfully between Mount Hunter to the south and 10,450-foot Mount Frances to the north. "Any landing you can walk away from is a good one," he reminds us. "If the plane still works, it's a great one." Soon the runners begin to bounce on the irregular surface of the glacier, and we skid for 300 feet before coming to a stop on the Southeast Fork of the Kahiltna. We have just gained nearly 7,000 feet in elevation—the largest single-day jump we'll make on the mountain.

As we exit the plane, some members of the RMI team that was pinned for seven cruel days at 17,200 feet queue up for their return trip to the world of hot showers, cold beers, and warm beds.

They are bone thin, and their exposed skin has been wind-lashed to a brownish red. There is little time for conversation—Jay hurries them and their gear aboard after dumping our bags onto the snow—but I study their faces, straining to register the depth of their suffering. As I do, I'm reminded of the opening scene from the movie *Platoon,* where Charlie Sheen's character and the other raw recruits exit the C-130 and file past a line of battle-hardened warriors bound for home, glimpsing in their countenances the transfiguring effects of war.

Within 10 minutes of landing, Jay's Cessna is screaming back down the runway. The three of us shoulder our packs, grab our duffels, and scamper toward the sidelines to get out of the way of incoming planes.

Within a few minutes, the second of the Hudson planes—this one piloted by Randy Smith—arrives bearing Kent, Matt, and Dick. Matt, whose face is the color of the surrounding snow, deplanes carrying his breakfast in a black plastic trash bag.

"I *hate* small planes," he says, tottering on unsteady legs.

It's clear that we've been granted a reprieve from Denali's brutal weather. It's close to 50°F, the reflected sunlight is blinding, and there's no hint of a breeze. My first act on a mountain renowned for some of the world's coldest weather is to break into a sweat.

"Over the next few days, while we're low on the glacier, the heat will be *unbearable,*" says Kent, slipping into his pack. "All these vertical surfaces turn the glacier into a huge reflector oven. In direct sunlight, it can get up to 90°F, and you just cook."

"Given the choice, I think I'd rather cook than freeze," I say.

"By the end of this trip, you'll do a little bit of both. In that regard, Denali is an equal-opportunity mountain."

In a single day on Denali, the temperature gradient can cover 110°F, from 90 above to 20 below. This inspires an endless process of peeling and layering as climbers strive for the perfect amount of insulation in a wildly fluctuating environment.

Kent explains that some expeditions attempt to beat the heat by sleeping through the day and climbing at night until they reach the upper mountain, where the altitude moderates daytime temperatures. But as I soon discover, the heat can be remarkably fleeting: An errant cloud passes in front of the sun, plunging the air temperature 30°F or more in an instant. The temperature rebounds just as quickly once the cloud has passed.

In a near-literal depiction of Robert Frost's "Fire and Ice," items stored in packs and sheltered from the sun remain frozen solid, while climbers clad only in a thin layer of polypropylene mill about camp, sweat trickling down their faces.

Following Kent's lead, I peel off my Gore-Tex jacket, unzip my fleece, remove my gloves, and slather on sunscreen. Each of us has packed four large tubes of SPF 45—which we'll apply 10 or more times each day—but the sun will still get through, baking faces, ears, and the backs of ungloved hands.

The faces of the veteran climbers here in base camp tell me that a mountaineer's most vulnerable spot is the underside of his nose. The reflected glare, combined with their constantly dripping schnozzes, makes it seem that they're all suffering from some dreaded flesh-eating disease.

Over the course of the coming weeks, the sun will create some dramatic effects. My salt-and-pepper beard, which is still predominantly brown, will be blond by trip's end. And my new navy-blue ball cap—bearing the slogan "Life Is Good"—will be bleached white by the sun. This happens because the intensity of ultraviolet radiation increases by as much as 250 percent above 13,000 feet—enough to sear the skin, blind unprotected eyes, and drain the color from vulnerable fabrics.

WITH KENT IN THE LEAD, we snake past half a dozen domed nylon homes set into the snow. Climbers—some shirtless—sprawl in camp loungers and call greetings to us as they cultivate tans and sip beers. The two-way radio in the Park Service ranger's tent is broadcast through speakers, and we can hear the ranger communicating with incoming pilots.

A plane lands and out climb two perfectly coiffed women in their mid-30s, dressed in sweaters, blue jeans, and city shoes. They slip and slide their way to the cluster of tents, locate a couple of weatherbeaten mountaineers and pose beside them for photos, then reboard the plane. The entire production takes all of 10 minutes, but they will return home with proof that they visited base camp on Denali.

Hundreds of bamboo wands—labeled with colored tape bearing official expedition names and numbers—protrude from the snow in the center of camp, giving the appearance that a gigantic porcupine has been interred just below the surface. The green wands, which are identical to the ones gardeners use to stake up tomato plants, mark the cache sites where expeditions have left behind unnecessary gear, as well as food stores to sustain them should a storm postpone their departure from the mountain.

Gary has told us stories of expeditions getting stuck at base camp for five or more days, awaiting a flight out. I've suffered through enough three-hour layovers at the Atlanta airport to begin to fathom the agony of enduring up to 30 days in grueling conditions, then drawing within 45 minutes of civilization—only to be condemned to five more days in filthy clothes and a crowded tent.

Despite the dramatic sweep of the surrounding mountains, the feature that rivets my attention is the plywood crapper. It stands just off the runway, in clear view of every base-camp resident—many of them women. A man in a red parka is seated on the perch, his bibs around his ankles, reading a paperback and watching the planes land. His private bodily functions have become a public spectacle.

In its effort to prevent human waste from fouling the mountain environment, the Park Service has placed privies—most without the privacy of protective walls—at the camps at 7,200 feet, 14,200 feet, and 17,200 feet. Along other sections of the route, climbers are responsible for collecting their fecal waste in plastic bags and hurling it into crevasses designated for that purpose. I make a mental note never to fall into that particular type of crack.

While forcing me to shed my last measure of modesty, the plywood loo will also serve as the site of a serious—and costly—miscalculation.

KENT LOCATES AN ABANDONED TENT SITE at the upper edge of base camp and proclaims it our home for the night. Such site scavenging is common practice on the mountain; arriving teams often hover about conspicuously while current occupants pack up to depart.

Though I'm inclined to plop down in the snow, rest, and orient myself to the surroundings, Kent has other ideas. He divides us into work crews. I am about to discover that climbing Denali is all about work, and that only a tiny fraction of it involves actually moving up or down the mountain. Though this is not Kent's intent—or maybe it is—activity helps soothe a churning mind.

Hewing a camp from the ice can take two or more hours, including the process of preparing platforms and setting up tents, erecting or reinforcing the four-foot-high ice-block parapets that shield tents from the wind, digging out a kitchen, and, higher on the mountain, constructing latrines. This is true even for sites that were recently occupied: Sun and wind work quickly to undo the painstaking labors of mountaineering teams, dissolving snow walls back into the glacier and consolidating tent platforms into pocked and pitted slabs of blue ice.

Armed with ice axes and shovels, half the team hacks tent platforms; others saw two-foot-square ice blocks from the glacier to fortify snow walls, or tape and label 200 four-foot-long bamboo wands. We will use the wands to mark our supply caches and flag our route up the mountain. Should a whiteout envelop us and force a retreat, the "magic wands," as I have come to think of them, will guide us back to camp after our boot prints have vanished beneath the blowing snow.

Kent, whose perfectionist bent first emerged during our exercises with the avalanche beacons on Rainier, makes it clear that an approximation of a flat surface simply will not do for our tent platforms. He orders the excavation team to continue hacking away with their ice axes until the surface is as flat as a tabletop.

"Remember, guys, we could be stuck here for a week," he says, "and you don't want to be sleeping on a lumpy surface. Let's take the time to do it right."

Catching Brad and me in an idle moment, Kent dispatches us on an errand to grab plastic sleds lying in a pile by the airstrip. The sleds had been left there by a departing expedition.

"Do we need to ask permission?" I ask.

"No," says Kent. "Just grab them. If someone tries to stop you, come get me."

"Who do they belong to?"

"In five minutes, they'll belong to us!"

As Brad and I slink downslope on our felonious mission, I'm thinking that there must be a sign-out sheet at the official Denali "sled rental" booth. It's unlike the regulation-happy Park Service to manage gear items so lackadaisically.

Determined not to linger near the scene of the crime, I grab a nested stack of 10 or 12 sleds and start sprinting back to camp. Brad's cooler head prevails.

"Hey, wait a minute—let's make sure we get good ones."

Some of the flimsy plastic sleds—$10 kids' models that you'd buy at your local hardware store—are cracked and gouged. Others are nearly pristine—remarkable considering the punishment they've endured on the mountain. After five minutes of sorting, we return to camp with a full complement of serviceable sleds, and no one tries to stop us.

Awaiting the arrival of the rest of our team, we join the others in erecting our tents. Ice axes and ski poles are buried as "dead men" to secure the guy lines.

Our ranks, I learn, have just been reduced from 12 to 11. Matt shares the news that his friend Doug has decided to bail; Denali wasn't in the cards for him this summer. While Jay was shuttling us onto the glacier, Doug was en route to the Anchorage airport and an early flight home, never mind the fact that he would have to forfeit the $3,800 fee for the guided climb, round-trip airfare from the East Coast, and the thousands of dollars he had spent on gear.

"The weird thing is," says Matt, "Doug's the one who talked me into this expedition. I wouldn't be here if it weren't for him."

"That guy seemed to be the toughest climber among us," I say. "It looked like he'd been living at the gym for the past six months, hooked up to a protein drip."

"Yeah, he's fit all right," says Matt. "But something else was obviously working on him."

Later on I will discover that Doug—despite being in peak physical shape—had not adequately closed the door on some pressing personal issues back home. "The timing just wasn't right," Doug tells me after my own return home.

As we will learn higher up on the mountain, all manner of obstacles can thwart a climber's summit bid, be they winds, storms, or simply a head and heart full of doubts. For Doug, the Denali summit would have been a Pyrrhic victory, eclipsed by the regret of having abandoned more important—and more meaningful—challenges back home in Pennsylvania.

Within two hours, the last two planes deliver the balance of our team, including Gary and Joe along with most of the group gear, which they've packed in G.I. duffel bags. Nearly half of the 115 pounds each of us will schlep up the mountain represents group gear, including three MSR-XGK stoves and one-liter fuel bottles; three heavy heat shields to insulate the stoves from the snow; two 10-quart cook pots; 275 breakfasts and an equal number of dinners (rations for 11 people for 25 days); eight three-foot-long aluminum pickets for setting running belays along exposed sections of the route (a running belay is a climbing rope threaded through carabiners attached to the top of pickets driven deep into the snow); and the five large scoop shovels and two ice saws that arrived with Kent. Added to that is the 20 gallons of stove fuel dispensed by the Park Service base-camp manager.

Kent gathers several of us and we walk to the ranger tent to pick up our disbursement of fuel. The ranger opens the tent flap, revealing hundreds of gallon cans of white gas organized in orderly stacks. As he hands over our supply, he labels each can with our expedition number. Before leaving the mountain, we will be obligated to return all empty cans and account for any that are missing—including those we've donated to other expeditions low on supplies—or face a stiff fine. This accounting system is one more facet of the Park Service's efforts to keep the mountain clean.

CAMP IS SET BY EARLY AFTERNOON, and Ken, Nat, and I lay out our sleeping pads and bags in the cramped enclosure of the tent. I've camped long enough to know that sleeping spots, once established, seldom vary for the duration of a trip; anxious to avoid the center slot, which would pin me between two sleeping bodies, I angle for a place on the side. I position my bag with the head toward the door—the easiest avenue of escape, should I suffer a claustrophobia-induced panic attack in the tent's tight confines. Ken and Nat, opting for the more traditional orientation, place their feet toward the door.

Once all our gear is stowed inside the tent, there isn't a square foot of surface that's not occupied by clothing, down booties, gloves and mittens, water bottles, nylon ditty sacks, or food bags. Even the mesh gear loft and side pockets are crammed full. It's hard to imagine enduring a single night in this crowded space, much less riding out a five-day storm in it.

Here in this tent, I suspect, I will wrestle more demons than any I'll have to confront on the open, airy slopes of the mountain. (The events of coming days will prove me right.) I envy Brad and Clay; in the wake of Doug's departure, they are flush with floor space in their three-person tent—even though they will have to haul the extra weight.

Gary calls us out to prepare our sleds and instructs us to tie lash loops through the holes around the outer edges. We attach carabiners to the front loops, then clip on our 20 yards of one-inch webbing. The webbing, tied into a long loop, will connect the sleds to our packs. Bungee cords hooked into the sleds' side loops will secure the gear in the bed.

Around 6:30 p.m., Kent turns his attention to preparing dinner. With his meticulous attention to detail, he seems perfectly suited for the task. He sends me out with a shovel and a plastic bag to gather snow. Melted snow will rehydrate our freeze-dried meals; it will also provide the gallon of water each of us will consume per day to hydrate our bodies and help stave off frostbite and altitude sickness.

"Make sure the snow is *clean*," Kent says. "In particular, avoid the *yellow* stuff."

I wander 30 yards from camp, fully aware that I'm walking above a chaos of hidden crevasses and that I could plunge through a fragile snow bridge at any moment. Finding a patch of snow that looks pristine and unmolested, I scoop the bag full and return it to Kent.

"Clean?" he asks.

"Well, I plucked out a used condom and a syringe with a broken needle, but other than that, yeah, it's clean."

"Very funny. Ever heard of the 'mung'?"

"Didn't Daryl Miller mention that in his orientation?"

"Yeah, he did. It's mountaineering shorthand for the shits. You drink water from dirty snow, and you've got the mung. That could end your trip."

Kent—whose penchant for caution and safety is notable, even among guides—has a fondness for cataloging the many events that could occasion an early departure from the mountain. Over time, these recitations will evolve into epic, Wagnerian lectures that encompass more warnings than the label on a bottle of prescription medication. They include (but are hardly limited to) altitude sickness, a wind-shredded tent, a crevasse fall, an unarrested slide down a slope, throwing a crampon, inadequate fitness level, frostbite, altitude-related anorexia or lethargy, penetration of a body cavity by any of an ice ax's sharp protuberances, noncompliance with a guide's instructions, improper use of alpine tools, heat exhaustion, snow blindness, insanity brought on by prolonged confinement, and now "the mung."

As Kent cooks, we gather around Joe Horiskey, who has become the target of our ceaseless questions about our route, conditions on the mountain, and identification of the prominent peaks around us. Joe's extensive knowledge of the mountain earned him an acknowledgment in James Michener's *Alaska;* some of the climbers on the team chose this expedition expressly for the opportunity to climb with him.

If there is a counterpart to Kent's cautious intensity, it is Joe's laid-back attitude about life in general and mountaineering in particular. To Joe, the alpine world is one big vertical playground. He seems determined to frolic rather than fret.

I had talked to Joe on the phone a couple of times prior to the trip, expressing neurotic concerns about the capacity of my backpack, the insulating qualities of my clothes and sleeping bag, and my level of fitness.

His responses were always the same: "Relax. No big deal. We'll make it work. You're gonna be just fine."

Unlike Gary and Kent, whose role on this trip is to lead, Joe, who just turned 50, seems to be climbing as much for himself as he is for his clients. As a co-owner of RMI, he is immersed in restructuring the organization and refining its mission in the increasingly competitive realm of guided climbing. Both tasks have tethered him to his desk back in the RMI offices. He therefore regards this expedition as a much-needed break from routine—and a chance to return to the peak that, in the world of Alaskan mountaineering, is as closely associated with his name as Everest is with Edmund Hillary's.

A black RMI ball cap rests at a skewed angle atop a dense shock of white hair cut in a straight line at Joe's eyebrows. A three-day growth of white stubble surrounds a toothy grin. But Joe's gut bears testament to his having eaten very well during the off-season.

One of the guides on the winter mountaineering seminar on Rainier had alerted me to Joe's easy nature and knowledge of Denali: "Joe's just a great guy; he understands Denali about as well as anyone, and he really knows how to have a good time on the mountain. Between you and me, though, he probably could have spent more time in the gym."

Joe may not be the picture of fitness at the moment, but his familiarity with this mountain is unassailable. He has climbed Denali so many times that he's lost count. When I ask him, he scratches his beard, shakes his head, and finally answers, "Thirteen summits? Fourteen? Hell, I don't remember. Let's just say a bunch."

On his inaugural climb in 1972, he spent 33 days on the mountain without summiting. The next year, he never got above 18,000 feet, but in 1974 he had the perfect trip: "Eighteen days to the summit and two back down. Classic. Just classic."

Joe visually guides us through the surrounding mountains with his finger, pointing to notable peaks and describing the events that he's witnessed on each one over nearly three decades of climbing in the Alaska Range. Eventually, he gestures toward Denali's summit. The sky is cloudless, a deep cobalt blue.

"*Perfect* summit day up there," he says. "It's zero, light wind. There are people on top right now. I guar-an-*tee* it. Denali climbers dream about days like this."

Though the eight clients on our team regard Joe with the utmost respect and would never dream of interrupting him when he's in the middle of one of his epic stories, the surrounding mountains are less deferential.

A deep rumble to the west draws my gaze toward Mount Foraker. There, a solid wall of snow and ice is sliding 5,000 feet or more down from the upper slopes, kicking up an expanding billow of white that obscures the entire upper half of the mountain. The thunder, which shakes the snow under our feet, continues for several seconds before the ice blocks come to rest at the margins of the Kahiltna Glacier.

I've witnessed smaller avalanches on Rainier, which were always worth a glance, but they were tame trickles compared with this cascade of ice that seems potent enough to grind a rope team into a few teaspoons of flesh, bone, and nylon. Avalanches, though spectacular, have killed relatively few climbers on Denali. The risk is minimal on the Washburn Route—our planned path of ascent—which deliberately dodges most of the mountain's avalanche-prone slopes.

"Wow!" says Joe, once the rumble stops. "That was a good one. A darned good one."

Over the coming weeks, these ground-shaking showers of falling snow and ice will become a familiar element of our surroundings. Unnervingly, I will never succeed in differentiating among three remarkably similar sounds: a passing jet aircraft, an MSR expedition stove roaring at full blast, or a potentially life-extinguishing avalanche.

"Hots!" Kent calls out from the kitchen, and the rest of us stare at him without the slightest notion of what we're supposed to do.

Kent responds to our inaction in typical fashion.

"Hots! Hot drinks! Grab your cups, and come and get it!"

Before Kent loads the cook pots with the makings of the evening meal, he heats the water to boiling for us to make hot drinks from tea bags or powdered cider or coffee. On Denali, "hots" are served morning and night. The morning regimen signals the start of the day and a much-needed infusion of caffeine for the coffee drinkers. The evening offering is the equivalent of cocktail hour back in civilization.

Tonight, still less than 10 hours from the restaurants of Talkeetna, we amble indifferently toward Kent, clutching our mugs. Higher on the mountain, we will lie awake in our tents, refusing to emerge into the frigid morning air until we hear Kent's call. After a long day of climbing, we will cluster eagerly around the cook tent, waiting for those telltale tendrils of steam to rise from the pot.

Half an hour later, Kent calls us to dinner. I am not the least bit finicky about what I eat; I tend to value quantity over quality, so I approach Kent's steaming pot of food with an open mind. This evening's fare is ramen noodles, canned chicken, and partially rehydrated green beans, corn, and carrots, all swimming in a thin sauce that's more gray than white. I lever out a spoonful of the stuff and ease it into my mouth expecting to be underwhelmed but satisfied. Instead I'm transported back to the cafeteria at Miami Hills Elementary School in Cincinnati, Ohio, where a bearded lunch lady is leering at me through cat's-eye glasses as she spoons out odious dollops of food unfit for a prison inmate.

When I say that expedition food is remarkably bad, I am being kind. In 22 years of eating camp glop, I have never tasted anything that even remotely compares to it—with the possible exception of the night in the southern Appalachians when I poured three ounces of peppermint camp soap into a pot of noodles, thinking it was cooking oil. To have lost my appetite at 7,200 feet does not bode well for me higher on the mountain, where the onset of altitude-related anorexia is almost guaranteed. I force down half a bowl of the stew, scrape the rest into the "spooge hole"—a square ditch carved in the ice near the kitchen for disposing of uneaten food—and grab two packs of salmon jerky from my food bag.

DURING THE IDLE HOURS AFTER DINNER, most of us eschew conversation in favor of watching the sun fade behind the western peaks. Then the magical colors of twilight emerge.

When the sun is high in the Alaskan sky, the snow becomes a monotonous, almost featureless expanse of white. It assaults the eye with such blinding intensity that you can feel your pupils draw down to tiny pinpoints, even though they're shielded by dark glacier glasses. The visual interest lies in the grandeur of the mountains, not in the subtlety of their features.

But late in the day, as slanting light blankets the slopes, a remarkable transformation takes place: The alpine world begins to exude a rich palette of muted hues and pastels. The hard ice that edges crevasses becomes an intricate network of turquoise veins, the cracked surfaces of glaciers glow soft pink, and deep-purple defines the sharp angles of jumbled seracs. Craggy gray and black rocks outline the spines of ridges and mottle vertical walls of ice. Deep in the shadow of overhanging cornices, a dozen shades of blue ice form fractured mosaics.

As a mountaineering photographer, Bill Hatcher has come to value the colors of twilight on the mountainscape. As the rest of us scamper to our tents to escape the plunging temperature, his attention is galvanized by the surrounding mountains bathed in evening light.

My tent mates, Ken and Nat, and I settle into a routine we'll repeat nightly for the next three weeks. Nat smiles at pictures of his wife and their infant son, Clark. Ken and I insert headphone buds into our ears and fish for FM stations on our mini-radios. I draw in an oldies station broadcast from Fairbanks.

The contact with the outside world seems ludicrous, laughable. I learn that the Godfather of Soul, James Brown, is coming to Anchorage, as is Jarred, the guy who supposedly cut his body weight in half by eating a certain brand of submarine sandwiches. A steakhouse is running a special on New York strips—the last thing I need to hear after my first run-in with ramen noodles.

Serenaded by the Righteous Brothers' "You've Lost That Lovin' Feelin'," I delve into a Ziploc bag that holds pictures and letters from my family. As I will every night of the expedition, I drift off to sleep thinking about home.

THE NEXT SOUND I HEAR is the sputter of expedition stoves coming to life. Though it's only 8:30 a.m., the sun has already cleared the eastern peaks and is lighting the tent walls. Above me, a half-inch layer of ice— the frozen respiration of three slumbering climbers—coats the nylon ceiling. I twist gently in my bag and bump the side wall, and a cascade of ice crystals falls onto my face. A tube of sunscreen and a water bottle lying forgotten on the floor beside me have frozen solid during the night.

I crawl from my sleeping bag and into the crisp air. Shivering, I pull on my clothes and boots and emerge into the sunlight. The temperature is now in the 20s. Kent looks like he's been up for hours, as does Bill, who's sitting on a block of ice, patiently clutching his camera.

I drop two coffee bags into my mug and head toward Kent's steaming pot. He fills my mug and food bowl with boiling water, and I stir in three packets of instant oatmeal. Breakfast goes down easy; it's impossible to screw up instant oatmeal.

I feel the coffee stimulate my digestive system and realize that my moment of reckoning has come. A short line has formed at the crapper, and I wait 10 minutes until the most conspicuous seat in the house is unoccupied.

Barring a bout with the mung, the two full rolls of toilet paper I've packed should see me through the trip. I grab a roll from the Ziploc and make my move.

At some point during the process, which seems to take much longer than it does in actuality, I notice that a woman has queued up and is watching me. I place the roll next to me on the plywood seat, stand to pull up my bibs, and then watch helplessly as my TP tumbles into the hole and hits bottom with a sickening splat.

I have just squandered half my reserves of a substance so highly prized among climbers that it is commonly referred to as "mountain money."

I return to camp, hoping that someone has brought a surplus.

I ask Brad.

After he stops laughing, he says, "Nope. Got just enough. Sorry."

I ask Ken and Nat. Same response.

Before long, the whole camp is enjoying a good laugh at my expense.

Then I remember Bill Hatcher's claim that whatever salmon jerky I don't eat I can use for barter. I grab three packs and head off to broker a deal.

The first climber I ask, like me, is heading up the mountain, so he's determined to hang onto what he's got. But he directs me to a guy who has just come down from the summit and is ready to fly out.

"He may be willing to deal," he says. "If he has any left."

I humbly approach. The climber is sprawled in the sun on his sleeping pad, looking like the mountain beat him up pretty bad.

"Through a chain of events I'd rather not elaborate on," I venture, "I happen to be short one roll of toilet paper. But I've got three packages of *very tasty* salmon jerky here to offer you in exchange for any extra TP you might have."

He responds with a hearty laugh.

"Well, that pretty much sucks," he says. "Tell you what. I've got half a roll that I don't need, and I'll give it to you for *one* pack of jerky. In a couple of hours, I'll have access to all the food—and toilet paper—I want. You're gonna need those calories up high."

"Deal. And thanks."

"No problem. Hey, good luck up there. I hope you make it."

"Me too. If I do, I'll commemorate your contribution in print. That's a promise."

When I return to camp, Gary, who has been monitoring my dilemma, asks, "How'd you make out?"

"Bill was right," I say. "This salmon jerky is solid gold."

TWO HOURS LATER, we've packed our gear and are standing in a circle around Gary and Joe, who are sorting the group gear into 11 more-or-less equal piles. Though no one's saying so, we're all eyeing the piles that contain the fewest awkward items—shovels and cook pots. Someone makes a premature grab.

"Hey, hold on a minute," says Joe. "Wait till we're done. They're all the same, for Christ's sake!"

"Yeah, maybe so," says Dick. "But some of them *look* heavier."

In a few minutes, Joe and Gary move out of the way, and Gary shouts, "Okay, grab a bundle!"

We dive on our preferred piles in a montane version of musical chairs. In the end, we all wind up with roughly 40 pounds of stuff and begin lashing it to our sleds. Since top-heavy sleds tend to turn over, the goal is to create the sleekest profile. I position my snowshoes on top, just in case I need them, along with my crampons and ice ax. We won't be using crampons until we reach the steep slope of Motorcycle Hill at 11,000 feet, and we'll set out using ski poles rather than ice axes.

The sleds—known affectionately as "pigs"—will have to be hauled all the way to the camp at 14,200 feet; beyond that, the steep terrain makes it difficult to tow loads.

The plan is to single-carry—move with full loads—to 9,700 feet. At that point we will begin double-carrying—dividing our loads in half, carrying half up and caching it under four feet of snow, then returning to lower camp to sleep. It's all part of a strategy to help us adapt to high altitude.

Though the West Buttress Route stretches only 16 miles from base camp to summit, climbing teams carry with them enough food, fuel, and gear for expeditions that can last as long as a month. The process of dividing loads and carrying them piecemeal up the mountainside makes the enormous equipment burden more manageable. It also allows climbers to spend a few hours at increased altitudes as they carry loads higher but return to lower altitudes to sleep. During sleep, the body's respiration falls, making climbers more susceptible to altitude sickness. Mountaineers have practiced this "climb high, sleep low" strategy since the early days of expedition climbing.

An hour later, we're positioned at the clip-in points along the three ropes. I take the slot right behind Kent. He may be intense and a marginal cook, but having seen him in action on Rainier I have the utmost respect for his mountaineering skills. Bill clips in behind me. Because we're down to 11 climbers on three ropes, one of the rope teams—ours—will consist of only three climbers. Bill will wear the excess rope coiled around his shoulder.

We clip the ropes into our seat harnesses and shoulder our packs. The rope runs behind me through a carabiner at the center of my sled and is attached by a prusik loop at the rear. In theory, at least, the prusik will keep the sled in line and prevent it from sliding laterally on side slopes.

"Ready to start climbing?" Kent calls to us.

"Hell, yes," we respond in unison. And at last we begin making our way up Denali. Ironically, the inaugural stretch of the "climb" involves *descending* 500 feet along a shallow slope known as Heartbreak Hill. Because hikers, climbers, and anyone else who sets his sights on a distant and lofty goal tends to obsess on ground gained, the surrender of even a few vertical feet inspires thoughts of mutiny.

Perhaps sensing this, Kent yells back, "You'll love this grade on the way up, but when we're humping back to the landing strip, worn out by three weeks of climbing, you'll hate it."

Lest anyone confuse us with skilled mountaineers, we have to stop every 100 feet or so to make adjustments to our "pigs" or to right them after they have flipped.

I can sense the frustration in Kent's voice as he calls out, "Okay, guys, are we *finally* ready?"

At the base of Heartbreak Hill, the ascending grade tames the careening sleds, but we feel the full weight of our loads for the first time. As we begin to move up the Kahiltna Glacier, following a well-worn path directly in its middle, I have to tug the sled into motion with every step. This gives me a painful cramp in my hips that will stay with me until we park the sled at 14,200 feet. The cramps I can live with. My thighs feel sturdy, and my breathing is regular and steady. The climbing is much easier than I had anticipated; all those training hikes up Frozen Head must be paying off.

Some of the other climbers are not faring as well. At one point we move off the trail to take a break, and the other teams pull up parallel to us. Matt is pressure breathing like a freight train, and Clay utters a phrase I will hear frequently over the next few weeks: "That sure was a long pull for a flatlander." Though Clay appears to be fit, the effort he's exerting on this gentle grade suggests he may be the weak link.

TODAY'S TREK to the base of Ski Hill at 7,800 feet will represent our smallest daily gain in elevation (600 feet) but our longest linear trek: 5.5 miles, or one-third the total distance from base camp to the summit. During our toughest days of climbing, we will ascend 3,000 feet or more but gain less than two linear miles in the process. This is why mountaineers prize vertical feet over linear distance in tabulating their progress.

By midafternoon the temperature has climbed to 80°F, allowing us to strip down to shirt-sleeves and bandannas worn Foreign Legion-style beneath our ball caps to protect us from the searing sun. Dozens of climbers—many of them schussing downhill on mountaineering skis with their sleds positioned in front of them—pass by. About a quarter of the climbers we see on the mountain will be traveling on such specialized skis—high-tech devices equipped with bindings that can be adjusted up or down to provide a horizontal platform for boots, regardless of the slope.

On the way up, the skis are outfitted with "climbing skins" that attach from tip to tail. The skins feature a textured nap that slides freely forward but grabs and prevents the skis from sliding backward. The devices are named for the sealskin strips that skiers attached to the bottoms of their blades before synthetic skins were produced. On the descent, the climber locks his heels down into the binding and schusses downslope like any alpine skier.

During our brief exchanges with the skiers, we find that the stable weather has increased the summit success rate. One skier describes 20 or more climbers occupying the summit ridge at one time two days earlier. Indeed, some of these skiers summited Denali as recently as yesterday; that means they have descended 10,000 feet from high camp in less than a day.

Near the base of Ski Hill, Kent starts rest-stepping like a robot in hyperdrive, and we soon pull away from Gary's and Joe's rope teams. Once we all stop for a rest break, Joe lets Kent know how he feels about the pace.

"My God, Kent, you're climbing like a gut-shot cougar!" he says between gasps. "How about slowing down a bit?"

"Okay, Joe," Kent answers, and with that we pull off the trail for a break. Though Joe is theoretically Kent's equal on this trip (and both are subordinate to Gary, the expedition leader), Joe outranks both Gary and Kent in the RMI employee hierarchy. That, combined with Joe's extensive experience on Denali, will obfuscate the trip leadership in some interesting ways.

Kent might have answered Joe's admonishment to slow down by urging Joe to speed up, but for the sake of group harmony he opts not to. Though the three guides will occasionally be at odds over various decisions, for the most part they present a unified front, comporting themselves like old friends and valued climbing companions—which, of course, they are. Joe has been with RMI for more than 30 years, Gary for nearly 20, and Kent for 5.

During our 10- to 15-minute rest breaks—observed by Gary religiously at one-hour intervals—we slip from our packs, pull on extra clothing layers to retain heat, and, at the guides' urging, eat and drink. From here we can see our day's destination at 7,800 feet, marked by a cluster of snow walls left by earlier expeditions. To our right, a lone climber skirts the base of mountains a quarter-mile to the east, navigating with a loaded sled through an eruption of large crevasses along the East Fork of the Kahiltna.

I've read that solo climbers sometimes tie aluminum ladders to their waists to span crevasses, should they take a fall, but I can make out no such device attached to this climber. Though we wonder what might have led him that far off course, we have little concern for his safety—a function of our ignorance of the mountain and its hazards.

Joe sees things differently.

"My God," he says. "That idiot is walking right into the Valley of Death. He's all by himself. If he falls into a crevasse, he's totally screwed."

We watch for a few minutes until the climber's form vanishes behind a rise in the glacier.

"He may be heading for the Cassin Ridge," Joe surmises. "Probably joining some other climbers. You don't solo on the Cassin Ridge."

The Cassin, an Alaska Grade V on a scale that tops out at V, is the most difficult climb to Denali's summit. It is also one of the most respected big-mountain routes in the world. This highly technical route—pioneered in 1961 by a team of Italians led by Ricardo Cassin—gains 9,000 vertical feet in a linear distance of two miles, accessing Denali's summit cone from the south.

We set up camp remarkably faster than we did the night before. Even after one day, we seem to know the drill. Gary fashions a crapper out of snow blocks and rigs a plastic bag open using wands. The set-up calls for precision and careful aim—qualities conspicuously absent in the climbers who use the device before me. Once I'm finished, I walk directly back toward camp. Bill stops me just before I reach the snow walls.

"Look out," he says, pointing. "Crevasse."

I look down and notice the telltale lips of blue ice bridged by packed snow.

"Thanks. I definitely wouldn't want that dump to be my last contribution to the world."

By the time the tents are erected, Kent is poised over his stoves. Tonight's offering: Mouse-gray chicken breasts, granite-gray powdered mashed potatoes, and a taupe-colored gravy laced with enough MSG to induce infarctions in otherwise healthy people. I am grateful that my toilet-paper benefactor deprived me of one, not three, servings of salmon jerky.

After dinner, Kent heads downhill to visit some friends we passed on the way up. Dick pops the top on a bottle of ibuprofen. "Ah, good old Vitamin I," he says, downing two pills. "Old guys like me need to take their vitamins."

GARY PREVIEWS OUR ROUTE for tomorrow: We will ascend the 1,000-foot Ski Hill and camp just below Kahiltna Pass, a notorious spot where weather from the north and south converge to form an almost perpetual storm system. Our cumulative gain will be just under 2,000 feet.

I lay my sleeping pad against an ice-block wall, facing west, remove my boots and socks, and lie back in the sun. It's 7 p.m., but I can feel my skin burning. I hang my bandanna from the brim of my hat to protect my face and doze off. An hour later I awaken to the sensation of freezing feet. The sun has vanished behind the western peaks, and the temperature has started its nightly slide.

An hour later I'm sound asleep in my tent, enjoying a common side-effect of altitude: a night of outrageous dreams. This is the first of numerous bizarre nocturnal side trips I'll take over coming weeks.

The night-long dream sequence culminates with me in the Alabama home of my former mother-in-law, where she is offering to set me up with my choice of her neighbors. One of the neighbors is blonde. The other neighbor is brunette. Both are beautiful young Southern belles.

I'm conducting exhaustive interviews with each one, asking what they have to offer that would be really special. The brunette says, "Here, honey, let me show you." She starts to peel off her shirt, revealing the most amazing set of—

"Hots!"

"Shit!"

"What's wrong, Brother Brill?" Ken asks, sitting up in his bag and rubbing his eyes.

"I was having the best dream of my life. If Kent Wagner had waited two minutes, I'd be the happiest climber on this mountain."

"That good, huh?"

"Un-be-*lieve*-a-ble. But very weird. My ex-mother-in-law was pimping for me."

"You must have had a very special mother-in-law."

"The best—but she never would have gone *that* far!"

Chapter Eight

A SHORT HISTORY
OF A TALL MOUNTAIN[1]

SEVERAL HUNDRED MILLION YEARS AGO, a Denali expedition would have required scuba gear rather than mountaineering togs: What is now the highest peak in North America began its life beneath the ocean with a clash of tectonic plates that heaved the seafloor upward, creating a dramatic arc of mountains that stretches 600 miles and divides southcentral Alaska from the interior plateau. The Alaska Range comprises a jumbled mass of ocean sediments and terrestrial lands, overlain with fractured granite that intruded during the mountain's chaotic inception and now forms the craggy spine of Denali's high ridges.

Eons after this geologic upheaval, the humans who populated the interior of ancient Alaska accorded Denali a central role in their creation myths and legends. One of the more striking, "The Second Making of Man," accounts for both the creation of Denali and the ancestry of modern humans. It was translated from the native Ten'a (DEE-nay)

---

[1] A number of excellent books provide detailed histories of climbing on Denali. Among them are Terris Moore's *Mt. McKinley: The Pioneer Climbs*; *Denali: A Literary Anthology*, edited by Bill Sherwonit; *Mount McKinley: The Conquest of Denali* by Bradford Washburn and David Roberts; and Bill Sherwonit's *To the Top of Denali: Climbing Adventures of North America's Highest Peak*. For additional sources, see the bibliography on page 243.

language by Julius Jetté, a Canadian-born Jesuit missionary who arrived in Alaska in 1898 and spent many years living with the Athapaskan Indians.

The myth, which has echoes in biblical accounts of Adam and Eve and Noah's Ark, involves a hopeful suitor who crosses an ocean expanse to court a woman on the opposite shore. Though she rebuffs his approach, a member of her tribe offers the man a baby girl to take with him on the return voyage. As he departs, the woman who had declined his advances gets swallowed up by mud at the edge of the sea, whereupon her vengeful mother sends a pack of bears in pursuit of the man's canoe. The bears churn the ocean waters so violently as to drown the inhabitants of the woman's village—and, presumably, those of the man's village as well). Attempting to quiet the seas, the man hurls his harpoon at the waves, then passes out and collapses into the hull of his boat. He awakens in a dense forest to discover that the wave crest pierced by his harpoon has risen to form a mountain: Denali, or "the High One." The baby girl, meanwhile, has magically blossomed into a woman, and she and the man repeople the Earth.

While this and other Native Alaskan myths undertook to explain the great mountain's origin, the Native Alaskans themselves did not venture too near the mountain nor feel particularly compelled to explore it. That distinction would belong to the white navigators, explorers, prospectors, and trappers who started to arrive in the 18th century; they deemed the mountain an object of conquest, the region surrounding it a source of riches.

Captain George Vancouver, who surveyed and charted the northwest coast of America for the British Admiralty in the late 18th century, was probably the first European explorer to study the profile of Denali. From his vantage point in Cook Inlet near modern-day Anchorage, Vancouver described "distant stupendous mountains covered with snow, and apparently detached from one another." He was likely glimpsing Denali and 17,400-foot Mount Foraker, the second highest peak in the Alaska Range.

A century passed without much exploration inland from Cook Inlet. Though settlements had sprung up along the coast, their inhabitants—primarily trappers and traders affiliated with the Russian American Company—showed little interest in the interior mountains. Indeed, most pioneers regarded the peaks primarily as impediments to travel.

In 1866, Boston-born William H. Dall traveled up the Yukon River and glimpsed the full arc of the Alaska Range from a distance of nearly 200 miles. Dall was the first to include the Alaska Range on a map, which he produced in 1870. But his distant vantage allowed him scant appreciation for the extreme height of the mountains. Not so Arthur Harper, an Irish-born prospector who traveled the Tanana River and viewed the Alaska Range from the north, near the site of present-day Fairbanks: Harper described Denali as "the great ice mountain."

The first American name for Denali is ascribed to prospector Frank Densmore, who viewed the mountain from the Kuskokwim River, less than 100 miles away, in 1889. So enthusiastic were his descriptions of the peak that his fellow prospectors came to call it "Densmore's Mountain."

Densmore's name stuck for eight short years before Princeton-educated prospector William A. Dickey lent the mountain the official designation it bears today. Dickey was also the first to arouse national interest in Denali by publishing an article, "Discoveries in Alaska," in *The New York Sun* in 1897. Defying fellow prospectors who supported Democratic presidential candidate William Jennings Bryan, Dickey proposed naming the mountain for the Republican presidential candidate (and later 25th President), William McKinley. The name Mount McKinley has persisted, despite a century of protest to restore the Native Alaskan name, Denali, as the summit's official designation. Dickey also accurately estimated the mountain's height—a remarkable feat, based as it was on a purely visual assessment.

"We have no doubt that this peak is the highest in North America," Dickey wrote in his *Sun* article, "and estimate that it is over 20,000 feet high."

Five years later, Alfred Brooks, working for the U.S. Geological Survey (USGS), became the first explorer to actually place a boot on Denali's flanks. Dispatched by the USGS to help map the Alaskan interior in 1902, Brooks produced a wealth of information on the mountain, including a *National Geographic* article entitled "Plans for Climbing Mt. McKinley."

Based on his survey of the mountainscape, Brooks proposed three possible routes for approaching the mountain. His favored route, which attacked the mountain from the north, was followed by most of the early expeditions and ultimately led the first climbers to the mountain's summit in 1913. The intervening years, however, would see folly, dashed dreams, and astounding feats of daring before man first trod on Denali's snow-capped apex.

IN 1903, TWO EXPEDITIONS—one led by federal judge James Wickersham, the second by explorer Frederick Cook—acted on the information provided by Brooks' article to set out for the Alaska Range. Neither came close to bagging the summit.

Following the Peter's Glacier, which reaches to the west of Denali's summit and flows north toward the McKinley River, Wickersham's team ascended to about 8,000 feet on the Jeffery Glacier before confronting (in Wickersham's words) "a tremendous precipice beyond which we cannot go." The wall, which rises nearly 15,000 feet in four miles and presented an insuperable obstacle indeed for the climbers, now bears Wickersham's name. The Wickersham Wall boasts one of the world's largest vertical rises—so monumental that it was not scaled until 1963, when members of the Harvard Mountaineering Club managed to inch their way up it.

Cook's team, which departed two months behind Wickersham, included a botanist, a photographer, a prospector, and a horsepacker—no one with even modest mountaineering experience. While Wickersham had approached the mountain from the north, Cook opted instead to follow the rugged route from Cook Inlet to the south of Denali. Robert Dunn, a reporter for the New York *Commercial Advertiser*, chronicled the trip—including the ineptitude, infighting, and constant bickering—in a series of articles he published in *Outing* magazine. He eventually published a book on the experience, *The Shameless Diary of an Explorer,* which remains in print to this day. The expedition succeeded in placing a climber at the dizzying height of just over 11,000 feet.

Cook returned to the mountain in 1906, this time with skilled mountaineers, including Herschel Parker, a professor at Columbia University, and artist and climber Belmore Browne. Again the team approached the mountain from Cook Inlet to the south, beginning in June. Two months later, they came trooping back homeward, defeated and for the most part convinced that the mountain was unclimbable from the south.

The lone dissenters from that view were Cook himself and expedition horse packer Ed Barrill, both of whom abruptly turned on their heels and headed back toward the Alaska Range. A few short weeks later, Cook returned, claiming to have reached the summit of Denali and insisting that he had the photo to prove it. The photo depicted Barrill holding an American flag atop the "summit."

In his book *To the Top of the Continent* Cook wrote, "We edged up along a steep snowy ridge and over the heaven-scraped granite to the top. AT LAST! The soul-stirring task was crowned with victory; the top of our continent was under our feet." As it turns out, both Cook and Barrill were standing knee-deep not in snow but in bullshit.

Though initially hailed as a conquering hero, Cook and his claim was later soundly debunked by Browne, Cook's former expedition mate, who insisted that Cook could not have reached the top in the time available to him. By then, however, Cook was basking in the celebrity of his 1908 claim (likewise subsequently discredited) of having been the first to reach the North Pole in 1908.

Browne cried foul after studying Cook's original summit photo. There, barely visible in the background, he detected a shadowy peak rising thousands of feet behind Barrill. In 1910, Browne and Professor Parker went back to the mountain, promising to return with proof that Cook's story was false. In the meantime, Barrill, who at first had stood behind Cook's claim, began to recant, admitting that the photo had been staged about 8,000 feet up the mountain.

Retracing the route Cook had described, which followed the Ruth Glacier (named for Cook's daughter) and approached the summit from the southeast, Browne and Parker identified a peak that looked eerily similar to Cook's ersatz summit. If Cook's improbably rapid ascent did not kill his claims, the two men's restaged photo nailed the coffin shut. Browne and Parker—not content to shatter Cook's feet of clay—went on to climb within a few hundred feet of the summit before retreating in the face of a blizzard. They rested at their high camp—about 16,500 feet— and made a second attempt on the summit the next day. Once again, however, they were driven back by a storm. (Unlike Cook's purported accomplishments, those of the Browne-Parker team were later substantiated by photographs and a detailed description of their route of ascent.)

As it turns out, the men's failure was fortuitous. During their descent from the mountain, a major earthquake shook the Alaska Range, destroying parts of the very ridge that Browne and Parker had followed toward the summit. Had they lingered high on the mountain, mustering their strength and resources for yet a third attempt, they very likely would have remained there forever.

FEW STORIES DEPICT a less likely troupe of would-be climbers: Outfitted with homemade crampons and ice tools and wearing bib overalls, long underwear, wool shirts, and canvas parkas, they achieved one of the most spectacular feats in mountaineering history.

"They" were a group of Alaskan miners, or Sourdoughs. Exasperated at the encroachment of mountaineering outsiders on their home turf, they launched the Sourdough Expedition in 1909. According to Bradford Washburn and David Roberts in Mount McKinley: The Conquest of Denali, the expedition may have begun as a barroom wager: In the fall of that year, a Fairbanks tavern owner named Bill McPhee offered $500 to the first person to scale Denali—and return with proof of the exploit.

Tom Lloyd, a Welshman who had been drawn to Alaska by the Klondike gold rush of 1896-1899, accepted McPhee's challenge. He organized a seven-man climbing party that left Fairbanks in December 1909 with packhorses, a mule, and a sled-dog team for ferrying supplies. The men also toted a 14-foot-long spruce pole and an American flag measuring 72 square feet. Their plan was to erect the pole and raise the flag atop the summit—where, they hoped, it would be visible from Fairbanks about 150 miles away, thus proving their claim of having reached the apex.

An altercation between Lloyd and a professional surveyor named Charles Davidson prompted the departure of three of the seven Sourdoughs. The remaining four—Lloyd, Billy Taylor, Pete Anderson, and Charles McGonagall—continued on, approaching the mountain from the north via the Muldrow Glacier.

In April, five months after the expedition set out, Lloyd showed up in Fairbanks, insistent that he and his three climbing partners had scaled the mountain. Not only had they reached the North Peak, Lloyd professed, but they had crested the 850-foot-higher South Peak as well.

As Terris Moore has recounted in his comprehensive *Mt. McKinley: The Pioneer Climbs*, the *New York Sun* picked up the story from the *Fairbanks Daily Times* and ran it on the front page. President William Howard Taft called from Washington, D.C., to congratulate the expedition leader. Within just a few days of their conversation, however, the *New York Times* published a Page 1 story headlined "McKinley Ascent Questioned." Frederick Cook, it seems, had not been the only one to embroider the details of his "conquest" of Denali. Prominent Alaskan explorers soon began to question Lloyd's claim as well.

Lloyd, acknowledging that his photos were no more convincing than Cook's, responded to these accusations by reassembling the team of Taylor, Anderson, and McGonagall—all three men had since had returned to mining their claims—and urged them to make a second attempt on the summit. In June the three prospectors returned to Denali—and came back home again in two scant weeks. Once again, they reported having gained the summit of Mount McKinley.

Though most listeners continued to dismiss Lloyd's claims as the fanciful products of an overactive imagination, his feat was validated three years later. In 1913 the Hudson Stuck team—the first to scale the 20,320-foot-high South Peak (and true summit) of Denali—examined the mountaintop with binoculars during their ascent. Sure enough, embedded in the rocks of the North Peak, they spied the unmistakable spruce pole that Lloyd and his Sourdoughs had lugged to the top.

Though the various members of the Sourdough Expedition undermined their own case by volunteering inconsistent and contradictory accounts of their climb, most Denali historians now accept the following as true: In early April, after Lloyd had been forced to abandon the climb (probably because of altitude sickness), Taylor, Anderson, and McGonagall set out for the summit from about 11,000 feet, hauling the spruce pole and the American flag with them. Just below 19,000 feet, McGonagall began to falter. Taylor and Anderson pushed on without him, reaching the 19,470-foot summit of the North Peak.

In 18 hours, the climbers had ascended more than 8,000 vertical feet to the North Peak, erected the flag, and returned to camp at 11,000 feet. Like snowflakes in a Denali storm, controversy continues to swirl around the team's choice of this false summit. Some accounts hold that they chose the North Peak rather than the South because the former could be more easily seen from Fairbanks; others say they mistakenly judged the North Peak to be the true summit. Either way, the Sourdough Expedition's achievement was a remarkable one: Modern mountaineering parties routinely consume 12 hours in making the round-trip from high camp at 17,200 feet to the summit—a vertical gain of only 3,120 feet.

THE UNDISPUTED FIRST ASCENT of Denali was notched in 1913 by amateur mountaineer (and Episcopal archdeacon of the Yukon) Hudson Stuck. Accompanied by outdoorsmen Harry Karstens, Robert Tatum, and Walter Harper, Stuck began his overland approach to the mountain from the north (via the Muldrow Glacier) in mid-March. Fifty days later, on June 7, the foursome nailed the summit.

Modern mountaineers marvel at the nearly 3,000 pounds of gear the Stuck party and its associated packhorses and dog-sled teams hauled on its 50-mile approach to the mountain. The equipment, as detailed in Stuck's *Ascent of Denali: A Narrative of the First Complete Ascent of the Highest Peak in North America,* included:

> ...one eight-by-ten "silk" tent, used for two previous winters; three small circular tents of the same material, made in Fairbanks, for the high work; a Yukon stove [a large metal wood-burning stove] and the usual complement of pots and pans and dishes, including two admirable large aluminum pots for melting snow.... The bedding was mainly of down quilts, which are superseding fur robes and blankets for winter use because of their lightness and warmth.... Two pairs of camel's-hair blankets and one sleeping bag lined with down and camel's-hair cloth were taken, and Karstens brought a great wolf rope, weighing twenty-five pounds, of which we were glad enough later on.

Beset by stomach woes brought on by their high-fat diet of pemmican (the human body struggles to digest fat at altitude), Hudson Stuck and company spent the night of June 6 at high camp around 18,000 feet. Though provisioned to endure three weeks awaiting their shot at the summit, the team found these extra supplies to be nothing but surplus freight; their summit push came the very next morning, which broke cold and clear.

After setting out at 5 a.m., the four men reached the summit by 1:30 p.m. Stuck, suffering from altitude sickness, confessed that he "had almost to be hauled up the last few feet and fell unconscious for a moment upon the floor of the little snow basin that occupies the top of the mountain."

The team members took a number of readings with the barometers and thermometers they had brought with them. Only after their scientific work had been completed did they allow themselves the luxury of savoring the view. Stuck described the sensation of gazing down upon the continent:

> [T]he chief impression was not of our connection with the earth so far below, its rivers and its seas, but rather of detachment from it. We seemed alone upon a dead world, as dead as the mountains on the moon. Only once before can the writer remember a similar feeling of being neither in the world or of the world, and that was at the bottom of the Grand Cañyon of the Colorado....

After an hour and a half (!) on the summit, the team turned to descend. Having logged a 12-hour summit day—and having just capped off a decade-long race to reach the highest point in North America—they arrived back in high camp about 5 p.m.

WITH THE SUMMIT CONQUERED, interest waned in climbing Mount McKinley. In fact, nearly 20 years passed before climbers returned to the mountain. In 1932, two expeditions made their way to the base of the mountain. The first, led by American scientist and engineer Allen Carpé, sought to establish a research facility on Denali to study cosmic rays. Carpé had conducted similar experiments on other major North American peaks, including 15,300-foot Mount Fairweather and 16,550-foot Mount Bona in Alaska and 19,850-foot Mount Logan in Canada. The second, headed up by Norwegian Erling Strom and Minnesotan Alfred Lindley, sought to be the first expedition to ascend the mountain on skis.

Both expeditions followed the route up the Muldrow Glacier and were supported by dog-sled teams furnished by the National Park Service. For the Strom-Lindley team, the park service provided two staffers as well: McKinley National Park superintendent Harry Liek and ranger Grant Pearson.

The Carpé team would enter the Denali history books on two accounts: They were the first climbers to be deposited on the mountain by an airplane—in this case flown by Joe Crosson, lead pilot for Alaska Airways—and they were the first to suffer a fatality on the mountain.

On May 7, Strom, Lindley, Liek, and Pearson reached the summit on foot, their skis strapped to their packs. On their retreat from the mountain, they happened upon Carpé's camp on the Muldrow Glacier. There they found an empty tent with two sleeping bags and packs, but no sign of Carpé or his climbing partner, Theodore Koven. About two miles below the abandoned camp, however, they discovered Koven's frozen body, badly battered from a fall. Farther down the mountain, they turned up an ice ax and a pair of crampons—evidence that Carpé had probably died in a crevasse fall. Thus did Carpé and Koven come to occupy the first and second slots on the list of Denali fatalities—which, as of July 2002, stood at 92.

FROM THE EARLIEST EXPLORATIONS of Denali at the turn of the 20th century until 1951, most mountaineering expeditions approached the 20,320-foot peak from Wonder Lake in the north. In 1936, however, mountaineer/photographer/cartographer/scientist Bradford Washburn had identified what he described as a "technically easy approach" from the west via the upper reaches of the Kahiltna Glacier and the West Buttress. Washburn had scouted out this easier alternative while flying over the mountain to shoot aerial photographs for the National Geographic Society.

No one acted on his discovery at the time because the overland hike of more than 50 miles from civilization to the upper Kahiltna Glacier seemed so daunting compared with the 35-mile trek from Wonder Lake. In 1942, while participating in a U.S. Army expedition designed to test Arctic military clothing and equipment in extreme temperatures, Washburn got a good look at the route during a climbing break on Denali Pass at 18,200 feet.

"As we spotted the Kahiltna Glacier 10,000 feet below us," Washburn wrote in a chapter that appeared in Colby Coomb's *Denali's West Buttress,* "we suddenly realized that almost all of that side of McKinley was nothing but a safe, steep, chilly scramble."

Washburn encouraged climbers to make that "chilly scramble" up to the top of Denali in a 1947 *American Alpine Journal* article entitled "Mount McKinley from the North and West." At the time the article appeared, Washburn and his wife, Barbara, were scaling the mountain to gather data for the Mount McKinley Map—still in use today—en route to making Barbara the first woman to reach Denali's summit.

Two years later, Washburn's friend Terris Moore, president of the University of Alaska, solved the problem of how to reach the Kahiltna Glacier. Moore, a pilot, had arrived in Alaska from New England in the late 1940s with a plane outfitted with retractable skis. In 1951, he flew Washburn and three other climbers to a flat patch of snow 7,650 feet high on the Kahiltna. There they were joined by four others who had trekked in from Wonder Lake. The eight climbers then followed the West Buttress route that Washburn had detailed in his journal article and reached the summit in just 21 days.

Today, more than 80 percent of climbers on Mount McKinley—including our own RMI expedition—follow the Washburn Route, as it has come to be called in his honor. It rates a II on the Alaska Grade, which tops out at Grade V in terms of danger and difficulty. Just as its pathfinder predicted, the Washburn Route has turned out to be the safest and easiest route to the summit of Denali.

Chapter Nine

THE TYPE-A TEAM

THROUGHOUT THE NEXT DAY, we continue straight up the middle of the Kahiltna Glacier, gaining 2,000 feet in 2.5 miles. From the base of Ski Hill, we spy a storm front churning up Kahiltna Pass at 10,320 feet, apparently plowing straight toward us. By day's end, however, we'll realize that it hasn't moved. This cloud squall at the pass persists for much of the next three weeks, even when the upper and lower mountain bask in sunshine.

Our first sustained climb comes on Ski Hill itself, which is so steep that even Kent has to slow his pace. We arrive at our hourly rest breaks soaked in sweat, but the 20-mile-an-hour wind cuts into us as soon as we stop moving, and we scamper to pull on additional layers.

The top of the hill rewards us with views of Mount Francis to the north and Mounts Hunter and Foraker to the south; the southern shoulder of the West Buttress to the northeast; and, beyond that, the south summit itself. Behind us, we can see the western edge of the landing strip and watch—and hear—the constant parade of planes making their drops.

Though we strive to settle into a rhythm on the climb, our sleds conspire against us. They have become the source of intense frustration, flipping over repeatedly on the uphill trek. A climber's first hint that he's pulling an overturned sled is the sensation that his load has just doubled—perhaps tripled—in weight, as snowshoes, ice axes, and criss-crossed bungee cords bite into the glacier's surface.

Righting an overturned sled stops a rope team dead. It usually involves a joint effort between the sled hauler and the climber behind him; as the two cajole their sleds back into proper position, they give the appearance of attempting to play jump rope.

The sleds torment us even when we're not in motion. Whenever we pull off the trail and remove our packs for a rest break on the steep incline, the sleds try to run downhill, pulling our packs with them.

The sleds are an irritant, but we don't yet loathe them enough to kick and curse them, nor to bash them with our ice axes and ski poles, as we've seen other climbers doing. It's apparent from watching the descending teams that the sleds will be even less manageable on the way back down.

I eavesdrop on a bizarre conversation between two climbers returning from the summit.

"My sled is messing with me!" the woman cries.

"It's not your sled," the man responds. "It's you!"

"What the hell do you mean by that?"

"I mean you're paranoid. You think your sled is out to get you."

"Are you calling me crazy?"

"Well, you're *acting* crazy!"

"Fine, you bastard. Just get me off this mountain!"

The man doesn't reply. Instead, he yanks his sled back onto the trail and continues down. The woman savagely kicks her sled, then follows.

This is not the last heated—or peculiar—exchange I'll hear between addled climbers on the mountain.

Mountaineering: Denali National Park and Preserve, a National Park Service booklet distributed to all Denali climbers, addresses the bizarre personality changes and grim fantasies that can occur at high altitude:

> Irritability can easily spring up between close friends during a stay at high altitude. A nagging fear, doubt, or feeling of guilt can easily grow in one's mind and prove

mentally exhausting as well as potentially dangerous. Leadership characteristics may undergo drastic change because of the stressful situation. Personality changes may bring out latent domineering tendencies in anyone and can be extremely upsetting to group relationships. Being on the mountain may precipitate a variety of phobias, including claustrophobia from living in close quarters, which can lead to panic with an overwhelming desire to run away.

I don't know the term for fear of sleds—Rosebudphobia?—but something is clearly at work on this woman. This in turn makes me wonder what sort of emotional transfiguration awaits us higher on the mountain. Will I hear someone shout, "Take me, Jesus!" and witness one of my climbing mates running naked through the snow at 17,000 feet? Will I or someone else in our party succumb to the paranoid delusion that his peers have hatched a plot to rob him of his food stores? Will we sleep with one eye open, clutching our Leatherman multi-tools, ready to fend off an ice-ax attack by a crazed member of our team?

The only domineering tendencies I've detected so far are a long way from latent. They belong to Kent—understandable, given that he's responsible for the health and safety of eight clients—and to Brad, our resident neurosurgeon. Brad's take-charge attitude has established him as a group leader, but it also manifests itself in a tendency to order the other climbers around. As Brad and his tentmate, Clay, set up their shelter last night, Brad constantly critiqued Clay's actions. Clay, with his quiet demeanor, seemed willing to acknowledge Brad's authority.

The very personality traits you'd seek in a brain surgeon—unshakable self-confidence, superior intelligence, poise under pressure—are prized on an expedition, but Brad's penchant for dominating the others troubles me. Perhaps his hours in the operating room, where his leadership and authority go unchallenged, have conditioned him to expect similarly deferential treatment from us.

Early in the day, during one of our breaks, Brad and I discuss personality types and the sort of person who is drawn to a Denali expedition.

"Every guy out here is a Type-A," he contends. "They may not have shown it yet, but wait until we're further into the expedition and the going gets difficult. That's when you'll really see personality types emerging. Think about it: Who else but a driven high-achiever would willingly subject himself to the conditions on this mountain?"

Before I met the other members of the group, I probably would have agreed with him. Though I didn't know the particulars of my fellow climbers, I could surmise a few things about them: They were very likely to be professionally successful—how else could they afford such a costly trip? They were no doubt sufficiently driven to risk their lives climbing a big mountain—no small commitment for fathers of young children. I knew they were middle-aged, suggesting they would take no guff when it came to being bossed around by their peers.

Yet the guys in this group seem even-tempered and laid-back.

Last night in camp I had a telling encounter with Brad. As we set up the tents and buried items in the snow to anchor the guy lines, I grabbed a snowshoe to use as an anchor and began digging a trench with my ice ax. The guy lines from Brad's tent and mine would tie into this anchor, which was supposed to be positioned halfway between the two shelters.

Brad approached. "That isn't going to be very effective, you know," he said. "Here, why don't you use this picket instead? It makes a lot more sense."

Brad was right: A sleek aluminum shaft is easier to set in the ice than a snowshoe and would create a more secure anchor. For reasons that may reveal as much about my personality as Brad's, however, I was not about to yield to his authority. I looked him squarely in the eye.

"Brad, we are using *this*," I said in a firm voice, forcing the snowshoe into the trench to punctuate the sentence.

"Sure, okay, fine," he said. Since then Brad and I have gotten on famously, and by trip's end we will be good friends. I don't know if that run-in made the difference: Did it signal the emergence of my own "latent domineering tendencies," or was it simply two male dogs pissing on fence posts?

Brad is not the only one whose personality traits have begun to blossom. Two days into the climb, a team dynamic begins to evolve; our personalities and operating styles dictate the roles we will play throughout the rest of the trip. Thus does the expedition become a microcosm of society as a whole.

Gary Talcott, the expedition leader, is so gentle and soft-spoken that I sometimes have trouble hearing his instructions. I have seen no evidence of the steely leadership qualities one might consider critical in this high-stress, high-risk environment. Should a showdown occur between Gary and one of his more-spirited clients over a judgment call, I can't picture Gary summoning the force of will necessary to prevail.

But Gary has been ushering RMI clients to remote summits for nearly two decades, so he must be doing something right. Ultimately, Gary will demonstrate to me—and to the rest of the clients—that leadership takes many forms; being brash, confrontational, and demanding is only one way to motivate men and women up mountains.

Already we've overheard guides on other expeditions loudly berating their clients for blunders born of inexperience. Earlier today, for instance, I heard a guide scream at a client, "Don't you *ever* fucking do that again on *my* expedition! DO YOU UNDERSTAND?!"

Had anyone said that to me, I would have retreated from the mountain, shamefaced and shaken. (That, or buried my ice ax in his head.)

I'm grateful to Gary that such abuse is not the price of a ticket to the top. For the next three weeks, Gary never raises his voice, never criticizes our lack of finesse, never suggests that tyros like us have no business being on a big mountain such as Denali. In the end, Gary's supple leadership style, keen judgment, and compassion for his clients will prove to be the perfect recipe for success in the face of some trying times.

Dick Bowers, with his facility for languages and his sincere interest in people, has become our toastmaster and social director. Though I'm sure Dick has had bad days in the past, he never succumbs to one on this trip. Opinionated and outspoken, he often jousts with the younger—and more liberal—men on the trip over issues such as recreational drug use and an American's right to drive a gas-guzzling SUV. Through it all, Dick seems more intent on engaging others in conversation that in hammering home his point.

Already Dick has hailed climbing teams from Taiwan, Spain, Russia, Slovakia, France, and Germany in their native tongues, probing for information on their home regions and previous adventures. In camp at night Dick makes the rounds, drawing the other climbers into dialogue and bestowing on them a measure of his irrepressible optimism.

Riper by nearly a decade than the next youngest climber on the team, Dick justifiably could have become the camp bitchmeister, venting about the aches and pains that plague a 61-year-old body in the midst of an extreme physical test. But even up high, when our chances fade for reaching the summit, Dick never does. He is living proof that will and attitude are as essential in mountaineering as strength and endurance.

Nat Brace, whose rigorous training at altitude near Seattle has established him as the fittest climber among the clients, becomes the camp Mother Teresa, selflessly endeavoring to make everyone's life easier. He seems indefatigably selfless in cutting and stacking snow blocks, shuttling water bottles from Kent's pot to climbers ensconced in their tents, or sharing supply items from his pack with others in need. Put a shovel in his hand and Nat becomes John Henry, efficiently excavating cache holes and refusing relief from his fellow climbers.

Nat's sense of wonder at the surrounding mountainscape never seems to ebb. He frequently directs our attention to something spectacular— a dramatic view, a cascading avalanche, a snowfield lit by alpenglow— by pointing and uttering his two favorite words: "Wow. Aw-w-w-wesome."

Ken Coffee, the quiet, reflective engineer, seems as interested in things as he is in people. He emerges as the expedition fix-it man, plying his craft to help teammates rig sleds, fashion knots, and use the tools at hand (duct tape, a hank of cord, sections of bamboo wands) to repair damaged equipment. So rife is equipment failure on Denali—snapped tent poles, popped rivets, shredded nylon, broken lace loops on climbing boots—that Ken could have profited handsomely by opening a repair shop on the mountain. While the rest of us stick to basics in preparing our sleds, Ken uses bungee cords to fashion an elaborate shock absorber on the webbing that tethers the sled to his pack.

Ken's greatest engineering triumph on the trip involves retrofitting his tiny FM radio to accept double-A batteries, rather than the triple-As on which it was designed to run. (In the whirl of preparations for the trip, he had bought the wrong kind.) In an odd twist, Ken will endure unsettling—and perilous—equipment failure of his own on the most technical section of the climb: the headwall above the camp at 14,200 feet.

The remaining clients, Matt McDonough and Clay Howard, seem comfortable in supporting roles. They internalize much of the experience, revealing little of how they're faring on the mountain. The two are vastly different—Matt has a dry East Coast wit while Clay is a gentle, slow-talking Southerner—but both are eager to pitch in whenever help is needed. Beyond that, they keep largely to themselves. There's an edginess about Clay that I interpret as apprehension at his ability to handle the mountain—a novel attitude for a former Marine. Matt and Clay's ragged pressure breathing when we reach each rest stop—to say nothing of their insistence on clipping onto Joe's slower rope—suggest they may be struggling already.

Meanwhile, Bill Hatcher and I devote ourselves to chronicling the trip. A proficient and experienced climber, Bill had initially seemed aloof—a trait I've observed in other photographers who fear sacrificing objectivity for camaraderie. Over the past few days, however, Bill has revealed himself to be a warm, often funny participant who's just as engaged in this adventure as the rest of us. The guides welcome his expert help in instructing the other clients.

THOUGH OUR DIFFERENCES ARE EVIDENT, we're unified both by our shared quest and by an unspoken but understood set of rules—let's call it a high-altitude social contract. Behavior that threatens our mission or our cohesion as a group is censured; conduct that moves us safely up the mountain is encouraged.

In a bid to stay hydrated, for instance, I've begun consuming 5 liters of water per day rather than the prescribed 4. This, Kent points out, is depleting the stove fuel required to melt snow for drinking water—which in turn may jeopardize the expedition's success.

One evening as I hover over the stoves, clutching my empty bottles, Kent says to me, "Dave, I want you to get as much water as you *need,* but keep in mind that little things often mean the difference between success and failure on Denali. We could be denied the summit because we run out of fuel, and that little extra we burned to provide you an additional bottle of water might have allowed us to hang on one more day."

After that, I take to topping off my fifth water bottle just before we depart each morning, when Kent normally dumps out whatever melted snow we can't pack up the mountain. It's a perfect compromise—one that enables me to maintain my daily water consumption at 5 liters without incurring communal disfavor.

Likewise, we realize that if one of us succumbs to severe altitude sickness he will probably be whisked off the mountain—even if a day or two of rest might have effected a full recovery. An incapacitated climber represents a risk—in safety as well as in summit aspirations—to the entire team. Higher on the mountain, we will have an opportunity to learn this lesson firsthand.

The guides voice their appreciation for our voluntary contributions to harvesting snow for water, starting the stoves in the morning, and cleaning the cook pots after breakfast and dinner. The overarching principle—one that the Rainier guides had articulated repeatedly—is to achieve the perfect balance between independence and interdependence.

The former goal involves a continuous process of self-evaluation: Am I taking in enough food and water? Am I getting adequate rest? Am I adapting well to the increasing altitude, or am I suffering the early symptoms of altitude sickness? Am I maintaining my gear—and keeping track of it all?

The latter goal involves contributing to the greater good of the expedition. As Daryl Miller had put it during the pretrip orientation:

"Commit yourself to giving more than you take. Practice patience. Don't let yourself succumb to frustration or anger, which are compounded by altitude. Don't let team morale break down."

The challenge is to give freely of your time and energy without giving so much that you become a liability to the team.

On Rainier, guide Paul Maier had described a fit young Denali client who emerged as the expedition workhorse when it came to performing camp chores. "This guy looked and acted like the toughest one in the group. He was always the first to volunteer for work duty. But at 14,000, he fell apart. He started developing symptoms of high-altitude pulmonary edema, and we led him off the mountain the next day. He had been taking care of the others, but he wasn't taking care of himself."

Just as each climber is responsible for his own self-maintenance, expeditions themselves are expected to achieve self-sufficiency. Requests for outside support—whether those entail hitting up another team for food or fuel, or calling in a rescue—are considered bad form except under the most extreme circumstances: Scamming grub and stove gas deprives other parties of their own essential supplies; rescues typically jeopardize the lives of the climbers who answer the call for help.

Mountaineering: Denali National Park and Preserve doesn't equivocate in addressing this principle:

> Search and rescue operations are conducted on a discretionary basis. The level and exigency of the response is determined by field personnel based on their evaluation of the situation. Rescue is not automatic. *Denali National Park and Preserve expects park users to exhibit a degree of self-reliance and responsibility for their own safety commensurate with the degree of difficulty of the activities they undertake.* (Emphasis added.)

By early afternoon, we arrive at camp at 9,700 feet, in full view of the storm raging above us at Kahiltna Pass. Should it creep down the mountain during the night, we could be enveloped by a classic Denali blizzard. The wind is blowing at 20 miles an hour. The sun is ducking in and out of drifting clouds. For the first time, we're all wearing our beefy summit parkas.

While the rest of us establish camp, Gary and Nat create an outhouse that would be the envy of all on the mountain. Three upright sleds form the side and back walls. A three-foot-square block of ice constitutes the ceiling. Gary uses his ice ax to fashion a bench seat, then digs a hole in the middle to receive the plastic bag. Lest anyone suffer a frosted bum while seated on this throne, Gary sacrifices half of his foam RidgeRest sleeping pad to the cause. The green pad, with a newly cut hole in its center, serves as a positively civilized seat warmer.

After dinner, we gather outside our tents. The rapidly shifting weather dominates the conversation, precipitating our first (but by no means last) enervatingly useless attempt to predict the future:

"The wind is from the north," Gary tells us. "That's a good sign. This is either a minor weather event or a blow from the Bering Sea."

Weather means everything on Denali, so it makes sense that we should invest hours of our time speculating on what the elements have in store. In the end, of course, the exercise always amounts to nothing. Even the nightly forecasts we pick up on our two-way radio from the Park Service are wildly inaccurate, as are the reports from the NPR affiliate in Talkeetna, delivered to Ken through his headphones.

The mountain—and its weather—will prove fickle to the very end. Joe's attitude seems to be the healthiest and best informed: "Stop worrying," he says. "We'll deal with it."

After clambering into our tents, we settle down to a lullaby of the buck and surge of nylon shelter walls and the sandpapery scraping of snow crystals filling the vestibules.

Chapter Ten

A WORLD OF WHITE

BLASTED BY OUR FIRST DENALI STORM

As a kid growing up in Ohio, I often awakened on winter mornings to find an odd white aura shrouding the bedroom window. Parting the curtains, I'd peer out and see a foot of fresh snow on the ground. The transformation was always dramatic: I went to sleep in one world and woke up in another.

So it is on the morning of May 31, our fourth day on the mountain, at 9,700 feet. Through the last few hours of sleep, conditions in the tent seem even more cramped than usual. Upon waking, as I slowly regain my senses, I realize I've gotten wedged between Ken's sleeping form on one side and a cinder-block wall on the other. I withdraw one arm from my sleeping bag, pound my fist against the tent fabric, and hear the dull thud of hardpacked snow. Zipping open the tent just enough to peek outside, I am greeted by a blast of wind and snow that blows into the enclosure, dusting everything in white.

An early morning invasion of windblown snow into otherwise snug sleeping quarters compounds the most excruciating aspect of camping just below the Arctic Circle: climbing from a warm sleeping bag and rising to greet the day—along with whatever jarring combination of cold, wind, and precipitation it has prepared for you.

If you've ever had the heady experience of dashing naked through the snow from a sweltering sauna into an icy lake, you just might grasp what I mean. Think about it: There you are, snug in your -40°F sleeping bag—which, at the current thermometer reading of zero, packs enough down to insulate you against a 40-degree plunge in temperature—despite the fact that nestled beside you in the bag are two full liters of water, a partially filled pee bottle, multiple tubes of sunscreen, your liner boots, and anything else you hope to keep from freezing.

Okay, things are tight, but all internal contents of the sleeping bag have, over the past 10 hours, been warmed to a uniform temperature. And the recent addition you made to the pee bottle feels as soothing against your skin as a heating pad. (If only you could enjoy the warmth without considering its source.)

The act of withdrawing from the sleeping bag—particularly, higher on the mountain, when the temperature inside the tent reaches -15°F—defies any instinct for self-preservation. In a matter of seconds, you emerge into freezing air from the down's warm embrace and, shivering in your thin thermal underwear, begin frantically looking for your sturdier insulating layers—which, through a night of tossing and turning, have vanished into the jumbled chaos of stuff spread around you.

Every clothing item you and your tent mates purchased at the outdoor specialty shop is navy blue, black, or dark gray. In the diffuse light filtering in through the tent walls before sunrise, you can't distinguish between a glove and a sock, much less distinguish *your* glove and *your* sock from those of your partners—who, by now, are also awake and engaged in a similar frenetic scavenger hunt.

So now you're slamming into each other in the chill morning air—your skin a blanket of gooseflesh, your nipples and nuts drawn up tighter than brass BBs—and bumping against the tent walls, which are layered with about an inch of interior ice from your agitated breathing through the night. Meanwhile, the ceiling is dropping goblets of snow down the nape of your neck. The ice crystals melt against your back, causing your body to spasm and contort as if you had been set upon by a swarm of hornets. The only sounds you can hear above the swish of tent nylon are chattering teeth and the occasional garbled expletive forced through numbed lips. At last, you lay your hands on a fleece jacket and hurriedly pull it on, only to discover that it is Nat's or Ken's, not yours. Once again, you surrender your body to the cold.

Though this process continues for no more than five minutes, it seems an eternity—and it gets repeated every morning you're on the mountain. Eventually, after plowing your shoulder into the snowpack at your door and worming your way through the vestibule—trying to ignore the snow that's blowing into the tent and drifting into the creases of your open sleeping bag—you emerge, fully clothed and with your metabolism cranking in high gear, to assess the day.

Which, in this case, looks marginal.

The mountain has changed overnight. Gone are the 50-mile views, the warm patches of sunshine, and any sense of our position on the mountain. Instead, we are in the grips of a storm—mild by Denali standards but still violent enough to shut down Atlanta for a few days. Walls of white edge us in on all sides, and the world in which we operate extends maybe 30 feet—just to the edge of camp, no farther. We've lost our visual connection with the greater community of climbers on the mountain, transforming us into an isolated clique of ants trapped beneath an opaque plastic cup on a huge frozen picnic table.

It's gusting hard. Sheets of windblown snow skitter across the surface of the glacier. Overhead, meanwhile, dense clouds rocket across a slate-gray sky, dropping their loads of snow as they pass. The sun occasionally penetrates the storm, permitting distant peaks to appear through the haze for an instant or two before vanishing behind a curtain of white.

Gary, Kent, and Joe—parka hoods cinched tight around their faces, backs to the wind—are talking, holding one of their daily powwows to decide our fate. If we move at all, we'll execute our first double-carry, shuttling gear items up to camp at 11,000 feet and returning here to sleep. After 15 minutes or so, Gary approaches.

"As you can see, the weather's kicked up overnight," he says. "We're not sure we want to push up the mountain and get trapped in a storm. Let's just hold up for a while and see how things look in an hour or so."

Two hours later, as the weather seems to be calming, Gary calls us together.

"Okay, we're going to do our carry, but we need to flatten the camp so nothing blows away while we're gone. Make sure you don't leave anything lying in the snow. It'll be buried by the time we get back."

Gary's advice comes a little too late for me. In my haste to crawl into my bag last night, I left my snowshoes lying out, and now they're buried under a foot of fresh snow somewhere in the 20 square yards that define our camp. Too embarrassed to acknowledge my mistake or ask for help, I surreptitiously stomp around camp, probing the snow with my ski pole and listening for the clack of metal on metal. After 15 minutes, I find the lost items and resolve never to make that mistake again.

We yank the poles out of tent grommets, collapse the tents, and weigh them down with ice blocks. The effect is striking: It looks as though the skies opened and a highly localized precipitation of ice blocks flattened four tents, with the occupants trapped inside.

As we're preparing to leave camp, I commit a second error. My sled has become such a nuisance that I decide to carry my full load—three liters of water, two gallons of fuel, and an enormous group-food bag—in my pack. I lash my snowshoes and a shovel to the outside. The combined weight is about 70 pounds, which approaches the load I carried to the top of Frozen Head during my training hikes.

The others, wisely, load up their sleds, letting the surface of the glacier, rather than their legs, bear most of the weight. Over the next few hours—grimacing, straining, uttering words I wouldn't want my daughters to hear—I will hoist and lower the pack eight times.

Our crampons and ice axes stay behind because we won't need them until we move above 11,000 feet. Up to that point the slope is shallow enough—and the snow soft enough—to kick steps using the lug soles of our boots or snowshoes. Other teams have passed unseen in the poor visibility, and we follow their trail, grateful that they have packed down the snow.

Gary plants a wand every few hundred feet as we climb, creating a trail we can follow back home later this afternoon. Like William Tell withdrawing arrows from his quiver, he pulls wands from the ski slots in his backpack with practiced efficiency.

In about two hours, we approach Kahiltna Pass. The weather, though windy, holds steady. To the west, we watch 12,525-foot-high Kahiltna Dome briefly materialize before vanishing into the clouds. After a rest break, we bend east and follow a gentle incline toward the basin at 11,000 feet. A wall of mountains looming 1,500 feet above us edges the route to the left, while a vast crevasse field lies to the right.

By midafternoon we top the last rise and arrive at a thriving community of 30 or more climbers who move purposefully within the fortified confines of their camps. Bundles of skis, planted to mark caches, sprout from the snow beside a labyrinth of ice-block walls. The less confident skiers have abandoned their skis here.

This basin at 11,000 feet provides a flat, sheltered niche that stretches about 75 yards from side to side and about 150 yards from head to tail. The residents cluster toward the center, away from the bus-sized chunks of ice that have broken loose and fallen from the upper slopes. An intricate network of crevasses, upthrust seracs, and overhanging cornices marks the point where the vertical walls of ice merge with the glacier.

Ahead, at the upper edge of the basin, the 400-foot slope inexplicably known as Motorcycle Hill looks impossibly steep, particularly for a team hauling sleds. I study the pitch—which includes a blue crack running horizontally across the face about 100 feet up—and think, "Damn, if I can climb this wall, I can climb anything."

Denali's West Buttress Route is perfect for novice climbers like me in that the technical difficulty escalates gradually the higher you go. Key sections along the route—particularly the headwall above 14,200 feet, the exposed scramble along the rocky ridge of the West Buttress, and the pitch that leads from high camp at 17,200 to Denali Pass—will forever reconfigure my definition of "tough going," and I will laugh at myself on the way down for regarding Motorcycle Hill as anything but a glorified bunny slope.

After we've dropped our loads, Nat-the-human-steam-shovel takes the lead in digging out a hole that's six feet square and four feet deep. Into this we deposit food stores, then hardware, and finally fuel cans. Marauding ravens are almost as proficient as Nat is at excavating cache holes; they've been known to pillage food stores three feet deep. We hope to thwart them by burying the food at the bottom, under the sturdier, inedible items.

Though we succeed, many others don't. A raven raid on a buried cache leaves ample evidence behind: the contents of Ziploc bags scattered widely on the surface of the snow in a way that reveals the ravens' preference for bagels, packaged meats and cheeses, nuts, and raisins. Even a famished raven seems to have little use for freeze-dried vegetables and ramen noodles.

As we turn to descend, I can't shake the frustration of surrendering the 1,300 feet in elevation we gained today, only to climb it again tomorrow.

On our way down, still an hour above camp, the storm gains full intensity. Within minutes, we are wrapped in a blinding blizzard. Ice crystals, borne along on 40-mile-an-hour gusts of wind, lash my raw cheeks and infiltrate my parka hood. The distinguishing features of the landscape vanish, heavy snowfall erases our boot prints, and we're left to navigate by following the green bamboo wands we planted on our ascent. Soon we're post-holing up to our knees in soft snow. Gary stops and instructs us to strap on our snowshoes.

I discover that my snowshoes, ancient relics from the RMI rental bin, feature one strap that's barely long enough to cross over my boot and slip through the spring-loaded clip, which has iced up and is frozen solid. I have to remove my gloves to work on them, and as my fingers come in contact with the cold metal, they go numb long before I can secure the bindings.

Crouching in the blowing snow, trying to manipulate intricate buckles and straps with fumbling hands that feel like frozen balloons, I experience my first bout with misery. I'm so consumed by the experience of being cold that I can't recall ever being warm.

For the first time, I begin to fathom the level of suffering that attends a Denali ascent, even under the most favorable conditions. I surrender to the notion that nearly all of life's amenities central to comfort and ease have been erased from my existence.

This experience in no way resembles the winter outings of my past, where I'd wander into the snow-cloaked Appalachian wilderness for two or three days, cognizant every instant that a car with a six-pack propped on the floor of its back seat awaited me at the trailhead a scant six to nine miles away. In a matter of three or four hours, I could be basking in the warm blast of the car's heater at the drive-through of the nearest fast-food joint, smugly celebrating my own fortitude and daring as I waited for some high-schooler to hand me a steaming sack of comfort food.

The few simple pleasures available on this mountain—a wet-wipe bath, a familiar old tune blasting through my ear buds, a mug of hot soup, the warm recesses of my sleeping bag, long minutes spent studying the photographs of my girls—provide fleeting distraction from the near-constant struggle against cold, wind, and altitude.

Dick brought a copy of *Killer Angels*, which recounts the Battle of Gettysburg in gory detail. It has turned out to be an informed choice, lending much-needed perspective to our discomfort. Compared with the experience of Pickett's men—gut-shot, crying out for water as they died in the hot sun—life on Denali isn't all that rough. Not only that, but we all detect strong similarities between Gary Talcott, our calm and composed Denali commander, and Lieutenant Colonel Joshua Chamberlain of the 20th Maine Infantry, the quietly competent stalwart who anchored the extreme left flank of the Union lines. Before the expedition is over, *Killer Angels* will be torn into multiple segments and passed around to the entire group.

Over the last few hundred feet to camp, the storm continues to hammer us, and we arrive to find that simple tasks have become major ordeals.

On hands and knees we wrestle the wind in erecting and anchoring our tents, and the chaos of the storm drives home how easy it would be for a sudden gust to snatch up a tent and blow it across the glacier like a tumbleweed. Yet this wind measures only 40 miles an hour—a mere zephyr compared with the full brunt of Denali's hurricane-force winds, which can pluck a mountaineer off her feet and send her sailing. More than once, an empty stuff sack or glove blows past me, its owner in hot—er, cold—pursuit.

Four of us are needed to erect the orange nylon kiva that shelters our kitchen: While Kent sets the center pole, three of us stretch the fabric against the wind and anchor the edges with ice blocks. In fair weather it takes us two hours to carve out a new camp; in the wind it takes us nearly twice that long to reestablish our existing camp. After a day spent battling the weather, even Kent's dinner—beef stew and instant potatoes—tastes good.

By morning the storm has cleared, leaving huge drifts piled against the windward sides of our snow walls and tents. Wearing light layers, sunhats, and generous applications of sunscreen, we ascend to the basin at 11,000 feet under blue skies. We arrive there primed for our first rest day on the mountain—and a chance to socialize with the global community of climbers ensconced here.

Chapter Eleven

GIMMESOME ROY AND GURU BABA FATS

IN THE BASIN THE NEXT DAY we meet Henry Webb, 26, and Joe Keen, 24, both from Juneau. Henry, who has stripped off his shirt and opened the side zips on his bibs, exposing his bare legs, is cultivating a wicked sunburn, but then both he and Joe are a little punch-drunk from their descent from the summit, which began at 4 a.m.—*this morning*. Round-trip, their climb will take just two weeks. Deprived of adequate time to acclimatize, it's no surprise they confess to having felt "a little green" on the summit.

"I just wanted to lie down and go to sleep on the ascent," says Henry. "But I have to say that watching the sunrise from the summit kind of perked me up."

The two depart for base camp a few minutes later.

Three diminutive women dwarfed by huge loads settle into the camp-site next to ours. They are Taiwanese climbers Yenling Lee, 27, Yihua Lin, 27, and Mei Liang Lee, 30, graduates from Ming Chuan University in Taipei. The trio has been climbing together for seven years; both Yihua and Mei Liang have also bagged Aconcagua.

Solo climber Dusan Golubic, a Slovenian, is rarely separated from his custom-made titanium skis—which, he insists, are among the lightest and strongest on the mountain. When Bill takes his picture, Dusan, with his ample beard and futuristic wraparound sunglasses, insists that the skis share the frame; that's when it hits me that he must have an endorsement agreement with the manufacturer. His plan is to ski down the 3,000-foot Rescue Gulley, a 40-degree chute that extends from high camp at 17,200 feet to 14,200 feet. The gulley is the chosen route for lowering injured climbers from high camp to the Park Service medical tent in the basin at 14,200 feet.

Another solo climber, Mike Clemens from Big Bend, Texas, is heading down after gaining the last—and most difficult—of the highest points in each of the 50 states. This feat has been accomplished by just over 100 climbers.

Dick Bowers, a fellow Highpointer, is on a similar quest; he lacks just 13 of the 50 summits. Dick recounts his trip to the highest point in Florida, Britton Hill, located on the state's panhandle about two miles from Florala, Alabama.

"It was a pain in the ass to get to," he says. "And I didn't hang around very long on the summit. The mosquitoes were killing me, and there wasn't a whole lot to see from the top—altitude 345 feet."

Rachel and Katy Garton, two animated sisters in their early 20s from Utah, arrive in camp later in the day. They exude a wholesome charm. If I were a betting man, I'd wager that they had served as president and vice president, respectively, of their high-school pep club. Their matching flesh-tone pee funnels, which allow them to urinate while standing, jangle from their packs.

Five minutes after meeting us, Rachel regales us with an inspired rendition of "The Perfect High," a 66-line poem by Shel Silverstein. For more than five minutes, she recites the poem from memory, barely pausing to gulp air between stanzas. The poem's main character, Gimmesome Roy, endures a punishing pilgrimage to seek out the guru Baba Fats, who lives high in the mountains, and to learn the secret of the perfect high. The dual message is predictable—drugs are a cop-out, happiness comes from within—but it seems eminently fitting coming from someone who seems to be enjoying a sustained high-on-life buzz:

"What's happening, Fats?" says Roy with joy,
"I've come to state my biz.
I hear you're hip to the perfect trip.
Please tell me what it is.
For you can see," says Roy to he,
"that I'm about to die,
So for my last ride, Fats,
how can I achieve the perfect high?"
"Well, dog my cats!" says Baba Fats.
"Here's one more burnt-out soul,
Who's looking for some alchemist to turn his trip to gold.
But you won't find it in no dealer's stash,
or on no druggist's shelf.
Son, if you would seek the perfect high—
find it in yourself."

Later, as I settle into my sleeping bag with my belly full of Kent's three-bean chili, I feel remarkably fit. In the wake of our first full day of inactivity, I'm anticipating a restful night's sleep. Instead, within two hours I'll be clawing at the tent door like a caged badger, convinced that I'm about to expire.

Chapter Twelve

THE TECHNICOLOR YAWN

AND OTHER NOTABLE EFFECTS OF ALTITUDE

WHEN DARYL MILLER ADVISED US that everyone has a bad day on Denali, I was certain mine would occur in the thin air and biting cold of the upper mountain above 17,000 feet. As it turns out, I have to climb only as high as 11,000 feet before the altitude begins to ravage my body's oxygen-starved cells.

I pass our first night at 11,000 feet in an interminable battle to catch my breath, waking up frequently in a sweat-popping panic. I don't think I'm suffocating; I'm absolutely certain of it. The accompanying sensation of confinement is so profound that I'm beginning to understand, on a very personal level, the park brochure's warning that the mountain environment can precipitate "a variety of phobias, including claustrophobia from living in close quarters, which can lead to panic with an overwhelming desire to run away."

Though I restrain the impulse to run away, in my struggle to breathe I tear the collar of my sleeping bag away from my face and fumble to unzip the tent door for some fresh air. After panting out in the open for two or three minutes, I get enough oxygen in my blood to ease back to sleep—only to awake a few minutes later and repeat the entire agonizing process.

My condition is known as periodic, or Cheyne-Stokes, breathing (named for Irish physicians John Cheyne and William Stokes). It's a bit ironic that the human body, rather than fighting the effects of altitude by increasing respiration, does just the opposite. After gulping air for several seconds, the climber drifts back to sleep and experiences periods of apnea—cessation of respiration—that can last as long as 30 seconds. Meanwhile, blood-oxygen levels plunge, and the climber awakens in the throes of hypoxia with his brain shouting, "Breathe, you bastard, BREATHE!"

Then there are the attendant nightmares, which usher me through Edgar Allan Poe's subconscious and culminate in unbridled panic. In one dream, I'm being stalked through the woods around my cabin in east Tennessee by a creature that makes the monster in *Alien* about as frightening as Macaulay Culkin. In another, I'm trapped inside a car that has punched through the guardrail of a bridge and is sinking to the bottom of a murky river. In yet a third, I trigger a slab avalanche and wind up pinioned beneath tons of snow and ice.

Another dream, just as vivid, is not so much macabre as it is mystifying. In it I decide to use an upcoming rest day to descend the mountain, travel by bus to Anchorage, and fly home to see my daughters. Only after I've arrived do I realize that I've spent my round-trip airline ticket, and no amount of impassioned pleading can persuade the ticket agent to fly me back to Alaska free of charge. I'm standing at the ticket counter in mountain togs and crampons, arguing my case while my teammates advance toward the top.

Most of these reveries, it hits me, revolve around various methods of suffocation; could this be my subconscious at work, attempting to spark my retarded respiratory system into action?

"A common nightmare at high altitude," write James Milledge, John West, and Michael Ward in *High Altitude Medicine and Physiology*, "is that the tent has been covered with snow by an avalanche and the subject wakes violently feeling suffocated and very short of breath." That's one dream I didn't experience, but its theme is strikingly similar to the ones I did have.

Though I seem to be suffering alone through the night, I find out later on that my misery had company: Had I been attentive enough to ignore my own death throes and listen to the goings-on in the next tent, I would have heard Dick in similar agony, tearing at his clothes and clawing for air.

My first bout with Cheyne-Stokes breathing had befallen me about a decade earlier, when I headed out to Aspen, Colorado, for a freelance magazine assignment. In less than 12 hours I had traveled from my home at about 300 feet above sea level to the summit of a 13,000-foot peak. Six beers and half a pack of unfiltered cigarettes later, I was lying in bed convinced that I had contracted rapid-onset emphysema. For the next two days, I shunned both drink and smoke in favor of superhydration and gulping liter after liter of spring water. By the third night, I was fine.

When I crawl from my sleeping bag "the morning after" on Denali, I discover a second symptom of maladaptation. The combined effects of altitude, insomnia, and overindulgence in Kent's salt-laden three-bean chili have left me feeling as bloated as Dom Deluise. The orbits around my eyes are swollen with fluid. My fingers are as fat as link sausages. My pulse pounds relentlessly in my temples. The slightest pinprick and my water-gorged tissues would explode, drenching the camp in a stinging saline mist.

I recall my mother lauding her "water pills" for their effectiveness in relieving her frequent symptoms of feeling "puffy." Mom, I finally understand what it feels like to store gallons of water in your eyelids.

This condition, known as peripheral edema, arises when fluids leak from your cells into the surrounding tissue. It explains why many summit photos of high-altitude mountaineers resemble portraits of prize-fighters on the losing end of the world heavyweight championship bout.

Despite years of intensive study, much of it by Dr. Peter Hackett at Denali's 14,200-foot-high medical station, altitude sickness remains a complex package of complaints that defy thorough clinical understanding.

This much we do know: Altitude illness is brought on primarily by the gradual decrease in barometric pressure as one ascends, combined with a reduction in the percentage of oxygen present in each lungful of air. (The amount of oxygen available at 18,000 feet is roughly 50 percent the amount available at sea level.) About half the residents of sea level who travel quickly above 8,000 feet experience some symptoms of altitude sickness. These symptoms can affect any—and sometimes all—of the body's systems, but they can generally be divided into two forms: disturbing or deadly.

As I learned on Mount Rainier, my symptoms, though unpleasant, can be attributed to acute mountain sickness (AMS)—which, despite its grave-sounding name, encompasses a wide variety of ailments that might otherwise stem from a nagging hangover. Among them are headache, lethargy, weakness, fatigue, fluid retention, anorexia, nausea, loss of coordination, cough, reduced urine output, and increased heart rate. They typically dissipate with increased acclimatization to altitude—or with immediate descent.

As these symptoms grow more severe, however, they can progress toward a more lethal form of altitude-related illness, which attacks the brain. In high-altitude cerebral edema (HACE), vessels in the brain begin to leak blood and the brain tissue begins to swell, pressing against the hard shell of the cranium. The swelling dulls mental functioning and causes sluggish, uncoordinated movements. (No need to elaborate on the mishaps this could trigger on an exposed ridge.)

In high-altitude pulmonary edema, or HAPE, body fluids leak into the lungs, compounding the challenge of extracting oxygen from thin mountain air. The symptoms first emerge in the form of a hacking cough, then progress to crackling sounds from the lungs, blue lips, and blood-tinged spittle.

For both HACE and HAPE, the most effective treatment is a rapid descent of at least 3,000 feet. If that doesn't occur, a climber stricken with either malady can die within 48 hours of its onset.

It's impossible to predict who will fall victim to altitude sickness, or under what circumstances. Younger climbers seem to be more susceptible than older ones. Physical fitness offers no protection, nor does previous experience at altitude: A climber may summit Everest without oxygen one year and succumb to altitude illness at 17,000 feet the next.

The Chinese may have been the first to describe the symptoms of altitude sickness in about 30 B.C., though they had no clue to its cause. Documents detail men growing pale as they passed over the aptly named Great Headache and Little Headache Mountains, most likely somewhere in the Karakoram Range of modern-day Pakistan.

High Altitude Medicine credits the first quasi-clinical account of the illness to a Jesuit priest who visited the Andes in the 16th century and fell ill at about 16,000 feet. In his *Naturall and Morall Historie of the East and West Indies,* Father Joseph de Acosta recounted his suffering at that altitude:

> When I came to … the top of the mountaine, I was suddenly surprised with so mortall and strange a pang, that I was ready to fall from the top to the ground … everyone made haste … to free himself speedily from this ill passage…. I was surprised with such pangs of straining and casting as I thought to cast up my heart too; for having cast up meate, fleugme, and choller both yellow and green, in the end I cast up blood with the straining of my stomach. To conclude, if this had continued I should undoubtedly have died.

After heaving up the green and yellow contents of his stomach, Acosta may have been the first mountaineer to describe the altitude-induced retching known as the "Technicolor yawn."

Paul Bert, a 19th-century French physiologist, conducted experiments in a decompression chamber demonstrating that decreased barometric pressure results in hypoxia. (This deficiency in the amount of oxygen that reaches the tissues of the body is better known as oxygen debt.) The symptoms could be reversed, Bert also showed, through the administration of oxygen.

The body's ability to adapt to increasing altitude—a process known as acclimatization—has been amply documented. Climbers have reached the 29,035-foot summit of Mount Everest without supplemental oxygen, yet a person flown directly from sea level to the top of that peak and deposited there would pass out in a few minutes. Death from oxygen debt would occur within an hour or two.

The breathing difficulties, of themselves, are troubling. Even more disturbing is the realization that I'm not even halfway up this mountain and already I'm struggling with the altitude.

"I'm fucked," I tell myself. "If this continues or gets worse, my trip is over. I'll return home having reached the lofty height of 11,000 feet— lower than a respectable Western ski slope."

The next morning, in an effort to kick-start my metabolism, I drink a dense, syrupy concoction of instant coffee, powdered milk, and hot chocolate. It succeeds only in adding nausea to my list of ailments. As I shuffle through the chill morning, I'm grateful for this rest day, which won't require us to move any higher. There's no question that I'm bloated; despite a normal intake of fluids, my kidneys have slowed my urine output to a trickle. I can hide my baggy eyelids behind my glacier glasses, but I fail to disguise my lethargy and growing edginess. At one point, Ken Coffee, who seems to sense my mood, asks, "You okay, Brother Brill?"

"Yeah, great," I lie. "I'm just having a little trouble processing Kent's chili."

"You just don't seem like yourself."

"I haven't been sleeping very well. I woke up every 15 minutes last night, feeling like André the Giant was sitting on my chest. I'm surprised I didn't keep you up."

"Nope. Slept like a rock. Hey, you take care of yourself, okay?"

"Yeah, sure. If this doesn't resolve itself by the time we move up, I'll talk to Gary."

"Maybe this is your 'bad day.' You're just getting it out of the way early."

Gary has instructed each of us to watch for signs of altitude sickness in our tent mates and to report any problems, so I pray that Ken won't rat me out. The last thing I need right now is to have Gary pay unwelcome attention to my symptoms—or, worse still, to have Kent launch into a lecture on the morbid outcome of untreated altitude sickness.

I know that masking my symptoms is exactly the wrong thing to do, but I also know I'm not the only one who's ever done it. The testosterone-soaked realm of high-elevation mountaineering attaches considerable importance to physical and mental toughness and self-sufficiency, and no one wants to reveal himself to be a blubbering wimp. Flagging mountaineers often keep mum, trying to tough things out until their symptoms disappear. Often they do, but sometimes they advance from bothersome to life-threatening. At that point the illness becomes a major drain on the expedition—particularly if the victim needs to be led off the mountain.

In my pack I carry a three-week supply of Diamox (acetazolamide). It's a tried-and-true drug that mountaineers have been taking for years, and it's particularly effective in combating periodic breathing.

Early in the trip, however, our resident physician—Brad Skidmore, M.D.—had voiced concern about its use. "If you haven't taken it before," he warned me, "I wouldn't use it on the mountain. An expedition is no place to start experimenting with drugs. You have no idea how your body will react. Beyond that, once you start taking it, you have to keep taking it for the duration of the climb. I just wouldn't risk it."

Despite Brad's professional advice and my desire to climb this mountain without the aid of performance-enhancing drugs, I vow that one more night of suffocation and freaky dreams will be ample cause to crack open the pill bottle.

I study the other climbers, hoping to detect a hint that they're struggling, too. They all seem full of energy, intent on making the most of our vacation day. I force myself to accompany them as they tour our immediate neighborhood.

Nat, whose exploratory forays have led him to the outer reaches of the basin since he climbed from the tent an hour ahead of us at 7 a.m., comes stomping into camp. There's something he wants to show us.

"You guys won't believe this," he says, leading us to the perfect icon of the world we've left behind: Idled climbers have sculpted a television set from snow and placed it on a large pedestal of ice. Two bamboo wands serve as the antenna. In front of a snow couch sits a snow coffee table; upon the latter is a handy channel-changing remote, likewise made of hard-packed snow.

We grab water bottles and a bag of food and settle onto the ersatz sofa. After a brief struggle over control of the remote, we tune in ESPN and watch some baseball. The only challenge is deciding whether to cheer for Nat's Seattle Mariners or Brad's Cincinnati Reds.

Embroidering the fantasy, we pass around Ziploc bags filled with snacks. Nat and Brad leap to their feet whenever their home boys turn a double play or loft a ball over the outfield wall. Eventually, I articulate the obvious: "The reception here is terrible—that screen is filled with nothing but snow."

We pass an hour or more in the warm sun, where I succumb to one of my increasingly frequent daydreams of home. At the moment, I can't imagine anything better than sitting in the bleachers of a real baseball stadium, drinking a cold beer and munching a bratwurst—not the healthiest regimen for a guy who's already retaining fluids.

Late in the morning, we switch off the TV and turn our attention to the extreme sport taking place—live and in real time—above us on Motorcycle Hill. We gather to watch climbing teams creep up the hill on their way to camp at 14,200 feet, their sluggish ascent a reflection of how hard they're working on the steep pitch. Sleds hang like pendulums from the climbers' waists. As I watch them tackle the slope, I brace myself, expecting to witness the inevitable fall. But it doesn't come; all reach the top safely and disappear from view. Tomorrow we'll follow in their footsteps to cache a load of supplies.

I spend much of the afternoon trying to offset my sleep deficit by going dormant. I lie on a foam pad angled to catch the sun, reading, writing in my journal, endeavoring to doze. When that fails, I retreat to the tent, climb into my sleeping bag, and practice a relaxation technique that has always been a guaranteed stress reliever in the past: I conjure up every love interest I've cultivated since the age of 17: "Kris... Karen... Tracy...."

Partway through the list, I realize that visualizing romance while poised on the lower flanks of the world's coldest mountain is nothing less than an exercise in mental torture. I might just as well picture tender meat ragouts and rich, savory sauces emerging from Kent's cook pot.

Shattering the fantasy for good, Kent calls us to dinner. I shudder to discover that the main menu item is Ramen Noodles Redux.

THROUGH A SECOND NIGHT OF FITFUL SLEEP and a cascade of suffocation dreams, I struggle to tame the emotional chaos rising inside me. Were I to surrender to these troubling (but thoroughly logical) impulses to flee, I could be off the mountain and back in civilization within a day. But then I'd have to explain my ignoble defeat to a world of people who have never felt the bite of Denali's cold, who have never been impelled by a senseless but powerful longing to stand on the highest point of ground and watch the surrounding world drop away in humbled repose. In my flight from the mountain they would see only weakness.

It takes every measure of discipline I possess to rein in my ragged, sleep-deprived mind. I focus on my breathing. I imagine my ultimate reentry to a world trembling with rich pleasures—my reward for punching through this invisible threshold of thin air. And I try to remind myself that altitude sickness is often transitory.

Though I cannot yet perceive it, I'm in the grips of a circumscribed mental and physical struggle; my battle against the debilitating effects of altitude will end here, at 11,000 feet. Throughout the rest of the climb, the altitude will often have me straining to infuse my shrunken lungs with air, but it will never again cause my emotions to avalanche nor threaten my resolve to reach the summit. I'll return home with those Diamox pills untouched.

At 8:30 a.m., I'm relieved to hear Kent's voice calling us to breakfast; it means I've made it through another night. I decline his offer of prepackaged cooked bacon in favor of low-sodium oatmeal and a couple of cups of stout coffee.

By 10:30, we're clipped onto the ropes and heading toward Motor- cycle Hill, dragging our sleds behind us. On each step upward, the sled pulls against me, demanding vigilance in planting the steel points of my crampons in the ice. But the combination of crampons and ice ax (the latter's shaft sunk deep in the snow) provides a secure anchor, and I gain confidence on the steep slope.

At the top of the hill, my full bladder forces us to stop. Then, for the next 1,000 feet of climbing, I serve as little more than a life-support system for my kidneys. Giddy with happiness, I piss like I've never pissed before, feeling the tightness ease in my bloated fingers and eyelids. The blessed experience of diuresis in itself is enough to lift my mood, and the outflow seems to carry my dark ruminations with it.

Above us at about 13,500 feet, Windy Corner, true to its name, is locked in blowing snow. Gary decides to bury our cache at 12,500 feet, rather than risk encountering winds higher up where the trail narrows and edges on a sheer drop of several thousand feet. We dig for half an hour, then inter our load of white gas and plastic bags of food. As we return to the trail and get ready to descend to 11,000 feet, we notice that Ken is standing at the lip of the cache hole. He looks forlorn.

"My ice ax is missing," he says.

"That's not good," says Kent.

"I think it's down there," Ken says, pointing toward the cache hole. In the frenzy of excavating the hole in the blowing snow and dumping in the supplies, Ken's ice ax got buried along with the rest of the gear.

Kent rubs his chin for a few seconds, then pulls from his pack a two-foot-long ice tool—more of a hammer—for driving pickets into ice.

"Use this," he says, handing it to Ken. "It's not ideal, but it might stop you if you start to slide."

I recall Kent's admonishment that the loss of an ice ax would end a climber's trip, and I sense Ken mulling that eventuality—it's his turn to brood. Without his ice ax, a climber is deprived of his primary tool for protecting himself. The diminutive ax that Ken now carries—clearly the product of a Lilliputian ironworks—reaches barely to his knees.

"If the ax is *not* buried in the cache," warns Kent, "we may have some tough decisions to make."

We use bungee cords to strap our now-empty sleds to our packs. They tower three feet above our heads and act like sails in the stiff wind, frequently pitching us off balance. Soft snow has obscured the trail, so we stop halfway down to remove our crampons and put on snowshoes. The adjustments I made during our rest day have paid off; the straps pass easily over my boots, and in three minutes I'm on my feet and ready to move. The wind is up, it's starting to snow, and my damp shirt chills my torso.

An hour later, we take a break at the top of Motorcycle Hill and reapply our crampons for the steep climb down. From this dizzying perspective, we gaze down upon scattered miniature tents hemmed in by walls of snow. Yet within 15 minutes we're back at the bottom, where we shed our packs and shovel a foot of freshly fallen snow from the tent vestibules.

The day's exertions have purged my system of salt and retained water. After dinner, I settle into my sleeping bag and spin the dial on my radio, fishing for a station. The only signal I'm able to tune in is Delilah's Love Songs. My tolerance for her syrupy dedications proves that my mental resilience has been restored. I sleep deeply through the night. My breathing is regular, my pulse is steady, and my dreams usher me to exotic rather than bizarre destinations; not one of them leaves me gasping for breath.

A storm blows in overnight, pinning us at 11,000 feet and granting us an unanticipated rest day. Though some of my climbing partners vent their frustration at Gary's decision to stay put, I'm grateful for the extra day to acclimatize. The forced immobilization here will teach crucial lessons in patience—which, if you believe Gary, is the cornerstone of climbing on Denali.

Higher up—and all too soon—we'll have multiple opportunities to put his philosophy to the test.

Chapter Thirteen

DOING CRACK

MY CLOSE ENCOUNTER WITH A CREVASSE

GREMLINS HAVE INVADED JOE'S GEAR KIT. A grommet attaching the cuff to his boot pulled loose yesterday, his backpack harness ripped this morning, and now he's in the grips of an acute case of the mung—which, as we ascend toward camp at 14,200 feet, forces him off the rope and out of formation just above Squirrel Point. There he suffers the indignity of squatting bare-assed over the snow in a stiff gale and letting things fly. We thank the mountain gods Joe had the presence of mind to point his butt downwind.

As we make our way toward Windy Corner, fate turns her attention to me. Gary motions us off the trail for a break. I take three confident strides, yanking my sled behind me. On the third, the foundation feels a bit spongy just before the snow gives way beneath my right boot. My leg disappears in snow up to my thigh.

Before my brain can register the fact that I've just *punched through a snowbridge and am about to slide into a crevasse*, a bemused smile crosses my face, and I absentmindedly brace myself with an outstretched right hand. The snow falls away beneath my glove, too, giving me a clear view into a blue-black crack with no discernible bottom.

Oddly embarrassed and still not fully aware of what's happening,

I mutter "crevasse" in the value-neutral tone with which I might ask some-one to pass the mashed potatoes. No one acknowledges. Then my adrenal gland starts pumping, my neural network crackles to life, and my survival instinct takes over. Buried in my brain must be an archetypal cluster of cells that understands the nature of crevasses—and the physical artic-ulations necessary to extract the body without further disturbing the snow.

For the next few seconds I watch someone else's body—I know it can't be mine—respond to the crisis. Initially I freeze, then slowly my weight shifts to the leg still floating on the surface of the snow. My left hand, meanwhile, starts probing for a solid base.

My movements may be discreet and cautious, but my verbal expres-sion most certainly is not. With brain, nerves, and muscles all now fully engaged, I bellow *"Crevasse!"* loud enough to trigger an avalanche.

Gary bolts into action. "Tighten the rope!" he yells, and my rope mates immediately take up the slack. The line cinches tight just as I ease back from the lip of the crack. I look up to find Gary wearing a nervous grin.

Among mountain guides who have seen crevasses mete out much more brutal punishment, my mishap is so minor as to barely warrant mention. Crevasse falls rank as Denali's No. 3 killer, behind unarrested falls (42 deaths) and exposure (19 deaths); crevasses have claimed 8 lives since climbers began exploring the mountain early in the 20th century. French alpinist Jacques "Farine" Batkin, to cite one of the better-known exam-ples, died when he fell unroped into a crevasse on the Kahiltna Glacier during the first winter ascent of the mountain in 1967. In addition, says Daryl Miller of the Park Service, hundreds of unreported—and nonlethal—crevasse falls have occurred over the past century.

In 1992, American climbing legend Terrance "Mugs" Stump lost his life in a crevasse fall on the Japanese Ramp route on the South Buttress. Stump, guiding two clients back down from the summit on May 21, approached a large crack from the uphill side. The crevasse lip gave way. Stump fell about 15 feet before the rope pulled tight, dragging client Nelson Max 20 feet toward the brink of the crevasse. Max executed a self-arrest, then felt the rope go slack. He cut the line, rigged a belay, and rappelled into the crevasse. There Max saw a jumble of ice and hard snow, but he could not locate Stump.

With the weather worsening, Max and the second client, Robert Hoffman, abandoned the search and went for help. A Lama helicopter returned to the accident site the next day, but rescuers failed to find Stump's body.

In the annals of mountaineering disasters, few accounts are as tragic or as heartrending as the death of Chris Kerrebrock on Denali in 1981. Chris, a guide on Mount Rainier, was climbing with Jim Wickwire, one of the first two Americans to reach the 28,250-foot-high summit of K2 on the China-Pakistan border. Wickwire and Kerrebrock were on a shortened rope on the Peters Glacier when Kerrebrock, in the lead, disappeared into a crevasse, pulling his sled—and Wickwire—in with him.

Wickwire suffered a broken shoulder in the fall. Kerrebrock, though pinned headfirst in the crevasse with the sled on top of him, had not been seriously injured. With his good arm, Wickwire struggled to attach his crampons. He then began chipping steps in the wall of the crevasse, which was "slick as a skating rink," and slowly climbed out.

For hours, Wickwire valiantly strove to extricate Kerrebrock. His efforts failed—as did his attempts to radio a distress call. In time, Kerrebrock's cries for help became less plaintive. Finally acknowledging that he would slowly freeze to death, Kerrebrock asked Wickwire (who had lowered himself back down into the crevasse) to convey some last messages to family and friends. Did Kerrebrock want his body to be removed from the crevasse or left on the mountain? Wickwire asked him. My father can make that decision, was Kerrebrock's reply.

Kerrebrock's final moments were later detailed in Jim Wickwire's *Addicted to Danger: A Memoir*:

> At about 9:30, six hours after we fell into the crevasse, Chris conceded, "There's nothing more you can do, Wick. You should go up." I told him I loved him and said a tearful goodbye.... Lying at the edge of the crevasse, I listened to my friend grow delirious from the

searing cold. He talked to himself, moaned, and, at
around 11, sang what sounded like a school song. At 2
a.m., I heard him for the last time. Chris Kerrebrock was
twenty-five. I was forty."

My own crevasse incident, though minor, has a major effect on me.
For the past nine days, I have had an abstract understanding that we were
crossing countless crevasses lurking beneath a winter's worth of accu-
mulated snow. Some of the bigger cracks telegraphed their presence
through subtle indentations on the surface of the snow. Others—among
them the one I stepped into—offered not a hint of warning.

Now, with every footfall, I anticipate a trapdoor effect and instanta-
neous plunge. I doubt that I would display the grace and poise of a
Kerrebrock in confronting my own demise.

Gary notices my tentative gait and tries to offer some reassurance:
"Dave, keep in mind that we're all hauling sleds, and the snow is soft.
Even if someone steps into a crevasse, the weight—and resistance—on
either end of the rope will quickly stop his fall. Just stay alert."

NAILING THE POINT AT WHICH ALERTNESS ENDS and paranoia begins has
always been a difficult task for me. Visual confirmation of danger tends
to leave me feeling paralyzed. Such was the case in 1995, when I watched
rescue workers pull a drowned man out of the Ocoee River near
Chattanooga. In a matter of a few minutes, the experience conferred an
enduring anxiety of entrapment drowning.

Until that day, I had no fear of big water. My grandfather was an
Olympic swimmer; under his guidance, I was doing flip turns in the
pool by the time I was six. Through high school and college, I had frequently canoed the Whitewater and Little Miami Rivers near my home
in Cincinnati, often sans life vest and with a cooler of beer wedged
between the gunwales. Years later, during a bachelor party for my brother,
Steve, on the New River in West Virginia, we rode Class V rapids.

Then, in 1995, I was assigned to write an article on the Ocoee River for a magazine for seniors. Photographer Robert Clark and I had cajoled five men and women—ranging from their mid-50s to 79—into boarding a raft with me so I'd have a story to tell and Robert would have some subjects to shoot. The 79-year-old, Polly, weighed all of 95 pounds.

"This is a harmless river," I had assured them. "Virtually no risk of drowning."

At that point, no one had drowned on the Ocoee since the late 1970s. It had been chosen as the site of the 1996 Olympic white-water competition because it was considered a safe but challenging run.

We set out on the river midmorning and quickly crashed through five miles of Class IV and V rapids. I had to pause regularly to pick Polly up from the bottom of the raft, where she tended to land whenever a wave knocked her off the gunwale.

Though we snagged on a few rocks, and though most of us "went swimming" at one point or another when the boat catapulted us out in the middle of a big rapid, we emerged at the take-out point with little more than bruised backsides and scraped knuckles.

The next day, Robert and I combed the river route, stopping to talk to rafters and spectators. At one point, Robert had a raft guide ferry us across the river so he could set up his tripod just below Table Saw, a tough rapid where a lone rock broke the surface. The effect was roiling water bisected by a saw blade.

As Robert shot pictures, boat after boat of happy rafters shot the rapid. Some of the boats swamped. Others tipped. We watched dozens of yellow-helmeted rafters laughing as they bobbed in the surf.

After Robert had exposed a few rolls, we ferried back across the river and headed up the two-lane road to gather our gear for the trip home. Within a couple of miles, traffic came to a halt. I eased the car to the side of the road and walked over to a crowd of people standing on the steep bank, peering down toward the river.

"What's up?" I asked a kayaker whose spray skirt dangled from her waist.

"Some guy's pinned under Table Saw," she said. "He's been down there for 45 minutes. These guys were in the boat with him." She pointed to a quartet of distraught men and women who hugged each other and cried.

The life squad had rappelled down the 75-foot bank and strung a line across the river. Now a rescue worker, suspended from the line, was easing himself toward the rock. Once in position, he worked at dislodging the body, which was pinned by the force of the water.

In a few minutes, he shouted: "He's free! He's heading downriver!"

I saw a human form, partly submerged, shoot downstream. Out of an idle curiosity bordering on the morbid, I followed it. A few hundred feet downriver, a second rescue worker snagged the body and pulled it into a boat. As he performed CPR, I got a look at the grotesque face, bloated and purple-black. The arms, legs, and bare torso looked the same way.

"Black guy, huh?" someone said to a man standing next to me.

"Nope. That's how drowning victims look."

The rescue workers continued to administer CPR as they loaded the body into the ambulance, but it was clear the man was gone.

The Ocoee River is activated by an elaborate "on-off" switch. Throughout the day, the Tennessee Valley Authority diverts water from the sluices that feed its power stations and shunts it into the river channel, creating a navigable waterway. By early evening, when the TVA returns the water to the sluices, the Ocoee dies. As I drove home, I realized the place where the boater had struggled and died fighting thousands of pounds of water would be a dry creek bed by sundown.

I've run the Ocoee River twice since then. Each time, an edgy vigilance replaced my once-cavalier attitude about the risks of white-water travel.

ON DENALI, I DEVELOP A SIMILAR CAUTION regarding crevasses. Just before we reach Windy Corner, Kent spies a crack running directly across the trail. He turns to shout instructions.

"Dave, put your feet *exactly* where I put mine as you move over this crevasse," he says. "Got it?"

"Yeah, I got it."

I step cautiously, trying to distinguish Kent's crampon prints from those of the dozens of other climbers who have passed this way. As I near the parted blue lips of the crevasse, I take an awkwardly large stride, lurch across, and land safely on the other side.

As soon as the rest of the rope team clears the breach, I call out to Kent: "Why don't we wand this crevasse to alert the climbers coming up behind us?" My personal fear of crevasses has evolved into an altruistic mission to save all mankind.

As Kent turns to face me, he sinks the shaft of his ice ax into the snow. I know that gesture: It means he's about to launch into a lecture.

"Okay, Dave, let's say we *do* flag this crevasse," he begins. "And let's say we flag *every* crevasse we cross on our way up and down the mountain. How many wands do you think we'd need? Five hundred? Eight hundred? *A thousand?* So now we've marked all the crevasses we can *see,* which has *significantly* slowed our progress, and the climbers coming up behind us are thinking, 'Okay, the team in front of us has marked every crevasse, so now we can relax.' And then some climber who's been lulled into complacency by *our efforts to do good* falls to his death. Now how are you going to feel about that, knowing that you had a hand in contributing to a *fatal* accident?"

"*Jeeeze,*" I say, affecting a look of shock and horror. "I see what you mean."

Fully acknowledging Kent's point, I realize, is the only way to repudiate what now strikes me as the world's dumbest question. As usual, Kent is right: Each climber on the mountain is responsible for his or her own safety and welfare.

Back in formation, we slog up toward Windy Corner, a wall of ice positioned between avalanche chutes to the left and a long, wind-scoured ridge to the right. Here the trail narrows to a 20-yard-wide ramp that turns left and wraps the base of the West Buttress.

This stretch exposes climbers to a double fall line: If a climber loses her footing here, gravity will pull her backward, downslope—the first fall line. But the narrow trail also pitches to the right—the second fall line—where a climber risks tumbling off the edge in a plunge of 3,500 feet.

Any fatal fall is tragic, but those of long enough duration to give the victim time to fully fathom the fate that awaits him are particularly cruel. A plummet from Windy Corner would provide an ample period in which a climber might consider his mistake before his body slammed into the upper reaches of the Kahiltna Glacier's Northeast Fork. If he were roped to other climbers, all of them would take the long ride down.

Gary drives in several three-foot-long aluminum pickets on the uphill side of the ramp. Each picket features a webbing loop and a carabiner— that is, a closed oblong ring of metal with a spring latch—into which we clip the climbing rope. Such devices, known as running belays, would arrest a sliding rope team before it went over the edge.

The running belays are good practice for the fixed lines that await us on Denali's headwall, just above 14,200 feet. They also require us to communicate with the other members of our rope team as we arrive at each picket. When a climber reaches a picket, he shouts "Anchor!" The team then stops while he clips the carabiner off the rope behind him and onto the rope ahead. Once the maneuver is complete, the climber shouts "Climbing!" and the team begins to move again. The pickets are spaced so as to ensure that a rope team is always clipped onto at least one anchor.

Clearing a bend in the trail, we sidle above a spreading field of crevasses large enough to swallow a fleet of 18-wheelers without leaving a trace. These yawning fissures provide our first glimpse deep into the blue bowels of a crevasse, revealing ice-glazed gashes and grottoes that penetrate to depths beyond the reach of sunlight.

The crevasse field stretches 1,000 feet above us, to the entrance of Genet Basin at 14,200 feet. The basin is named in memory of Ray "Pirate" Genet, who took part in the first winter ascent of Denali in 1967. In 1979, at the age of 48, Genet reached the summit of Everest. Forced to bivouac without shelter on the descent, he froze to death.

The sight of the sprawling, sun-drenched bowl entices us through two more hours of painfully slow glacier travel. Finally we arrive at our destination—a protected basin at 14,200 feet. The same distance on the Appalachian Trail would have taken us 10 minutes.

Chapter Fourteen

THE WAITING GAME

WE ARRIVE AT THE BASIN at 14,200 feet late in the afternoon of June 5, our ninth day on the mountain. Some 6,100 feet above—three days' climbing, under ideal conditions—lies the summit. At this pace, we're on schedule to nail the summit and return to base camp in two weeks.

Gary congratulates us on our progress, but he tempers our optimism by reminding us that the mountain is always in charge. Once again, he counsels patience. To reinforce Gary's point, Joe tells us about an expedition that got stormed in and never rose above Kahiltna Pass at 10,000 feet. We've also heard accounts of storm-buffeted expeditions that never left the landing strip.

"This mountain never makes things easy on you," Joe says. "One day you're baking in the heat; the next day you're pinned in your tents by hurricane-force winds. Some Denali storms can last a *week* or more, and you gobble up your supplies going *nowhere*. You just never know."

Though Joe bases his comments on past events, he might as well have been peering into our future. Before we depart the basin, nine days will pass, lingering storms will dump nearly four feet of snow, our ranks will be reduced by two, and weather reports will predict a fierce Arctic blast—the worst to hit the mountain in a decade.

For now, however, we are content simply to be here, whiling away our time in this sun-drenched palace of the ice gods.

A WALL OF 16,000- TO 17,000-FOOT MOUNTAINS rims the basin to the north and defines the West Buttress, the rocky ridge that leads to high camp. To the south, the basin abruptly ends and falls away more than 3,000 feet to the Northeast Fork of the Kahiltna Glacier. Nearly 20 miles beyond, the snow-cloaked shoulders of Mount Foraker command the horizon.

The camp stretches about 200 yards square. Like the mountain's other big settlements, it features an intricate network of snow-block parapets, with dome tents nestled in the lee. Dead center in the camp sits a plywood privy—convenient, yes, but even less private than the crapper at base camp. Shortly after we arrive, I notice a woman seated on the plywood seat carrying on a casual conversation with the leader of a rope team moving through camp. Ten feet from the crapper is a yellow-tinged vertical shaft in the ice large enough to consume an unwary climber. The pit has been excavated over the preceding month by hundreds of bladder loads of warm urine.

Stout National Park Service cabin tents cluster on the southeast edge of the basin beside solar panels that power the radios. Occupying the tents are Park Service climbing rangers, who execute rescues and recoveries, and a volunteer medical staff. Both crews cycle through the season. The medical tent boasts the requisite medical supplies for diagnosing and treating victims of altitude, cold, and injury.

Dr. Peter Hackett, a high-altitude medicine specialist, established the camp in 1982 as part of the Denali Medical Research Project. "I chose Denali for four key reasons," Dr. Hackett tells me a few months down the road. "First, if I wanted to study all aspects of altitude illness, I had to go to a place where people were getting severely ill on their own. I couldn't ethically take people to altitude just to get them sick so I could study them. I needed to go where the action was."

Second, says Dr. Hackett, National Park Service Ranger Robert Gerhard asked him to come to Denali to help the park staff contend with the increasing number of altitude-related evacuations and deaths. (Hackett's previous work in Nepal had significantly reduced the number of evacuations and deaths in the Everest region.)

Third, the University of Alaska in Anchorage had money available for cold-related research.

And fourth, says Dr. Hackett, the wide basin at 14,200 feet on Denali provided the perfect site for a research and rescue camp.

As Dr. Hackett had surmised, the site was ideal in terms of access to test subjects; by the end of the first year, he and his crew had treated more than 100 climbers. Over the next several years, as Dr. Hackett's team stabilized more and more stricken climbers before they were led down the mountain under their own power, the number of emergency evacuations declined dramatically.

During its tenure in the basin, Dr. Hackett's team also significantly advanced the field of high-altitude medicine. They were the first to demonstrate (but not the first to publish, Dr. Hackett points out) that HAPE can be prevented and treated through the use of nifedipine—a vasodilator that reduces pulmonary artery pressure. They also showed that the synthetic cortisone known as dexamethasone can effectively treat acute mountain sickness, or AMS—as can acetazolamide, or Diamox, which until then had primarily been used only to prevent the condition. Athough the Denali Medical Research Project ended in 1990, the medical staff on-site continues to assist sick and injured climbers.

Hanging on the outside wall of one of the tents is a large dry-erase board that "broadcasts" twice-daily weather reports. The reports detail current conditions at 14,200 and 17,200 feet, including temperature and wind speed. In a personal flourish, these forecasts often feature hand-drawn (and highly expressive) faces. The frowning countenances that will predominate throughout our stay signal impending storms and dangerous wind conditions; the smiley faces, which we will rarely glimpse, denote improving weather trends and safe climbing.

The community of climbers here—50 men and women milling about in light layers and down booties—seems more like a frosty Club Med than a high-altitude encampment. Despite conditions that would wither the manhood of all but the most virile young climbers, I'm certain that some brief (if not meaningful) male-female relationships have been consummated here. Raise the temperature by 40 degrees, remove the deadly hazards, and I'm certain that the basin—with its resident population of high-energy thrill seekers—would sustain a lively fluid exchange.

Tibetan prayer flags and national banners affixed to wands flutter above snow walls, defining the fiefdoms of at least 15 international delegations. On the edge of camp, a man and woman bobble a hacky sack on hardpacked snow. Others embellish their frozen homes by sculpting elaborate arched entryways or hewing kitchen benches from blocks of snow. The smell of cooking fish wafts from the cluster of tents occupied by the large contingent of Taiwanese climbers.

Among them are our friends from 11,000 feet, Yenling, Yihua, and Mei Liang. I'm a tad disappointed when, after greeting us warmly, they ask to have their picture taken with Brad, "the American doctor," rather than with me, "the American journalist." Perhaps they're well aware of the income disparity between American surgeons and writers.

Nor is this my first chance to develop an inferiority complex. The day before, an earnest man in his 30s approached me and asked, "Are you with National Geographic?"

Through all my years as a journalist, I had fantasized about the moment when I could honestly tout that affiliation.

"Yes, as a matter of fact, I am," I said, swaggering like Barney Fife.

"Gosh, I've always wanted to meet a National Geographic photographer," he said.

"Oh, I'm a writer, not a photographer."

He looked disappointed.

"I'm really not that interested in the writing part of it. Will you introduce me to the photographer?"

Feeling like Bill Hatcher's advance man, I responded, "Sure, follow me." Then I led the man to where Bill was busily snapping pictures.

As I wandered back to camp, I could hear Bill's newest fan gushing, "I've always wanted to meet a National Geographic photographer!"

Also here in the basin are the sunshine sisters, Katy and Rachel. They arrived an hour ahead of us after speeding past our sluggish, middle-aged rope teams on the way up, their urine funnels a jangling, flesh-tone blur.

Four police officers calling themselves "Cops on Top" are camped in the middle of the basin. Rumor has it they're carrying the ashes of James Saunders (a Washington state cop killed in the line of duty in 1999), which they hope to deposit on the summit. I suppose the familiar no-trace camping admonishment to "leave nothing but footprints" sufficiently covers the issue of discarding human remains in a natural area— if the strict National Park Service policy on the matter leaves any doubt. The expedition leader—Sergeant Keith McPheeters of the Farmington, New Mexico, Police Department—does his best to debunk the rumor: The team is carrying only a plaque and some "personal effects," he insists. Few items, it occurs to me, could be more personal than human remains.

McPheeters launched the Cops on Top project in 1998 to memorialize officers killed in the line of duty by hauling plaques inscribed with the victims' names to the summits of notable American peaks. McPheeters and a Cops on Top team were on Denali in 1998, but the weather kept them from ascending above Washburn's Thumb on the West Buttress. The climbers therefore erected a small stone cairn at the upper edge of the Rescue Gully, 2,000 feet above the basin, and left a plaque there dedicated to Dale Claxton—an officer shot and killed that year in Cortez, Colorado, while attempting to stop the driver of a stolen truck.

"It just seemed fitting that a memorial to an emergency service officer would overlook the Rescue Gully," McPheeters confides. "And I think the tribute really helped the family heal. Claxton's father sat in a rocker for weeks after the funeral, just looking at a picture of his boy. He told me he finally snapped out of his grief when he knew we were on the mountain."

Climbing with McPheeters are Officer Rocky Fails, also of the Farmington, New Mexico, Police Department; Officer Charlie Newman of the Jefferson County, Kentucky, Police Department; and Trooper Stu Frink of the Washington State Patrol.

Though I'm sure these guys exude a strong "command presence" back home, up here—sans guns and badges, and bundled up in standard-issue fleece and down—they are indistinguishable from every other climbing hopeful.

WE'VE OCCUPIED AN ABANDONED CAMP at the upper edge of the basin, 200 yards from the bottom of the headwall—the steep slope that rises from the lower part of the mountain and leads to the ridge above. The site makes us front-row spectators at the drama unfolding on the slope above.

Separating the upper and lower mountain, the headwall represents the only truly technical stretch on the West Buttress Route. As Gary puts it, "Once you reach 14,200 feet, the walking ends and the climbing begins."

After dinner, we observe a nightly ritual: We form a semicircle, grip mugs of hots, talk in staccato bursts, speculate on our future—a thoroughly futile exercise—and study the 2,000-foot sweep of snow and ice that rises from the basin to the ridge at 16,200 feet.

At first glance, the slope looks deceptively short. But then, as we discern small dots moving almost imperceptibly upward, we realize we're watching climbers spaced at even intervals along 165-foot ropes. Half are moving up; the rest are descending. From our viewpoint, the distant climbers look like tiny beads strung on invisible threads.

About halfway up, the ascending climbers converge and cluster at the base of the fixed lines, which lead the final 800 feet to the top. At the beginning of the climbing season, National Park Service rangers anchor two parallel ropes in the snow about 20 yards apart. In deference to most of the world's drivers, the right rope leads up and the left leads down. Onto the ropes the climbers clip their mechanical ascenders, which are tied into their seat harnesses. An ascender slides freely as the climber moves up, but clamps tight on the rope should he fall on the steep, slick surface.

Though descending skiers and snowboarders cut wide turns on the outer edges of the slope, I'm initially much more interested in the ascending climbers; they are following the same route we will take to reach high camp at 17,200 feet—and, beyond that (we hope), the summit of Denali.

Two descending climbers capture my attention. They stagger away from the base of the fixed lines and move erratically for a time before deciding that climbing down is too much work. They slip from their packs, sit down in the snow, and execute an uncontrolled glissade all the way to the base of the slope, their packs dragging behind them. The two forms lie motionless for several minutes; eventually they rise, shoulder their packs, and advance toward camp.

"Damn," says Ken, "those guys looked wasted!"

"Based on their technique, it looks like they went to the same climbing school," I say.

"Kind of makes you wonder what the mountain is doing to people up there," says Ken.

"We'll find out soon enough," says Nat. "We do a carry up to the ridge day after tomorrow."

"I've been dreading this stretch since I first found out about it," I admit. "Eight hundred feet of steep snow and ice. This is where we get to pretend to be real mountaineers."

"The fixed lines may be steep," says Nat, "but it's the West Buttress that has me jazzed. Joe describes it as 'a 1,000-foot continuous pucker.' Exposure on both sides, narrow ledges, and a 1,000-foot drop to the Peters Glacier."

"Just to keep us from getting bored," someone ventures, "we're going to climb both the headwall *and* the ridge in the same day."

"From here up to high camp is supposed to be the second toughest day on Denali," says Nat. "Some say it's even harder than the summit."

Kent arrives and encourages us to focus on ourselves rather than the climbers struggling up and down the headwall.

"We made a big jump in altitude today," he says. "You guys need to drink lots of water and take it easy until you adjust. If you don't, you're gonna wake up in the middle of the night in a world of hurt."

He, too, studies the slope above us.

"That's one place you don't want to experience equipment failure," he says, pointing toward the fixed lines. "The last time I was up here, a guy threw a crampon on the headwall. By the time we got him fixed up, he was in tears. The next day he was heading back down the mountain."

THE SUN DISAPPEARS behind the western slopes by 9 p.m., whereupon the temperature begins its deepest plunge since the trip began. By morning, it will be -12°F. Nat, Ken, and I have worked out an orderly system for entering the tent. I go in first, and immediately pull off my plastic boots in the one-foot-deep "stoop" we've dug in the snow at the door. The stoop allows us to sit in the tent door, with our knees bent, in the shelter of the vestibule. I then scoot inside the tent, peeling off layers as I go, and wedge my liner boots into the bottom of my sleeping bag (a "long" bag I've purchased for that very purpose). Instantly I detect a horrid stench reminiscent of the elephant house at the city zoo on an August afternoon. The smell is fleeting, so I forget about it.

Once I'm in my bag, I call to Nat, who enacts the same ritual. Finally, Ken climbs in and zips into his sleeping bag. I notice that Ken is sniffing the air like a Labrador on the trail of a leftover. My feet are separated from my head by approximately 65 inches, so I'm safely out of range, but they lie about six inches from Ken's nose. Evidently their aroma is potent enough to pass through eight inches of lofted down.

"Uh, Brother Brill, are you going to change your socks at some point?" he asks. Ever faithful to his gentle nature, Ken is straining to be nonconfrontational, but he has clearly passed the threshold of disgust.

"You think after nine days it might be time?" I say. Though plastic double boots are a marvel of modern technology, they are notoriously poor at venting perspiration. I can wring a teacup's worth of sweat from my socks at the end of the day, but if I sleep in them, they will be relatively dry by morning. Dry, but not clean. The socks are beginning to feel—and smell—more like catfish skin than wool.

"I know we all stink, but it's just that your feet are right next to my head."

"Tomorrow. Fresh socks. I promise." For some reason, I've been hoarding clean socks. Though I have four pairs in reserve—including two fresh pairs for summit day—I've worn the same pair since the trip began. Dry socks are a must on summit day because any residual moisture they contain can lead to frozen feet in subzero temperatures.

When it comes to backcountry hygiene, Ken could teach me a few lessons: He gives himself a bath with Wet Wipes nearly every night. He never goes to sleep without first brushing and flossing his teeth. Most amazing of all, the white polypropylene shirt he's been wearing since the trip began is still recognizable as that color. Before leaving home, I purposely outfitted myself with black underwear just so I wouldn't have to confront visual evidence of my filth.

Other indicators are tougher to ignore. My hair, for instance, feels like someone has glazed it with Crisco. When I peel off my wool cap in the morning, greasy plaits are matted against my scalp. Then there are my fingernails, inexplicably packed with black dirt from my passage through a pristine environment of snow and ice. The bare skin of my torso feels slimy, as if I had rubbed myself with aspic, and globs of coagulated sunscreen are lodged in the creases of my nose and ears. Were I to mingle with the homeless crowd living under the bridge in downtown Knoxville, I'd fit right in.

GARY'S VOICE ROUSES US from sleep the next morning.

"You guys feeling okay? Any problems like headache?" Gary makes the rounds, stopping at each tent to check for symptoms of altitude sickness, which often sets in overnight (as respiration ebbs) after a long ascent. I'm feeling great, but Nat complains of a headache, and I notice swelling around his eyes. Ken wakes up looking like a J. Crew model. How does he keep his hair so clean?

Today we descend to recover our cache—and, we hope, Ken's ice ax—at 12,500 feet. It takes us 45 minutes to reach the cache, half an hour to dig up the goods (there's Ken's ice ax, sure enough, buried beneath the cans of white gas), and three hours more to climb back up. Late in the afternoon, we return to find the basin largely abandoned. With the forecast calling for clear, calm weather, there has been an exodus of climbers taking advantage of the weather window to move up.

Their departure may have been ill-timed. Despite the favorable weather predictions, we awake the next morning to a foot of fresh powder on the ground, then watch as sheets of snow whip through camp all day. We're concerned about the climbers above, but the timing of the storm dovetails with our plans; today is a scheduled rest day before we carry a load to 16,200 feet tomorrow.

I spend most of the day reading in the tent, then participate halfheartedly in Kent's seminar on the proper use of an ascender. The instruction I received on Rainier is still fresh—besides, practicing on a limp, horizontal rope does not even begin to approximate the conditions we'll encounter on the headwall.

Later in the day, I wander over to the Park Service camp and meet Dan Cosgro, a bearded, pony-tailed physician's assistant from Bend, Oregon. He is manning the 6-by-10-foot medical tent, which holds an arsenal of medical devices worthy of the M*A*S*H 4077th. Two cots—one of them supporting a green oxygen tank—occupy the end walls. A propane tank and heater sit on the floor. A chest whose several dozen drawers overflow with drugs shares a small table with other medical supplies. A stethoscope snakes across the tabletop beside a two-way radio.

Cosgro, who flew onto the mountain nearly a month ago, will be rotated off in another few days. I take a seat on one of the cots while he shows me a battery-operated sensor that registers pulse rate and the amount of oxygen in the blood. He invites me to try it out.

I clamp the device onto a fingertip and brace for a reading that will have Cosgro on his radio in seconds, calling in an immediate evacuation. Instead, the digital readout displays my pulse rate at 68 and my hematic oxygen level at 89 to 90 percent.

"Those are very good numbers," Cosgro informs me. "Average oxygen levels at 14,200 feet fall in the low to mid-80s." Over the next few days, curiosity will lure all eight climbers on our team to the medical tent to get their numbers checked. Clay, with a reading of 92 percent, will emerge as the aerobic cyborg among us.

In the three weeks that Cosgro has been here, he has called in two helicopter evacuations: one for a young Swedish climber who blew out her knee skiing down from below the fixed lines, and a second for a victim of HAPE.

"The climber's oxygen level had dropped to 62 percent," says Cosgro. "Even at sea level he would have been near death with those numbers, but he was actually pretty sharp for a guy in that condition."

Cosgro has treated numerous cases of frostbite and snow blindness, but the most common illnesses afflict those patients he refers to as the "worried well."

"Anxiety is rampant up here," he says. "A lot of climbers overreact to the normal effects of altitude and wind up with diarrhea from frayed nerves and stress. Many of the people I see are physically fine but mentally shot."

"I know just what you mean," I say, but I spare him the details of my crazed nights at 11,000 feet.

Chapter Fifteen

ABSURD INCONGRUITY

YEARS EARLIER, while interviewing Dick Bass—the first man to climb the highest peak on each continent and co-author of *Seven Summits* with Rick Ridgeway and Frank Wells—I had learned the value of humor in negotiating tight spots on big mountains. Paralyzed by fear high on Mount Everest, Bass had defused the crisis by recalling the definition of humor—"the juxtaposition of incongruous elements"—that his Yale English professor once scrawled on a chalkboard.

Webster's defines humor as "the mental faculty of discovering, expressing, or appreciating the ludicrous or absurdly incongruous." The scene on the headwall at 15,400 feet certainly qualifies. Yesterday's storm has blown itself out, and though the winds are scouring the ridge above us, Gary is leading us up to cache a load. After about two hours of tough but efficient climbing, we arrive at the base of the fixed lines.

For a time, it seems like nothing can possibly go wrong. But as soon as I clip onto the fixed lines, I realize I'm perched on a slope that might have served as the ramp for the Olympic ski jump. The front points of my crampons have a precarious hold on a near-vertical bulge of hard ice marking the *bergschrund*—the point where the lower glacier cleaves away from the upper slope. Above me, Kent nimbly scales the pitch.

I'm sure I'll enjoy a good belly laugh when I fully grasp the "absurdly incongruous" qualities of a neophyte mountaineer and middle-aged father of two clinging to one of the world's great peaks. For the moment, however, the only emotions I'm able to register are fear and inadequacy.

With my right hand gripping the mechanical ascender tied into the fixed line, I use my left to drive the ice ax into a surface harder than steel. The tip bounces harmlessly off the ice.

Ahead of me on the rope, Kent Wagner—the toughest human being I've ever met—shouts gentle encouragement over the wind and blowing snow: "You *WILL* keep up!"

Because angering Kent is the only thing that frightens me more than sliding off this mountain, I redouble my efforts, hammering my ice ax into a crack to help pull myself up.

So much for the incongruous elements. Fate then adds the ludicrous part: Feeling a sharp tug on the rope from below, I turn to see that Brother Ken has thrown a crampon and is sliding downslope. Ken had not yet clipped onto the fixed line, so the only thing halting his slide are me, my ascender, and the self-arrest skills of Nat, who is clipped onto the climbing rope below him. It must be an effective trio, because Ken comes to a halt, with the rope pulled taut.

Over the screaming of my Achilles tendons I hear garbled expletives rain down from above. Finally, Kent manages to articulate the obvious: "We *CAN'T* stop here!"

Nat rushes to Ken's aid from below, speedily reattaching the step-in crampon (the bulky fabric of his overboots had kept the crampon from fully grabbing the indentations at the front and back of his climbing boot). At the end of an interminable two minutes, the tension on the rope eases. I begin to creep upward, convinced that the crisis has passed.

Then it happens again.

As I feel the oddly familiar tug on the rope, I realize the worst that could befall us here is a short tumble culminating in a badly bruised ego. That's when the situation's humorous qualities emerge. Above me, a type-A guide is bellowing his disapproval of our unique climbing style.

Below me, the hapless victim of equipment failure is kicking with his single cramponed boot against the tug of gravity, evoking Robert Shaw sliding into the gaping maw of the great white shark in *Jaws*. And below him, a dozen climbers wearing identical hats are pointing up at us and conducting an animated assessment of our predicament in Chinese.

As before, Nat helps Ken secure his spikes—this time the repair holds—and at last we're moving again up toward the tight gap at 16,200 feet. Just when it seems our troubles are over, Kent notices that a second dozen Asians—this group climbing above us—are clipped onto the fixed lines not with failsafe ascenders but with utterly useless carabiners.

Though the fixed lines are anchored every 40 yards or so, Kent's quick appraisal has revealed that a single falling climber above us would trigger an avalanche of Asians that would knock all of us down to the next anchor in a tangled clot. Kent, the most cautious climber I know, commands us to wait, our steel points dug into the ice wall and our leg muscles quaking, until the entire contingent above us advances beyond the nearest anchor to the next stretch of rope.

Kent also ranks as one of the most assertive men I know. When we arrive at the gap, spent and breathless, he dumps his pack near the Asian climbers, who are now seated, and launches into a loud critique of their climbing style.

"These guys are practicing unsafe climbing techniques!" he shouts at us (but entirely for their benefit), "and they have *endangered* my ENTIRE TEAM!!"

The other team may not be up to a literal translation of Kent's remarks, but they understand his fury is directed at them. They respond by nodding their heads, shrugging their shoulders, and departing for high camp.

Gary cautions us about the steep drop-offs on both sides of the narrow spine we will have to negotiate when we make our move to high camp. His caution seems entirely unnecessary; right now my mind is cycling through the myriad falling scenarios that could result from a single misplaced boot step. A tumble to the north would deposit me 1,000 feet below on the Peters Glacier. A fall to the south would send me tumbling 2,000 feet past the fixed lines all the way back to camp in the basin.

To tether our bodies to the mountain, we drive the shafts of our ice axes deep into the snow, with the leashes still clipped into our seat harnesses, and settle in for a rest break. Kent sets a picket for additional security, and we all stay roped.

Fatigued and a bit shaky, I start to stand, but the ice-ax leash pulls up short. I totter for a terrifying instant before returning to my seat. So thoroughly exposed is this tight patch of snow that I'm reluctant to move—much less dig a cache and bury supplies.

Sixteen thousand feet up a mountain may not be the best place to discover you have a latent heights issue. I look above, following the line of the West Buttress to where it disappears behind a wash of snow, and spot a remarkably narrow spine of boulders poised above sheer vertical drops on both sides. Once again, Denali has upped the ante; we have surmounted the headwall only to encounter the dizzying features of the West Buttress.

JUST ABOVE US, two middle-aged climbers bicker over the effectiveness of a belay made from a rope section passed several times through a pair of carabiners attached to sunken ice axes. I'm no ace at climbing technique, but even I can detect that one end of the rope is lying unanchored on the snow.

"Where in hell did you learn your climbing skills?" demands one of the men. "This is a pathetic excuse for a belay."

"What's wrong with my belay?"

"Nothing, except that the rope *isn't tied to anything!*"

"No, it'll hold."

"Like hell it will. Watch this!"

The first climber tugs smartly on the rope. It glides freely through the carabiners until he is holding the entire coil in his hands.

"Oh, shit. Sorry. Maybe I should let you do it next time."

"You are *dangerous.*"

"Hey, I said I was sorry."

"We could have *died!*"

"Yeah, but we didn't."

"Nope—not this time!"

They move on, feuding as they climb, but I sit tight, hoping my malingering won't be noticed. The others grab shovels and dig a cache, deposit our supplies, then check for misplaced ice axes before filling the hole.

I'm delighted when Gary starts to lead us back down. Two hours later we're back in camp, where the West Buttress quickly supplants the headwall as my demon du jour.

Chapter Sixteen

TOUCHING THE VOID—OR NOT

THOUGH I HAD BEEN ABLE TO HIDE my newly hatched fear of heights from my climbing mates up at the pass, a seemingly innocent exploratory hike the following day—a rest day—telegraphs my weakness to the entire party. After breakfast, Kent leads us to a rocky promontory on the southern edge of the basin. It is aptly named the Edge of the World.

Roughly the size of a Volkswagen but studded with teetering rocks mixed with crusted snow, the outcropping juts out over a sheer 3,000-foot free fall to the glacier below. In much the same way that you can't go to Washington, D.C., without seeing the Lincoln Memorial, visiting the Edge of the World is de rigueur for Denali climbers. It's worth noting, however, that no one has ever fallen to his death from the steps of the Lincoln Memorial.

We approach the point in two rope teams, and Kent instructs us to queue up for our turn to gaze down from the edge and pose for pictures. Dick goes first, stomping confidently out to the very brink. He turns to face the camera, then stands studying the interlacing rivers of flowing ice below. The others follow, and finally—inevitably—it's my turn. I take one step. I can feel rocks, buried beneath the snow, twisting under my crampons. Two steps. I hit a patch of soft snow and plunge in up to my shin. Three steps. My crampons scrape on solid rock. Four steps. I'm halfway out and glance down to see the world fall away on either side. I stop.

"Hey, great view," I say, trying to hide the quaver in my voice. Then I quickly begin to retreat.

"Oh, come on, David," says Dick. "Go on out to the edge. The rope will stop you if you fall."

Suddenly I'm 11 years old, standing atop a bluff 30 feet above a lake in southwestern Ohio, trying to persuade myself to jump. My friends, who have jumped before me, are in the water. At first they cajole. Then they badger. Finally they heckle, but still I stand frozen on the ledge. Finally I back up five paces and sprint toward the edge. Then I'm falling for what seems like minutes before my feet crash into the water. I take the plunge only once—just enough to halt the heckling.

"David, do you have a heights issue?" Dick shouts.

"Do I have a healthy aversion to tottering on wobbly rocks above a 3,000-foot drop? I'd have to say yes."

"Come on, David, confront your fears," says Dick. "Prance right out there. We've got hold of the rope."

I force my stiff legs to carry me out to the edge. I turn, muster an artificial smile, and shout to Bill, who's got my camera: "Take the fucking picture!"

Back on terra firma an instant later, I let out a long sigh. Kent pulls me aside while the others continue to scramble on the rocks.

"Oh, shit," I think. "I've revealed a fatal flaw to the one man I know who *has* no flaws, at least when it comes to mountaineering."

"Hey, Dave. Let's talk," Kent says, affecting the soothing tone of a major league manager who's about to tell his aging shortstop he's being sent down to play triple-A ball in Pulaski, Virginia. "If you've got a problem with exposed climbing, I need to know about it right now. The West Buttress is 1,000 feet of extreme exposure, and the summit ridge is about two feet wide, with a 9,000-foot dropoff on one side. I need to know that you're going to be okay higher on the mountain."

"Kent, this may sound like bullshit," I say, "but when it counts, I'll be fine. Venturing out onto that rock was not essential to my trip up the mountain, so I saw no reason to force myself to do it. I want the summit as much as any guy out here, and I promise you I'll be right on your heels all the way up. I may be fearful, but I'm even more willful. No worries, okay?"

"Okay," he says. "But I'm gonna be watching you."

EVENTS OF THE NEXT FOUR DAYS, though yeilding virtually no gain in elevation, converge in a way that refocuses our expectations and dramatically reconfigures the character of the expedition.

First, on June 9, our 13th day on Denali, an RMI team led by Everest veteran Brent Okita catches up to us, even though his expedition set out a week after ours. Capitalizing on good weather, Brent has covered the 7,000 feet from base camp to the Genet Basin in six days to our nine.

Brent has spent the previous few weeks on Everest searching for the body of Andrew "Sandy" Irvine, who disappeared while climbing the mountain with George Mallory in 1924. The two climbers were last seen through a telescope somewhere near the summit. Mallory's body was discovered in 1999 by a team led by Conrad Anker, but Irvine's corpse is still up there, locked somewhere in the ice. Locating Irvine's body is of particular interest because he was very likely carrying a camera; the film, once processed, could resolve nearly 80 years of speculation over whether the two men made it to the summit 29 years before Edmund Hillary and Tenzing Norgay officially accomplished that feat in 1953.

After a short stopover at his home, Brent lit out for Alaska with an abundance of oxygen-carrying red blood cells still coursing through his veins. He is driving his team hard—but then, Brent is known as a strong, accomplished climber whose aggressive style of guiding differs radically from Gary's softer approach, which is designed to put the maximum number of clients on the summit. By the time Brent reaches 14,200 feet, the seven clients and three guides who started the climb have dwindled to five clients—two of them severely ill—and one subordinate guide. One of the ailing clients, a young woman, lies curled on a sled in the fetal position, unable to move.

Kent glances at her and says, "That's the *worst* thing she could do. She needs to get up and move around."

The woman will head down the day after tomorrow, along with the second sick client, thinning Brent's ranks to three climbers. Joe volunteers to lead them down. As a company owner, Joe is willing to sacrifice his shot at the summit to make sure the ailing climbers are evacuated safely from the mountain. Seeing Joe leave will be hard on all of us. We'll miss his jovial, carefree attitude and his stories from three decades of climbing in Alaska.

Gary had planned for us to move up to high camp on June 10, but we awaken to see an ominous lenticular (UFO-shaped) plume blowing off the West Buttress—an indication of harsh winds and cold temperatures. At 10:30, just as we're preparing to strike camp, Gary tells us to hold off.

"The wind is way up, so we'll stay put for the time being," he says. "We've been here longer than anyone expected, and you guys are dealing with the toughest aspect of mountaineering—the mental part. But we're all strong and healthy, we have plenty of food and fuel, and I think we all have a shot at the summit."

A collective groan meets Gary's cautious assessment. We've been stuck here long enough to regard ourselves as the official Camp 14,200 Welcome Wagon.

Now the week-long storms that Joe alluded to become reality. Over the next few days, if we're not dealing with feet of fresh snow, we'll be contending with the wind. In several instances, we decide not to move based on rumors of approaching storms. One weather report predicts a storm that will rival the Arctic blast of 1992, which dumped 60 inches of snow in 24 hours and led to the deaths of seven climbers.

Joe, who has seen just about everything in his months on the mountain, pauses to reflect on our situation. "Ah, hell," he says, scratching a growth of white stubble. "No big deal."

Trying to cushion the blow, Gary adds: "We want you to go home with all the fingers and toes you arrived with."

"I need these fingers," says Ken. "I just bought a new guitar."

Though the wind is blowing hard up high, the sun is baking the basin, so I spend much of the day socializing and scrounging for food. A team of descending Danish climbers pulls a sled loaded with surplus supplies into our camp and invites us to take all we want. I grab several Baby Ruth bars and a can of sardines. Dick, undeterred by the fact that it's frozen hard as marble, snatches a five-pound block of Havarti cheese. I see him sawing off chunks with his Swiss Army Knife and letting them melt in his mouth.

As the climbers lead the sled away, I glance up and see a towering red-haired man clad in a baggy orange coat that resembles a relic from a 19th-century polar expedition. The threadbare, knee-length garment seems to be held together by two dozen hand-stitched patches. Below it, antique lace-up SMC crampons wrap over white rubber boots—standard-issue footwear for U.S. soldiers dispatched to the Arctic in the 1950s. A red beard and a dense shock of hair frame a middle-aged face.

The climber's anachronistic appearance suggests that, having been left for dead on the mountain half a century ago, he has just stumbled up out of a crevasse to confront a world gone mad with Day-Glo plastic boots, Gore-Tex parkas, and fleece.

Joe, who hasn't yet descended, treats the figure with a respect bordering on reverence. He pulls me aside.

"Don't you know who that is?"

"No idea, but he looks a little underdressed."

"That's *Dave Johnston!* He was on the first winter ascent of this mountain back in 1967. He's a Denali *legend!*"

Johnston's feat is chronicled in the book *Minus 148,* named for the estimated temperature extreme Johnston and two teammates experienced while wedged into a tiny snow cave at 18,200 feet for seven days—by some estimates, the harshest conditions that humans have ever endured on a mountain.

If Johnston's quirky outfit isn't shocking enough, a rosy-cheeked child munching a candy bar walks up a few minutes later and stands beside him. Johnston drapes his arm around the boy's shoulders.

"This is my son, Galen," he says, introducing his son to the growing throng of mountaineers clustered around them.

"Galen, how old are you?" I ask.

"Eleven."

"You're a year younger than my daughter Challen!" I say, straining to visualize my little girl in Galen's place, stomping around in crampons, looking like she absolutely belongs up here.

"If Galen makes it to the top," Johnston says proudly, "he'll be the youngest climber to reach the summit of Denali."

Also climbing with Johnston is his wife, Cari. The Johnston family trio moves off toward its tent.

I glance upslope to see a skier ascending the 4,000-foot Orient Express. (The deadliest place on Denali, it got its gruesome name after three Japanese women fell to their deaths on it in 1972. Since then, 16 other climbers have met their fate on the Express.) When the skier reaches the top, he steps into his skis and slices turns back down, skiing directly over narrow crevasses and straddling the fine line between skiing and falling. By now I've come to recognize the daredevil alpinist as Mike Gajda, a ski patroller from Whistler, British Columbia, whom we have dubbed the Crazy Canadian. Mike seems more determined to ski than to summit. Over the past few days, as the storms have kept us from moving up, we've grown accustomed to seeing his lone figure scaling impossibly steep slopes only to schuss back down them.

Though we're staying put for now, others—including the Taiwanese women—have opted to defy the raging winds and make their move toward high camp. We can see some of them working their way up the headwall. High above, the windchill drives the summit temperature as low as -60°F—cold enough to freeze exposed flesh in five minutes.

Driven by dwindling supplies, looming return-to-work dates, inflated self-confidence, or impatience induced by inactivity, these climbers have chosen to ignore the weather and push for high camp. The mountain will punish many of them for this lapse in judgment. During our time at 14,200 feet, in fact, dozens of tortured climbers attest to the wisdom of Gary's decision to stay put. Throughout the day, long, languid lines of mountaineers emerge from the swirling clouds at 16,200 feet, clip onto the fixed lines, and creep downward. At the base of the fixed lines, as they draw closer to us and we begin to make out their features, we can read the depth of their struggle in their bent postures and wobbly steps.

We watch the Taiwanese women descend unsteadily after four days at high camp. Brad, Ken, Nat, and I grab Kent's pot of boiling water and a few packets of cider mix, then rush over to provide them hot drinks and help them settle in.

"I wonder if they made the summit," I say, and Kent overhears me.

"Dave, whatever you do, don't ask them that," he says. "No question will sting a mountaineer as much as that one if she didn't make it to the top."

I've made that mistake in the past and noted the shamefaced responses from those who answered no.

Once the climbers have hot mugs in their hands, I ask a simple "How did things go?"

The language barrier and the women's fatigue make communication difficult, but we learn that they spent four days in their tents at 17,200 feet, never daring to go higher.

Though the women's descent wasn't particularly spirited, they executed it with much more grace than some others we've seen. Many descending climbers wobble two or three paces and then collapse onto the snow, sliding 20 or 30 yards downslope like inert scarecrows, their arms and legs listlessly flopping about. Soft snow eventually brings them to a halt. They lie still for several minutes, muster the strength to stand, then repeat the process until they reach the base of the slope. From there, deprived of gravity to power their progress, they rise to their feet, their packs hanging at awkward angles away from their bodies, and stagger four or five steps before bending at the waist and leaning on their ice axes, gasping for breath and struggling to stay erect.

The ones who have suffered frostbitten hands and feet totter directly to the medical tent for aid. Others creep toward their tent sites, resigned to the reality that their ordeal isn't yet over and that they still have to erect shelters and build snow walls. Even as I hurry to assist them, I yield to a perverse fascination with the visible effects of the climb etched into their features.

Triangles of black skin on their cheeks betray the vulnerable gap between goggles and balaclavas. Lips have become red and swollen bands of blisters and cracked skin, coated in gobs of white zinc oxide. The rest of the skin is rust-red from exposure to wind, sun, and cold. The eyes, sunken into hollow cheeks, are fixed in dull stares that focus on nothing. Reedy, exhausted voices speak in an economy of clipped utterances: "Four days at 17," "no shot at the summit."

Gary, though sympathetic to their condition, uses their experience as a teaching tool.

"It's tough to watch this mountain beat up on people," he says. "And it's easy to get so frustrated by the wait that you're ready to go higher at all costs. But look at these climbers coming down and ask yourself: Is it worth it?"

We arise at 14,200 feet on June 13, our 16th day on the mountain, to clear skies and blowing snow. Our luck has returned, Gary tells us; the latest forecasts have downgraded the storm, so we're heading up.

Or so we think. After a quick breakfast of oatmeal and hots, we break camp—a process that consumes three hours—shake snow off stuff bags and shove them into packs, slather on sunscreen, and strap on our crampons. By 11 a.m. we're roped up and crunching steps to high camp at 17,200 feet. Brent Okita's team, having carried a load to the top of the fixed lines, is taking a rest day and will join us tomorrow.

Five hundred feet above camp, we pause for one of our hourly rest breaks. Seated on overturned packs, we pull on wind layers and take in food and fluids. The whomp of rotor blades rises from last night's camp—now just a tight cluster of tiny dots below—where a helicopter is setting down with supplies for the Park Service high-altitude patrol.

On our feet again, the grade steepens. Ahead of me on the rope, Clay—a former Marine and college athlete, the guy who set the team record when his pulse and oxygen levels were measured in the medical tent—begins to falter. He stops abruptly and leans on his ice ax. I can see his chest heaving as he struggles to breathe in the thin air. He calls out to Kent, who's leading the rope, in a frail voice. "I"m not feeling so good," he says. "I need to rest for a while."

"Clay, take a few minutes," Kent says.

We wait five.

"You ready, Clay?" Kent asks.

"Yeah, I think so."

The rope pulls tight, and we're moving again. Within a few minutes, Clay, who is now staggering, stops again.

Kent jettisons his pack, clips off our rope, and rushes downslope to take the load off Clay's shoulders. Our upward progress stops here, and the guides begin to reveal the decision-making savvy for which they're noted. The rest of us know what's coming: Because altitude sickness has only one sure cure, for Clay the climb is over.

We move to a flat patch of snow at the base of the fixed lines. Kent tries to raise Brent on the radio, hoping he can come up to get Clay so we can continue on. Brent declines, invoking a curious Park Service rule that forbids guides from traveling alone on the mountain.

According to Daryl Miller, the Park Service can't forbid mountaineers from attempting to climb Denali solo, but it discourages such undertakings because of their extreme risk. And because Denali guides are licensed by the Park Service, the organization exerts some control over them; hoping to set a good example for other climbers on the mountain, it requires every guide to travel in a team of two or more.

"We don't want to see guides—or anybody else, for that matter—un-roped on the mountain," says Miller. "In the interest of safety, teams should consist of two or more climbers. Solo climbers pose a risk to themselves. If they get into trouble, they can also endanger the lives of rescuers."

The rule, if applied to our situation, would allow Kent or Gary to lead Clay down, but neither guide would be allowed to return alone and rejoin us.

Gary feels Clay's pulse and does his best to lead Clay to the proper—and only—decision.

"This kind of problem can hit anybody at any time," he says. "The route from here on up is tough, and we're only a couple of hours into an eight- or nine-hour day. If you're feeling sick here, you'll probably only feel worse the higher you go."

"Maybe if I rest here awhile," says Clay, "I'll feel better. I don't want to fuck things up for the rest of the group."

And that's when Kent intervenes. He pursues a different—and decidedly less subtle—tack.

"Clay, if you're hurting here," says Kent, "there's no way you're going to make it to camp at 17,200 feet. You have to go down."

WE ARRIVE BACK IN PURGATORY AN HOUR LATER.

"Hey, something about this place looks familiar," says Brad. After dumping his pack, he approaches me and offers his professional medical assessment: "As tough as this is on Clay, there's really no other option. Maybe he'd be okay in a day or two, but the guides have to think about what's best for the expedition." The day before, Brad reveals, Clay told him he hadn't urinated in nearly 18 hours.

We all feel bad for Clay, a kind, gentle soul who has become an integral part of our mountaineering family. I am particularly sympathetic, having had my own bout with altitude sickness back at 11,000 feet.

By the next morning, attrition has suddenly become a problem. Clay will descend with Brent's only remaining guide—who, when we see him at breakfast, is none too happy about ending his first trip to Denali at 14,200 feet. He grumbles about the injustice of it all as he sloshes hot water into my food bowl.

We're savvy enough to realize that Brent won't take a shot at the summit without the assistance of another guide. To do so would be unsafe.

Furthermore, if one of his clients flags on the ascent, the whole team will have to descend.

That means one of two things must happen:

Brent, who will likely forgo a rest day in high camp if the weather on the summit is clear, will "borrow" one of our guides for the day, forcing us to wait an extra day to let that guide rest after his first summit day. That's a troubling possibility: We're down to our last few days of food and fuel, so if a storm blows in at 17,200 and we lack the reserves needed to get us through three days of weather, we will probably have to descend.

The second option is to merge the two expeditions, ensuring a guide-to-client ratio of 3 to 10. Should that occur, I wonder whose leadership style—Gary's kind, nurturing approach or Brent's balls-to-the-wall tactics—will prevail. Brent's three remaining clients are strong young climbers who seem to thrive at altitude. I'd hate to have them pacing me to the summit.

Chapter Seventeen

ONE OF OUR GUIDES IS MISSING

TRUE TO HIS WORD, Kent keeps his eye on me as we make our way from the basin at 14,200 feet to high camp another 3,000 feet above it. I fully understood his intent when he asks me to clip in right behind him on his rope. Throughout the day I often catch him glancing back at me, making sure I have not been immobilized by the extreme exposure along the ridge.

Though Clay's departure was a significant loss, the timing actually benefitted us. Had we not been forced to retreat and delay our move to high camp by a day, we would have had to scale the ridge in the teeth of wind and blowing snow. Over the years, hundreds of climbers have fallen on the West Buttress; 27 of them died as a result. The victims include RMI guide Chris Hooyman, who was blown off the ridge in 1998 when he unclipped from the rope to aid a struggling client. Hooyman's body was found a few days later, and Gary was on the mountain as the recovery helicopter passed overhead.

Struggling beneath our full loads, we reach the top of the headwall by noon. The fixed lines, by now familiar, have shrunk from terrors to irritants in my imagination. Then it's time to work our way along the West Buttress—a ridge so ruggedly dramatic that our entire route bears its name (this despite the fact that the feature constitutes only 1,000 feet of a 13,000-foot climb).

Even under ideal conditions, the West Buttress presents countless points at which the slightest lapse in judgment can be disastrous. Before we begin, Kent reminds us that we are entering a "no-fall zone": Despite the relentless tug of gravity, the dizzying effects of hypoxia, and the numerous exposed ledges, we are not allowed to fall. I don't know about the others, but I respond to Kent's warning by mustering a level of mental vigilance so intense that nothing can disrupt my focus.

Or so I think.

Shortly after we begin climbing, we weave from left to right along the ridge—in some places no wider than 10 feet—meandering around and sometimes between bus-sized boulders. Short sections of fixed lines lead up the steeper pitches. It soon becames obvious that if one of us takes a fall, the entire rope team will be plucked off its feet, so we loop the rope behind boulders on the uphill side—an unorthodox form of protection, but it's the best we have. The technical challenge of picking my way along the ridge, with its chaos of jumbled rocks and patches of ice and snow, so thoroughly engages me that fear never disturbs my calm or sense of purpose—until the French arrive.

About halfway up the ridge, as I cling to the corpus of a large boulder, standing on an icy ledge no wider than two feet, leaning out over a 1,000-foot drop, I hear a lilting feminine voice say, *"Excusez-moi, s'il vous plaît."*

I look behind me to see that a pert woman—*unroped* and carrying ski poles rather than an ice ax—has infiltrated our line and is moving along the ledge toward me. She has passed Ken, behind me on the rope, and I can see the stunned look on his face. She moves purposefully along the ledge, our rope sliding across her shoulders or against her back, and draws within three feet of me before repeating, *"Excusez-moi, s'il vous plaît."*

Hoping for guidance, I look ahead at Kent. He shrugs his shoulders, then shakes his head in disgust. The location and timing of the intrusion so completely violate my calm that my legs begin to shake as I press the whole of my being against the rock—endeavoring to make myself as thin as possible—and feel the woman brush against me as she wriggles past.

A few seconds later, her partner, a man, follows: *"Bonjour. Merci. Merci,"* he says as he, too, squeezes past. The incident reinforces a sentiment I had heard expressed lower on the mountain about European mountaineers and their cavalier approach to safety. I could understand the climbers' decision to shun caution and expose themselves to unnecessary risk, but here they have jeopardized my life and the lives of my three rope mates. Had the woman slipped on the ledge, she very likely would have grasped for our rope in a desperate attempt to save herself. In so doing, she would have carried us down with her.

The West Buttress consumes more than three hours. The effort and concentration required to negotiate the ridge far exceed those of the fixed lines, but the views amply reward our struggle. During a rest break, I gaze down upon a scene of such power that it almost brings tears. Hundreds of jagged mountains sweep in an endless panorama all the way to the greening Alaska tundra. Directly above us looms Denali's south summit, some 3,500 feet higher. For the first time, it appears within reach.

Amid the rigors and fear of expedition life, there are instants like this one when you lift your gaze from the patch of snow before you—away from your crampons, your ice ax, and rope—to behold perfection on the grandest possible scale. The fatigue, the biting winds, the bitter temperatures all temporarily melt away as you savor the beauty of the scene. Such moments lead men and women to risk pain—even their lives—to stand atop high mountains.

THE COMPLEXITY OF THE TERRAIN along the ridge forces us to move slowly, which in turn protects us from the full effects of the altitude. When we reach the end of the West Buttress and enter the wide, secure terrain of the basin at 17,200 feet, however, Kent picks up the pace. Suddenly my lungs feel shrunken and useless. We snake past a dozen or so tent sites before locating Brent Okita's team. Having arrived three hours ahead of us, they've already erected their tents and built their snow walls.

My gait upon arrival at high camp can best be described as a drunken stagger—I'm grateful that the Cops on Top don't demand I walk a straight line—and as I stumble toward Brent, who's proffering hot water, I nearly lacerate one of his tents with my crampon points.

"Hey, watch out!" he says. His tone is firm but not cross. "Have you seen what crampons can do to a tent?"

I immediately sit down and remove my spikes, not particularly troubled by the apparent synaptic breakdown between the commands my brain is sending and my body's efforts to execute them. The altitude notwithstanding, I don't feel bad—though the process of breathing demands a huge effort—I just feel *stupid*. As Daryl Miller had explained during our pretrip orientation back in Talkeetna, "At 18,000 feet you have only 50 percent of the oxygen saturation at sea level, so you're only half as smart."

If Miller is right, and average IQ is 100, then high camp on Denali is populated by idiots; at sea level we might hope to find work packing Christmas ornaments. Yet here we are, equipped with all manner of sharp objects and surrounded by an astounding array of unpleasant ways to die. This sobering reality occurs to me only later, on the descent, when the denser air reoxygenates my brain.

At the moment, I feel giddy—euphoric even—and completely unfazed by the fact that hypoxia has reduced me to a mental midget. I'm 17,200 feet up a frigid mountain rife with hazards. The hidden blessing of stupidity—be it conferred by thin air or heredity—is that you're blissfully ignorant of possessing the mental acuity of a box of finishing nails. Once you've experienced the fog of altitude, it's easy to understand why compromised decision-making plays a key role in many—if not most—mountaineering accidents.

THE PROCESS OF MAKING CAMP consumes several hours, and I pause frequently to rest as I fortify snow walls. Blocks of snow that once seemed featherweight now feel ponderous and heavy. The 300-yard trek to the open-air privy—a plastic device with a sliding lid—requires rest-stepping and pressure breathing; upon reaching my destination, I couldn't care less if a major network broadcast the procedure. At this point, I'm more concerned about my dwindling roll of "mountain money" than I am about exposing my backside to queued-up mountaineers.

Back at 14,200 feet, necessity had prompted one desperate climber to use the pages of a stout Dickens novel to meet his needs. (Up until then, I had thought a scathing review was the worst indignity any book can suffer.) If our summit push is delayed by even one day, I realize, I'll have to choose between defiling *The Professor and the Madman* or the section of *Killer Angels* now in my possession.

FOR A MAN WHO HAS ALWAYS LOVED TO EAT, altitude-induced anorexia is a novel experience. My climbing pants have started sliding off my hips, and several extra inches of rope now dangle from the cord lock I use to cinch it around my waist. Upon my return to civilization, I'll discover that the expedition has relieved me of 17 pounds.

I know that my body desperately needs both fluids and food. Regardless of what Kent serves for dinner tonight, I resolve to eat some of it. My stomach turns when he ladles the loathsome ramen noodles and vegetables into my bowl. On the brink of nausea, I eat with tiny bites, grimacing each time I swallow. I've lost my appetite even for the chocolate bars now frozen in my pack.

At 17,200 feet, we have entered the "death zone"—the rarefied precinct where humans simply cannot survive for long periods of time. Our bodies are dying, our muscles withering, and each hour we spend here hastens our physical decline. Brad, lean to begin with, resembles an Auschwitz survivor. All of us look hollow-cheeked and weary.

With the perils of the West Buttress behind us and a day of rest ahead, I manage to sleep soundly through the night.

❖

HIGH CAMP ON DENALI is one of the Earth's least hospitable places. Even during the relatively warm spring and summer climbing season, night-time temperatures regularly plunge to -50°F—sans windchill. Frequent storms blowing in off the Gulf of Alaska from the southwest can pack 100-mile-an-hour winds and dump massive amounts of snow. We have already witnessed the devastating effects of such storms on the beaten climbers descending from high camp to 14,200 feet.

The camp's reputation for frigid temperatures seems not to faze our neighbor, Dave Johnston, who arrived with his wife Cari and son Galen a day ahead of us. While my six climbing mates and I shuffle around in multiple layers of fleece, Johnston has stripped off his shirt and is culti-vating a tan as he fortifies the snow walls around his tent. To a guy who has endured temperatures of -148°F, the current conditions—20 above in the sun, no wind—must seem downright tropical.

"In more than a decade of climbing Denali," remarked a Park Service ranger camping here this morning, "I've never seen such calm, warm weather at 17,200 feet." The comment only heightens our concerns about squandering such a perfect day idling in camp. But after the long, rugged climb from 14,200 feet—and given the urgent gasping that attends the slightest effort at this altitude—a 12-hour slog to the summit (a cumu-lative elevation change of more than 6,000 vertical feet) is unthinkable without a day of rest beforehand.

All morning long, we watch dozens of climbers leave camp and move up the shadowed bowl that leads to Denali Pass (18,200 feet) and the gateway to the summit ridge. The Cops on Top are kicking steps up the mountain and will place James Saunders' personal effects on the sum-mit. (Climbers leave all sorts of mementos atop Denali.)

Among those climbers is Kent, who left high camp at 8:30 this morning with Brent and his team. Last night, Brent and Kent—both head-strong alpha males—tangled briefly after we had entered our tents, and though we couldn't make out their acrimonious words, we gathered that the heated exchange had something to do with Brent's asking Kent to accompany his team the next morning. (Brent, an RMI supervisor who is technically Gary's and Kent's boss, could have pulled rank and demanded that Kent assist him. Instead, we suspect, Brent phrased his request in the form of a question and Kent grudgingly assented.)

Like every other RMI guide, Kent regards safety as paramount; his inclusion in Brent's team will help ensure the safe passage of its three remaining clients. But Kent doubtless shares our concerns that he will return from his summit push with Brent too exhausted to repeat the feat with us the next day. No one has ever questioned Kent's devotion to our team, and I think I know him well enough by now to understand that he will push himself to the brink of his endurance to guide us to the top—even if that means back-to-back summit days.

Earlier in the trip, Joe acknowledged that bagging the summit twice in the course of Denali's four-month climbing season would be regarded as a major achievement. Kent has demonstrated extraordinary physical and mental toughness in the last three weeks—but is he strong enough to climb this mountain twice in two days?

DAVE JOHNSTON MAY THRIVE AT THIS ALTITUDE, but his 11-year-old son, Galen, seems to be suffering from the effects of the altitude and the cold. Last night, the temperature dropped to -20°F, the coldest it's been so far. Gone are the beaming smile and rosy cheeks that Galen displayed at 14,200 feet. Wan, pale, and listless, he rarely leaves his tent throughout the day.

All of us are suffering similarly. Hypoxia turns the 100-yard trek to the ledge of granite boulders edging the high-camp basin into a battle to breathe. If we can just make it there, however, the compensation is a dramatic topographic summary of where we've lived and worked for the past 19 days. Nearly 10,000 feet below us to the southwest flows the long, tapering arm of the Kahiltna Glacier, its arched fingers probing deep into snowy pockets outlined by upthrust crags and granite ridges.

Using Bill's telephoto lens, I can make out tent clusters marking successive stages up the mountain. The camp at 14,200 feet sprawls directly below. Though only a day behind us, it looks remarkably distant. The enormous scale of the West Buttress dwarfs the forms of climbers ascending its spine. We study the ridge for motion, pointing excitedly whenever we spot a climbing team moving antlike among the maze of boulders.

THE EASY BANTER that characterized our morning meals lower on the mountain has been replaced by sparse and efficient exchanges communicating only essential information. Even the loquacious Dick Bowers has grown almost taciturn. Though we don't say much to each other, our minds sustain an internal dialogue fraught with doubts and fears about our chances of reaching the top. Conditions and circumstances have converged in such a way that tomorrow may mark our one and only shot at the summit.

Through our rest day, these tormented musings resist any efforts at distraction. We try to occupy ourselves by sorting summit gear, reading in the sun, or studying the climbers moving up toward the pass. In reality, we're focused on a small patch of snow perched above us at 20,320 feet.

Katy and Rachel stop by for an afternoon visit. Just a few hundred feet from the top, they report, they had been turned on their heels by an emergency bathroom break—and the frosted backsides that resulted from it. Now they're heading back down without having bagged the summit.

By evening, the day's calm gives way to rising winds and subzero temperatures, and 8 p.m. finds us squirreled away in our sleeping bags, listening to the wind lash the tents and straining to catch the familiar sound of Kent's voice.

A short time later, Kent and the other climbers can be heard returning from the summit. There's happiness in their voices, and as I listen to the wind piling snow against the tent walls I give in to envy.

"The wind's picking up," I say to Ken and Nat. "We're screwed. We missed our shot."

For the first time since I've known him, Nat offers not a word of encouragement. Ken stares straight ahead, listening through his ear buds for the nightly weather forecast from the NPR affiliate in Talkeetna.

"The weather report calls for 30- to 50-mile-an-hour winds on the summit tomorrow," he says, eventually. "It's supposed to blow for the next couple of days."

My irritability gives way to summit fever—the judgment-clouding ailment that has contributed to the deaths of more climbers than falls, avalanches, and mountain sickness combined. In my jaundiced mood, I begin to regard the entire undertaking as a meaningless black hole— a waste of time, energy, and money—without the summit.

My mind swirls with contingencies and counterplans. If the team chooses to descend, I'll offer Kent $1,000 to stay on the mountain with me a few more days. Or I'll hook onto someone else's rope—it really doesn't matter whose—and beg a ride to the top.

Just as our reserves of food and fuel have dwindled, the difficult conditions on the mountain have eroded my strength and resilience. My yearning for the summit aside, I'm flat-out bone-tired. I've been wearing the same clothes for 19 straight days. My fingertips and toes are constantly numb. The odor of camp food clinging to my gloves makes me sick.

For nearly three weeks, I've endured conditions harsher than any I've experienced before. I've strained to hold myself together in the face of warring emotions that have pushed past the angle of repose and now threaten to avalanche. Even the toughest humans were not meant to live at this altitude. We're all operating on borrowed time.

Then I delve into the Ziploc bag that holds pictures and letters from home, and suddenly I gain perspective. I may sport the clothing of a mountaineer, but at heart I'm just a middle-aged father who misses his preteen girls.

Chapter Eighteen

UNWELCOME WINDS
ON THE WAY TO THE MOUNTAINTOP

THE NEXT MORNING, we dig our way out of our tents through the wall of snow that has blown into the vestibule during the night. Kent is poised over his stoves, seemingly none the worse for having covered 6,240 vertical feet over 12 hours the day before.

The wind whips through camp, keeping all but the most foolhardy climbers from moving up toward Denali Pass. The windchill has driven the temperature down to nearly -40°F. Climbers cluster in camp, their bodies layered in their warmest combinations of fleece and down, talking and scanning the ridge above them through a haze of blowing snow.

Though we're all edgy and eager to ascend, we can tell that the disintegrating weather conditions have probably robbed us of our shot, especially if they persist longer than a day. The two-foot-wide summit ridge is notoriously exposed; if a sudden gust blasted a climbing team off its feet, its members could slide nearly 9,000 feet—the fatal plunge that Daryl Miller describes as "the whole ride down."

Here we are gripped by mountaineering's great conundrum: deciding what we're willing to risk in order to reach the top. I recall George Dunn's words from the Rainier seminar: "You need to continually ask yourself: Do I want to continue on and die or go home and try again?"

I'm so fully bewitched by the summit, I realize, that I'm willing to wager far too much to achieve the goal at hand; I'm on the verge of making a sacrifice I could never expect my daughters to accept or understand. I can't imagine paying the financial, physical, and emotional costs necessary to return to Alaska in some later year, starting the long slog up from 7,200 feet, then enduring these horrid conditions for another three weeks only to face the same depressing 50-50 odds of reaching the summit. Yet I know that if I don't reach the top, this peak will haunt me the rest of my life.

In this crazed state of longing—exacerbated by the distorting effects of altitude—I cannot grasp how climbers just a few hundred steps from a summit (even in the face of a potentially deadly storm) could muster the will to turn around and descend. In 1912, Parker, Browne, and La Voy did just that, though their ascent to Denali's crest would have made them the first men to stand atop the mountain.

Fortunately, the responsibility for making this difficult decision resides with Gary, who has been bargaining with mountains for access to their peaks for nearly 20 years. Confirming what we already know, he advises us to hold off on packing our summit gear.

Dave Johnston, now clad in his cold-weather gear, walks over to talk with Gary and Kent. "I think we're going to wait and see what the weather's like tomorrow," he says.

Brent and his three clients are already on their way back down; they will descend 10,000 feet to the landing strip today, then spend the evening celebrating in Talkeetna.

The envy I feel toward Brent, his team, and their success degenerates into loathing. Black emotions that I've never felt before overtake me. I've retained enough mental acuity to realize that mountaineering is not a zero-sum game—the success of others has no bearing on my own—but this newborn resentment eclipses any efforts on the part of my logical mind to regard circumstances for what they are: We have climbed high on a magnificent mountain, we are all safe and relatively healthy, and our inclination to define the summit as the ultimate measure of success is nothing more than a perverse outgrowth of Western man's obsession to conquer the natural world.

We mill around camp as the morning elapses, talking little, gulping air, peering up at Denali Pass. Will we ever get there?

At 10:30, Gary calls us together.

"It's blowing pretty hard right now," he says, "but let's pack our gear and get up to the pass. This may be nothing more than a training climb, but we won't know till we get up there and put our noses into the weather."

Suddenly, our movement gains purpose. Though I face risk and a level of exertion more extreme than any I've confronted, I'm giddy with anticipation. We stow water bottles in our packs, insert chemical heat packs into our boots and gloves, double-check to see that goggles and face masks are accessible, cinch tight our crampon straps, don bulky down summit parkas under our Gore-Tex windshells, and finally pull on heavy mittens and shells over liner gloves.

Around 11:30, we commence the slow slog up the shadowed basin to Denali Pass at 18,200 feet. Ahead, Gary leads the rope; behind me climb Brad, Nat, and Ken. Dick, Matt, and Bill have hooked in with Kent and are bringing up the rear.

From the perspective of high camp, the slope to the pass looks deceptively gentle. Once we gain the two-foot-wide trail on the upper lip of the bowl, however, we discover we're suspended above a steep, icy ramp that plunges 500 feet into a crevasse field. More climbing accidents have occurred on the incline below Denali Pass than on any other section of the mountain. The pitch acquired the macabre name "the Autobahn" after 1976, when a European climber fell to his death here, becoming the first of six climbers to die in similar circumstances. The Autobahn has been the site of up to 200 falls, estimates Daryl Miller, but only about 50 of them were officially reported as incidents.

In the basin at 14,200 feet, I had met a climber who took a 300-foot fall here on his descent from the summit. Thoroughly unhinged by the mishap, he opted not to return from the summit to his tent at 14,200

feet (where his summit push began) because it would have meant enduring the exposure of the West Buttress en route. Instead he holed up, with
no sleeping bag, in a vacant tent at high camp.

Gary stops frequently to drive in pickets and set running belays—
welcome pauses that permit me to lean on my ice ax and breathe. We
arrive at the gap in three hours, where a frigid wind from the east belts us
in the face and billows our parkas. Gary, I know, is about to turn us back.

Instead, he gathers us together.

"Boys, this is our summit day," he says, grinning. "Pull on your face
masks, put on your goggles, and cover every inch of skin. Anything
exposed will get frostbitten."

I pull on a thick windproof fleece balaclava over my mouth and nose,
then adjust a pair of goggles over my eyes. The balaclava muffles the sound
of the wind but amplifies my desperate gasping for air. Even at rest, the
force of my breathing is such that, as I exhale, the balaclava balloons out
from my head; as I inhale, it draws tight around my face. Higher on the
mountain, I fear, I will face a difficult choice: Suffocate or freeze.

Some of the climbers have duct-taped foam over the grips of their ice
axes to combat the conductive cooling that is strong enough to pass
through all three layers protecting our hands: liner gloves, dense fleece
mittens, and nylon shells.

The visual transformation is dramatic. Vanished behind protective
shields are the faces I've gazed upon for the past three weeks, conjuring
in their place a band of generic mountaineers. The facial expressions that
once so effectively communicated how each of us was faring will remain
masked for the remainder of the day. Brad, with his iridescent green goggles, has been reborn as an enormous insect.

Soon we're climbing again, pushing into the wind, and passing the
South Peak's notable landmarks: the weather meter maintained by Japanese
meteorologists at 18,900 feet and the rocky knob of Archdeacon's Tower
at 19,650 feet. The struggle to breathe forces me to pull the balaclava
below my chin, inviting the moisture from my breath to freeze my beard
to the collar of my parka.

We descend into the broad expanse of the Football Field at 19,500 feet, drop our packs, and take the last of our rest stops. The water in the bottle I've carried inside my down parka is still liquid, but the two additional bottles, bundled in insulated covers and stowed in my pack, are frozen solid. Before leaving high camp, I intentionally bashed to fragments the Baby Ruth candy bar that I had snatched from the Danes at 14,200 feet, knowing that otherwise my teeth would break on the hard-frozen mass.

Once again, Gary has demonstrated his extraordinary gift for decision-making. The howling wind has eased to a moderate bluster. If we fail to reach the top, it won't be because of the weather.

Above us is the jutting spur of the Kahiltna Horn. To the left of it, the headwall leads to the summit ridge. A faint trail in the snow meanders from the Football Field toward the horn, and the tiny forms of climbers can be seen moving toward the summit. Although the summit ridge looks to be only minutes away, Gary informs us we won't reach the top for nearly two hours.

On our feet again, we leave our packs behind and begin kicking steps toward the summit ridge. Seven hours have passed since we left high camp, yet I have lost track of the passage of time. Instead, soothed and entranced by the rhythmic crunch of my crampons, the rasp of my breath, the sound of my ax piercing ice, I flow through the frozen landscape. The totality of my perception falls on the three feet of snow directly in front of me.

The world seems thoroughly uncomplicated. I cannot recall another moment in my life when my purpose seemed so clear, my goal so close at hand. So complete is the sensation of tranquillity and peace that not a single worry or concern intrudes upon my thoughts. In the midst of the most dangerous stage of the climb, even the specter of death fails to faze me.

Descending climbers, equally focused on the snow beneath their feet, pass like ghosts. Occasionally a pair of us glance up and acknowledge each other. Just before we attain the summit ridge, I emerge from my reverie long enough to ask one of them a question:

"How far?"

"Less than an hour," he replies. "And if you don't make it, I am personally going to kick your ass!"

I smile at his response—the kindest and most encouraging words I've ever heard, given the context. Soon I'm planting my boots on the foot-wide trail of the knife-edge that leads to Denali's crown, strangely unconcerned that I might fall. Then, after what seems like an instant, I glance up and see Gary ahead on a tight patch of snow, coiling me in. As I reach out to shake his hand, I feel warm tears on my cheeks. It's 8:30 p.m. on the 16th of June, 2001, and I am standing on top of North America.

The others come up. I dig into my parka and unfurl a sign I had fashioned with a fat-tipped marker and a white garbage bag at 14,200 feet. Dick has his picture snapped—first with the American flag that graced his limousine during his ambassadorship in Bolivia, then with a sign proposing marriage to his girlfriend, Kay. Not every man can claim to have climbed the continent's highest peak for the woman he loves.

Once the hugging and backslapping subside, we stand silent, savoring the view. As my eyes sweep the endless expanse of ragged mountains that sprawls around us, it occurs to me that in the context of 20 days of hauling huge loads and waiting out weather and stomping in snow with numb feet, 20 minutes of standing on the highest point of ground would not amount to much—if it didn't mean everything.

For me, Denali is an endpoint, not a stepping-stone to higher and more celebrated peaks. I've promised a few folks back home that once I return from this mountain, I'll hang up my crampons for good. For that reason, this moment marks a literal and figurative high point in my life. As we begin our descent, I realize, with some sadness, that I will never again stand with steel points in ice and view the world from this vantage point.

WE STOP FOR A REST AT DENALI PASS, where Kent—who seems to be drawing strength from his back-to-back jaunts to the summit—reminds us that the trip is far from over.

"This is a very dangerous stretch," he says. "Focus on your feet. You *cannot* fall here. Is that clear?"

We mutter our acknowledgments. Then Gary gets to his feet and asks me to help slip a picket into the waist belt of his pack for the trip back down. If I felt stupid on our arrival at high camp, I feel absolutely imbecilic here: I'm exhausted *and* hypoxic. I've curled my cramponed boot under my butt, tangling the spikes in the prusik lines attached to my harness. I respond to Gary's request by attempting to stand. Kent, spotting the brewing disaster, moves toward me and gently pushes me back down.

"Sit still, Dave," he commands, extricating my boot from the snarled rope. "You're scaring me."

Over the past days, I have come to treasure Kent's vigilance, friendship, competence, strength, and commitment to our team. As long as he's around, I know I'll be okay. His gruff demeanor, it hits me, is merely a manifestation of his deep concern for us.

As Kent frees my boots, I have to resist the emergence of a whole new altitude-induced issue: With the coveted summit behind me and my access to beer and good food imminent, my heart swells with sappy sentimentality. I rein in my emotions picoseconds before I would have thrown my arms around Kent and yelled, "I love you, man!"

The fact is, I do feel like embracing everybody. I can just see the incident report now: "Nine climbers fell to their deaths below Denali Pass this evening after executing a high-altitude group hug."

We're back at high camp by 11:30 p.m., where I collapse in the snow. My hands and feet are freezing but I'm too weak to stand. Ultimately, somehow, I stagger to my tent, slide into my sleeping bag, and lapse into a dreamless sleep.

Chapter Nineteen

EIGHT VIEWS OF MOUNT McKINLEY

THE TEAM SUMS UP THE SUMMIT

NAME: Gary Talcott

OCCUPATION: RMI Guide, ski coach

FAMILY STATUS: Single

BORN: July 6, 1953

HOMETOWN: Ashford, Washington

PREVIOUS SUMMITS: Denali, Rainier

CONDITIONS ON SUMMIT DAY shifted from marginal to some of the best I've seen, although I usually don't attempt to move when the weather is unsettled. The wind was a factor, and getting up to Denali Pass is one of the key parts of the climb. After we reached the pass, the wind started to ease up, and I felt that everyone had a good chance for the summit. I really enjoyed the day, particularly looking back at the team and seeing everyone moving along so well. It means a lot to an expedition leader to see his group working together efficiently and making great progress.

The nine days we spent at 14,200 feet are typical for a Denali climb, largely because weather on the mountain is hard to predict, with storm systems coming from several directions. Toward the end of our stay there, the harsh winds above us were a continuing problem.

It would have been unfortunate for us to have turned around at that point and headed down, because that's where the "walking" ends and the real climbing begins. If you have to turn back, it's better to give the team the experience of ascending the fixed lines and a look from 16,200 feet. Many teams make it to high camp and get some real action with weather. After five days or so, they've had enough.

I think Clay just had a bad couple of days prior to our move to high camp. Any one of us could have been in that situation, and all of us can remember some days that were harder than others. Clay didn't pick a good day to have problems, though, because we were approaching the fixed lines—the most technical stretch of the whole route. I was surprised to see Clay in that condition, and I hoped that if we descended, he'd feel stronger the next day, but he didn't. Moving down 1,000 feet can make a lot of difference for someone with altitude sickness. Clay is strong, and I'm sure he'll be back to summit Denali. I'd like to be there when he does.

Our team worked together from day one. Everyone did his job and assisted the guides. The climbers were taking care of themselves, which made for a safe and successful trip. While we were stuck at 14,200 feet, I sensed that some in the group were eager to move, but I knew that, in time, they'd see some of the climbers struggling back down after having made the wrong decision—not a pretty sight.

Then there was the risk we'd get slammed by the big storm the Park Service predicted. The storm of 1992 was quite an experience, with extreme cold and high winds. There were rescues going on constantly, and we heard all the activity on the radio. Loss is always tough on a mountain. It's doubly difficult if you know people who die. The loss of RMI guide Chris Hooyman in 1998 really affected me. He was coming off the mountain on the West Buttress and was blown off the mountain when he tried to help a client. I was at base camp when it happened. A climbing ranger woke us and gave us the news. Joe flew off the mountain that day, and the rest of us continued the expedition. They found Chris's body a few days later, after the storm. We knew it could have happened to any one of us. Chris was just doing his job.

The winds we experienced before starting for the summit were considerable, and I knew we risked frostbite and someone being blown off his feet. But I also knew there was a chance for the wind to ease later in the day, as it had in previous days.

After we got through Denali Pass, conditions seemed to improve, and the group was setting a good pace. As we neared the summit, everyone was tired and feeling the effects of altitude, and I was thinking "climbing this mountain sure doesn't get any easier." (I still marvel at Kent for pulling off those back-to-back summit days.) Then there are the pioneer climbers, who scaled the mountain wearing wool blazers and leather boots, with no idea of what was ahead of them. Those climbers are true Denali heroes.

One thing that really got my attention as we worked toward the summit was the snowboarders heading to board down the Messner Couloir. I just wondered if they really knew what they were getting into.

The Alaska Range is an amazing place, and many parts of the West Buttress are just as exciting as the top: Windy Corner, the fixed lines, the ridge that leads to high camp, and Denali Pass. And then, of course, there's the arrival back at base camp—hearing the mosquito drone of Hudson Air coming to pick you up and returning you to Talkeetna and all the joys of civilization.

NAME: Kent Wagner

OCCUPATION: RMI Guide, Colorado River Raft Guide

FAMILY STATUS: Single

BORN: January 28, 1963

HOMETOWN: Boulder, Colorado

PREVIOUS SUMMITS: Aconcagua (Argentina), Ixta and Orizaba (Mexico), Kilimanjaro (Africa), Rainier

AFTER MY FIRST DAY ON THE SUMMIT, I talked with Gary about my ability to go up again the next day. Much earlier in the expedition, I had promised Gary that I'd be there for our team when the time came, but I wasn't sure if I'd be physically able to make it to the top again without slowing everybody down. I recall thinking that night, "There's no fucking way I'm gonna be able to go up there again in just a few hours."

A few days earlier, Brent Okita had asked me if I'd be willing to go up with his team if needed. Because that seemed so far off, I said I didn't see a problem if we could work out the timing. The night before his team's summit attempt, it became apparent that he *would* need my help, since he was the only remaining guide on his team, and we got into a heated exchange. I felt I was no longer being given a choice in the matter. Rather, it seemed like a direct order, and I resented it in part because I was tired at that point.

As much as I wanted to help him out, and as much as I wanted to get to the summit, I wanted foremost to get there with the guys I had struggled with for the previous 19 days. I surprised myself when I woke up on the morning of my second summit feeling great.

While we were en route to the top, I went into autopilot. I just put one foot in front of the other, trying to focus on the moment. I listened to the crunch of snow beneath my crampons. I watched the spindrift rolling by. I saw the light on the ridgelines. I felt the other climbers behind me on the rope.

As we climbed, I focused on seemingly small things and tried not to get tunnel vision; it's so important for a guide to keep tabs on the whole group. I really wanted to see everyone get to the top, and I was walking very softly, hoping that nothing would go wrong. My senses were heightened, and I was fully alert. A fall on the summit ridge could be a very bad thing. It's no place to get cocky. I became preoccupied—almost paranoid—with how everyone was doing.

When we finally reached the top, I wasn't in a celebratory mood; I never am when I get to the top of anything. Topping out is only half the climb. We had to get all the way back down, and I knew the climb wouldn't be over for several days. But that doesn't mean the summit wasn't important to me. Sure, we're supposed to focus on the journey, rather than the outcome, but in reality, we're all hungry for the summit.

The reality of a McKinley climb is partially about all the hopes and expectations of everyone on the team, all of whom have made great sacrifices. I suspect most people assume they will get to the top, but getting everyone back home safely—with or without the summit—is my priority. I'd been on the mountain twice before and never got to the top.

The dynamic of this group was special—and rare. It was great to see that everyone seemed to be handling the physical challenge well, but it was even more gratifying to watch us evolve into a "team." Rarely have I seen this so concretely. Sometimes groups just gel and come together. This was one of those times. To randomly throw these individuals together and see them work so well was a lucky break and fundamental to our trek to the summit. Each one of them was an asset to the team as a whole. Being in a place with people I truly enjoy is what makes it worthwhile for me. I'd rather reach the summit of Mount Sunflower in Kansas with people I love than get to the summit of K2 with a bunch of assholes.

It was tough to see Clay go, but in his condition, he had no choice. It could have been any one of us. As it turned out, it was an unfortunate event, but the timing was good. We had the manpower to cover the situation and the time to reorganize after the loss.

There were many high points along the climb, and I remember in particular laughing my butt off about the stupidest shit with Joe and Gary while we were tentbound. I feel so lucky just to have been able to spend a few weeks with them.

NAME: Brad Skidmore

OCCUPATION: Neurosurgeon

FAMILY STATUS: Single

BORN: March 15, 1961

HOMETOWN: Fort Thomas, Kentucky

PREVIOUS SUMMITS: Cerro Huayna Potosí

and Nevado Illimani (both in Bolivia), Rainier

CLIMBING DENALI WAS THE NEXT LOGICAL STEP for me and is just a midpoint in my climbing career. I intend to go to the Himalaya and climb

Cho Oyu (26,750 feet) and who knows what after that. Because I had been to fairly high altitudes in the past (21,700 feet on Aconcagua), the altitude of Denali did not concern me as much as the extreme cold and the expedition style of travel. Carrying huge loads, both on your back and with a sled, was new to me.

When I showed up at the airport and met the other climbers, I felt like the "little guy." Because of my slight build, I take great care in packing extremely lightly. I know that my body frame and muscle mass can handle only a certain amount of weight.

Our time at 14,200 feet was filled with a great deal of boredom. The first trip up the headwall to cache our load at 16,200, though not bad, inspired me for what was to come. But then weather forced us to wait another week before even attempting the climb to high camp. It seemed that the weather would never break, that we were going to be stuck at 14,200 feet forever. I began to suspect that we'd never go higher. Oddly, the one thing that bothered me most wasn't that we'd leave 14,200 feet without a summit attempt—it was the reality that we had cached a load at 16,200 and that some or all of us were going to have to climb back up there to retrieve it. It's bad form, and a violation of Park Service policy, to abandon a cache on the mountain. But climbing up to retrieve it would have been a terrible expenditure of energy for no gain.

Clay was behind me the second time we attempted the headwall. I hadn't realized that he was struggling until we got to the steeper section just below the fixed lines. He started to drag on the line, and every step I took, I felt his weight. I kept turning around to encourage him. His pace triggered a chain reaction. When he stopped, I had to stop, which stopped Kent, who was at the head of the rope. Clearly, Clay was making no friends that day. It was obvious by the time we got him up to the base of the fixed ropes that he couldn't go much farther. He was clearly getting sick; he was deteriorating. He hadn't been able to eat or drink for a couple of days—in fact, I found out later that he hadn't voided in more than 18 hours—and was clearly exhausted. I wanted him to go higher and make it, but I knew that in his condition he would be a burden to our group and could endanger the entire expedition.

Though our holding pattern at 14,200 feet was difficult mentally, I was grateful that we were staying out of the storm up high, especially when we saw all those beaten climbers struggling down from 17,200 feet. I remember watching people come down, and it seemed to take them hours to reach camp from the base of the fixed lines. Some of the Park Service rangers headed up to check on the climbers who seemed to be in the worst shape. The climbers would take several steps, fall, roll and slide down part of the mountain, sit on their pack for 20 minutes, before rising and doing it all over again. I couldn't help wondering if, as we went higher, I'd be one of those out-of-control climbers.

High camp was a whole different experience from the basin at 14,200 feet. There was less oxygen, it was harder to move around, harder to breathe, the wind picked up faster, and the nights were colder. The first night we were there, it was so cold and windy that Gary moved the cook stove into the vestibule of our tent. He sat on a piece of coiled rope and melted snow for all of us. The next night, the wind was really beating on the tent and sounded like it would never stop. I was concerned with our low reserve of fuel and food—we didn't have more than a couple of days' rations left.

The weather on summit day was reasonable but far from perfect. We started up Denali Pass to, as Gary put it, "put our noses into the weather." When we got to the pass, the wind was tremendous. We all put on balaclavas, stout summit mitts, and our heaviest winter gear. Goggles were a must, and any exposed skin was destined to become frostbitten. Once I had put my goggles on, I felt like an astronaut on the moon—I was entering an area where few others go. I could hear the crunch of my crampons as they hit the hard snow, barely piercing the hard-frozen surface. By the time we got to the Football Field, I knew I was going to make it. It was now just a matter of time. That awareness had a powerful emotional effect on me. I knew then that all the hard work, both on the mountain and through months of training, had paid off.

On the summit ridge, I was a little surprised about the exposure, though I had seen pictures. The drop-off to the right was extremely steep; a slip would have resulted in a fall of several thousand feet. I took small, careful steps and snapped a few pictures. I kept my camera inside my parka; the cold was sapping the lithium batteries. Every time I took my hands out of my down mittens, they'd stay cold for 45 minutes.

Success on Denali is measured in terms of the summit, despite what anyone tells you. The group went through a lot together, and we became part of an exclusive fraternity. No one else will know what we really experienced up there. People can read about Denali in a book, and they can look at pictures, but those are poor substitutes for actually living on that mountain for three weeks.

NAME: Charles Richard (Dick) Bowers

OCCUPATION: Retired. Former U.S. Ambassador to Bolivia

FAMILY STATUS: Married

BORN: May 26, 1940

HOMETOWN: Louisville, Tennessee

PREVIOUS SUMMITS: Cerro Huayna Potosí and Nevado Illimani (both in Bolivia), Rainier, Whitney, and 38 of the 50 U.S. high points

WHILE WE WAITED OUT THE WEATHER at 14,200 feet, I reflected on the German phrase, *"Alles gut."* Essentially it means "All's well that ends well." The longer we languished there, I realized, the more we would acclimatize and the easier the rest of the climb would be. Once we had climbed that high, I really didn't think that getting to the summit would be all that difficult—provided the weather cooperated.

The only other issues that concerned me were our dwindling food and fuel supply and the attitudes of some of the climbers on our team, who seemed to be growing impatient and ready to quit and head down. But if the bad weather had kept up, we might all have gone stir crazy and welcomed the chance to head back to Talkeetna.

When Clay got sick, I was sad and disappointed for him, but his departure really got my attention. From that point on, I really focused on taking care of myself and my tent mates to make sure *we* didn't bonk, too. Over the preceding days, I had learned valuable lessons on how to deal with extreme cold, how to tweak my gear for maximum efficiency, how to pace myself, and how to keep my head clear and focused on the task at hand, knowing that, if things went well, each step would lead to that magical moment on the summit.

On the morning of our summit push, I really wasn't fearful, but I did have some pestering concerns about the weather. It was so cold and windy when we left high camp, and I kept fussing with my balaclava, trying to achieve the perfect balance between covering exposed flesh and allowing myself to breathe in the thin air. Eventually, I yanked the balaclava under my chin and used my free hand to cover the skin around my mouth to protect it from frostbite. When we got to the narrow summit ridge, and the wind was kicking up snow, I kept reminding myself that the climb wasn't over until we were safely back in Talkeetna.

Kent reinforced that when he gathered us together before we started up the ridge and yelled, "This is a no-fall zone! Stay focused and alert, and we'll make it to the top." Before I left for the expedition, my then-fiancée had given me a prayer from the Bible to take with me: "May the Lord watch between you and me, when we are absent, one from the other." That prayer served as my mantra all the way up, and I mentally recited it in time with my rest-stepping. It helped me block out the cold and the pain.

I remember passing a group of descending climbers, and they graciously stepped aside to let us pass. They were so supportive. "Way to go," they said. "You're almost there. Your buddies are already on top." When we did arrive, I was a little puzzled why our first rope team seemed to be hogging the confined space, and it was hard to get our summit pictures. I had an important message I wanted to communicate to my fiancée. I proposed to her via a hand-written sign from the summit. When I got home, I showed her the picture. We were married in April.

Descending from the summit was almost ethereal. The wind was increasing, and the snow was whipping off the cornice above the Football Field. I remember being intensely focused on the placement of my feet and watching the snow blow over the tops of my boots as I stepped.

When we finally arrived back in high camp, I knew I was dehydrated—I had long ago drunk my last bit of water—so I helped Kent get the stoves going to melt snow. And to fully celebrate the occasion, I broke out the bag of Fritos and teriyaki turkey jerky I had carried in my pack for 19 days. I shared them with my tent mates.

Getting to the top of Denali was an important accomplishment for me, but then I've always tried to set and achieve goals that stretch me and allow me to grow. The expedition really validated for me the notion that, while age is a factor—remember, at 61 I was the old man of the team—it doesn't have to be a show-stopper. Age is no excuse to stop reaching and stretching and growing and doing. Beyond that, the climb affirmed and reinforced some important lessons I'd learned earlier on in life: the value of a positive attitude, the importance of teamwork, the role of patience, and most important the beauty and power of God's grandeur.

NAME: Matt McDonough
OCCUPATION: Commercial Real-estate Broker
FAMILY STATUS: Married, three children
BORN: May 6, 1960
HOMETOWN: Mendham, New Jersey
PREVIOUS SUMMITS: Rainier, Baker, Hood, Adams

MY GOALS ON DENALI weren't so much about the summit as gaining climbing experience in a major mountain range. But as we waited out the weather at 14,200 feet, I began to realize it would be disappointing if we had to turn back before we experienced the open ridge of the West Buttress and reached high camp. As the days dragged on, I did begin to doubt our chances of getting any higher than 14,200 feet. On Denali, weather is always the deciding factor, provided you're in good shape.

The night before our summit attempt, I was apprehensive about getting all the specialized gear together and organized. There wasn't anything we could do about the wind, so I didn't worry about that too much. Besides, I had achieved my goal of ascending the ridge up to 17,200 feet and would have been satisfied if we had stopped there. Anything higher was a bonus.

I was a bit confused when Kent was "pulled" off our team. I didn't understand why Brent's team wasn't joining our team, which is how I understood the original plan. I thought we were going to go up together. If we failed to make the summit because of weather or lack of strength, that was one thing. But if Kent had been too tired to go up the next day and thwarted our hopes, I would have been angry. Beyond that, I think Brent's move compromised our cohesion as a team. But Kent *was* strong enough. In certain climbing circles he is now known as Kent "Do-It-Again" Wagner.

Just before we started to move on summit day, my concerns were mostly practical: Will I be able to keep my feet warm? Will I have enough food with me? What gloves should I bring? I quickly realized that these concerns were really just manifestations of overall anxiety. Eventually, I got these issues under control; all I really had to worry about was getting enough air, and I pressure-breathed every step of the way.

When we got under way, the wind had subsided significantly, so I anticipated that we would keep going. In my experience, it's rare that you go up for a "look-see" and don't keep going. When we arrived at Denali Pass, the wind hit us in the face. When we moved out of the shadows and encountered exposed rock and wind-scoured snow, I got a feeling of real altitude.

It's interesting: When you're at home you think about the mountains, and when you're in the mountains you think about home. As I approached the summit pyramid, I experienced nostalgia and a longing for home, but I also felt a surge of joy and well-being.

I don't remember too much conversation on the way up. But I remember Kent collecting our rope team at the base of the summit ridge and explaining that we were entering a "no-fall zone," which meant, of course, that we were not allowed to fall. The summit ridge was spectacular. I remember seeing the rope teams stretched out along the knife edge, with the snow blowing over the back of the cornice, and thinking, "Now, this is really something."

By this point, the summit was a foregone conclusion, and I savored the experience of walking along the ridge, with its extreme exposure, and reaching the proper little summit cone. It didn't look like much—a clump of snow the size of your desk—but as each of us walked across it, there was Gary waiting just to the side, to congratulate us as we arrived.

The thing I remember the most is pulling into high camp after returning from the summit. It was near midnight, and the sun dipping below the ridge to the west cast long shadows, silhouetting the other climbers against the orange sky. The temperature was starting to plunge, yet I was soaked in sweat—and completely spent and satisfied.

As time has passed, I've gained more of an appreciation for our time on the mountain. The cliché that you tend to minimize the negatives and accentuate the positives holds true in this case. I've tended to forget some of the struggle and remember all the great times we had.

The mountain has had some lasting effects on me. When I first got home, it was easier to be more patient and courteous. It's all too easy to revert back to the hectic ways of the workaday world, but I remind myself often to take things more slowly.

NAME: Nat Brace

OCCUPATION: Former Group Manager, Microsoft

FAMILY STATUS: Married, one son

BORN: July 7, 1960

HOMETOWN: Seattle, Washington

PREVIOUS SUMMITS: Kilimanjaro, St. Helens, Rainier, Adams

AFTER FOUR DAYS AT 14,200 FEET, I felt very anxious—almost a sense of mild panic—that we wouldn't go any higher. The clues were all there: We could see high winds raging above, Robert Link's team had already descended beaten from a week at high camp in horrific conditions, and it looked like the storm developing over eastern Siberia was tracking over the Bering Strait and coming right at us. Later that day, I remember reasoning it through: We were all strong, we had adequate food supplies to last a while, we were relatively comfortable (unlike Link's poor team), and we were all in great spirits. I couldn't control the weather, so I stopped agonizing over it. After that, I enjoyed my time there and realized that the longer we stayed, the better acclimatized we'd be if we advanced.

Clay's departure was one of the most disappointing moments of the trip. Everyone had seemed so strong up until that point. That's the tricky thing about altitude—you can't really train for it, you never know when or how it's going to hit you.

I also found it helpful to continually refine my "system" for managing my gear, food, and water. I had different-colored bags for each category of clothing (insulation: hands/feet, head; technical stuff: goggles, ascender, extra prusik slings). I kept them in roughly the same place in my pack, so if the weather got bad, I could quickly find my fleece hat and stow my sun cap. And drinking water day and night was something else I think that really helped out—even though I knew the half-liter I drank at 11 p.m. would be waking me up at 3 a.m. for disposal.

I remember lying in our tent in high camp and hearing the wind come up. I felt a creeping sense of disappointment, but I quickly thought, "Hell, we just spent nine days at 14,200, we dodged what was supposed to be the biggest storm to hit the mountain since 1992, and we're all strong. We can't do a damn thing about the weather and brooding over it isn't going to change anything." With that, I put it out of my mind and had a great night's sleep.

I was annoyed at the apparent politics at play behind the scenes that resulted in Kent going up with Brent's team, but again, it wasn't something I could do anything about, so I just tried to put it out of my mind. In a selfish way, I thought that Kent's attempting back-to-back summits might jeopardize our chances. Brent's move was especially galling, given that Gary and Kent had been so effective in getting all but one of our team to high camp.

I had two key concerns about the summit: Would the weather give us a break? Would anyone—myself included—get sick? After our second break above Denali Pass, I was confident we'd make it. When we got to the Football Field, we could see pretty strong cross winds and a plume blowing off the summit ridge, and I thought we might get turned around.

On the way up, I remember chatting with Ken who was right in front of me on the rope team. At one of the hairier spots on the summit ridge, I remember joking, "Hey, if you fall left, I'm going to jump right."

When I was about 20 yards from the top—I could see the colorful wands and some of our guys already up there—I felt this intense feeling of accomplishment and was almost giddy. I was so proud of our group. We had been through the ups and downs of the weather, Clay's sickness, losing Joe, and the distraction of Brent's dysfunctional climb, but we were going to make it. It was great to be standing on the top of North America, but to be there with such a great group of people made it even more meaningful.

I kept my expectations low about making the summit so I wouldn't be too disappointed if we didn't make it. I have been weathered off mountains in the past and have adopted this strategy so that I don't get too emotionally committed to making the top and make a stupid and dangerous decision. That said, several times, I did reflect on how I would explain that we hadn't made the top, given that, in our culture, the implicit definition of mountaineering success lies in gaining the summit.

When I set out on the expedition, I was curious to see if I could enjoy an extended period on snow and in bitter cold. As it turned out, I enjoyed it immensely. The 24 hours of daylight felt a lot less claustrophobic than typical winter camping where you have to deal with 14 to 16 hours of darkness and have only a narrow window of sunshine to move.

The most valuable lessons I learned on the mountain had to do with patience. Surrounded as we were with such awesome beauty, I found myself impatient to get around the next corner or make it to the next camp. But Gary's methodical, restful pace was the very key to making it up the mountain. Besides, it gave us time to savor our surroundings and journey through them, as opposed to charging blindly toward the top. I now believe you really have to take the mountain at its pace rather than yours.

Modern life seems so fraught with issues that seem important in the moment but from the perspective of Denali are pretty trifling—rushing here and there, technology that won't work, burning your toast in the morning. Living on Denali is pretty elemental; you don't have much of an opportunity to become preoccupied with the superficial. Yet nothing matches the savage beauty, the sense of camaraderie, the amount of learning that you experience within yourself and with others.

NAME: Ken Coffee

OCCUPATION: Engineer, Company Owner

FAMILY STATUS: Divorced, one daughter

BORN: September 5, 1961

HOMETOWN: Tulsa, Oklahoma

OTHER SUMMITS: Rainier (four times), Cotapaxi and Cayambe (Ecuador)

OUR TIME AT 14,200 FEET, watching those damned weather boards predict the Siberian storm's arrival, was difficult. Every time we walked down to the ranger's tent to check the weather board we were hoping for a change. I only remember going down there to read the board in a group. It was as if I couldn't face that bad news alone. As the storm days piled up, I doubted we'd make it.

It was difficult watching other climbers go up, but it was even harder watching them come back down, beaten. Intellectually, I knew we were acclimatizing, but that's the thing about that mountain: It really creates an enormous divide between your intellectual and your emotional self. When things are easy back in civilization, the distinction isn't there. On Denali, there were two very distinct, very different Kens. There was the Ken who dealt with the mountain on an intellectual or rational level, and the Ken who was constantly processing the emotional difficulties we faced. It is something I have never felt before, and haven't felt since.

Initially, on the way up the mountain, I asked every climber headed down whether he or she had made it to the top. Most hadn't because of the brutal weather conditions. They often hung their heads and said, "No."

I remember a group that was really bickering coming down. One climber from the group insisted that they had pushed up too fast and she had gotten sick. The group seemed to be playing the blame game.

Kent said something at 14,200 feet that really stuck with me. He said, "No question you could ask will sting as much as asking those on the way down, who never got to the top, if they reached the summit." I didn't want to face that question myself and have to say, "No." I never again asked that question. Instead, I would simply ask people how their climb was going.

Before you get to Denali, intellectually you know the mountain lets only half the climbers reach the top. You have a 50 percent chance, you tell yourself, yet you never imagine that you will be among the 50 percent that doesn't make it. But once you get on the mountain and start to contend with the difficult conditions, you understand the odds. Knowing that, the emotional part of me was damned worried. We had pushed so hard over so many days; I didn't want to come off the mountain without having tagged the summit. Part of it was that I didn't want to have to go through all that was necessary to get back on the mountain and try again: all the training you put in and organizing your life so you can be completely out of touch for a month.

I missed my daughter and my girlfriend terribly. Not being able to talk to them was hard. Some guys got hold of a cell phone at 17,200 feet on the way down and called home. I couldn't have done that. I knew if I talked to my girlfriend, Misty, or my daughter, Megan, I would turn into a blubbering baby. I just had to keep the emotional Ken in check.

Clay called me a few months after the climb, and I felt really close to him. It hurt to see him go down. I've never seen a Marine cry, but Clay had tears in his eyes that day. Man, that was tough: him hugging everybody as we were about to head up and he was heading down.

The fact is, Clay just had a bad day, and everyone has a bad day on Denali. The low point on the trip for me was when my crampon fell off just below the fixed lines. "Fuck this," I thought. At that moment, I just thought my being on the mountain was a big mistake—completely senseless. As mountaineers know, one crampon equals no crampons. And Dave was perched up there on the icy pitch. I knew I was hurting him, but I was helpless. I might have just fallen out of the womb at that point. I wanted to cry. I wanted to go home. Then that gigantic smile that was Nat came up to help. God, what a great human being!

Climbing Denali is all about taking care of yourself: Don't burn yourself out. Keep a good attitude. Drink tons of water. Eat as much as you can. Tend to your feet. I remember also trying to take care of my tent mates. But they did a better job of taking care of me. The little things meant so much: good food, a liter of Gatorade, crackers. Being pinned in the middle of the tent was tough from the perspective of claustrophobia, but that kept me real warm. I'm grateful for that.

The night before our summit attempt I was fitful; my mind was frustrated, and my body became my outlet. I remember looking at my watch constantly and listening to the wind blow. I checked the time at around 4:00 a.m; I had not slept up until that point. I slept less than two hours that night. I *knew* we weren't going up, and I was unbelievably pissed off. I wrote in my journal that mountain climbing is nothing but complete frustration. I was surprised the next morning when Gary told us to get ready to ascend.

When Brent pulled Kent off our team, I was a little angry but mostly jealous. I had initially wanted to be on Brent's climb. For weeks, I had begged Joe Horiskey to put me on that climb because of Brent's rock-solid reputation. In retrospect, I honestly don't know if I could have maintained Brent's pace. I felt that he had burned through his team just to get home early. When the climbers returned from the summit, I was consumed with envy—an emotion I rarely experience.

Once we started climbing, going up the pass took everything I had; I had to fight to keep from feeling dizzy. I felt like falling over with every step I took. I felt okay in terms of strength, but was having some serious vertigo. After the pass, the climb just seemed exhausting. I had to concentrate on every step just to keep my breathing up. Once we reached the Football Field, I knew I could make it, but when we got to the summit ridge, I thought, "Shit, this is really scary!"

On the way, I remember Bill Hatcher saying he was cold and that the breaks were too long—he wanted to keep moving. He had this flimsy little down jacket, and I kept kicking myself for not suggesting he grab Clay's before he went down. I have pictures of the summit day, and there is Hatcher—you can tell he is just trying to stay warm.

Gary turned out to be a great leader. When Gary suggested we regard the ascent to Denali Pass as a training climb, I thought he was just trying to burn some frustration out of us. I thought it was a good move as a leader, but I *knew* that this was what he was doing; there was *no* way we were going to the top. When we reached the pass, and he told us to put our goggles on, I was stunned. I thought he was going to let us push into the wind for about 30 minutes just to show us how tough it was. Then he'd turn us around. As a result, I didn't have my summit mojo going at all.

At that point, the meaning of the summit was still beyond my grasp. I think in some ways it still is, but over the past months, little moments reveal the meaning bit by small bit. I meet people now who find out casually that I was born in Alaska. If they have been to Alaska as a visitor, they most likely have been inside Denali National Park and Preserve. They will ask me if I have been to the park and if I was able to see the peak. I smile and tell them, yes, I was lucky enough to see the top. I rarely elaborate—it's my little secret.

Once we reached the summit I was with my team, and I was very happy. In the pictures I have of myself at the top, I look like a 70-year-old man. I looked like shit, but I was happy.

For now, Denali is an end point for me. No other summits cry my name. But I have to say that life, in general, is much easier for me now because Denali was so tough. My "difficult" meetings at work aren't nearly that difficult anymore

Before I arrived on the mountain, I surmised that just "being there" would have been enough. Bullshit to that notion after you step on Denali. Getting to the top is incredibly important once you are there. Being zen-like and philosophical is for the living room, not the mountain.

Over our three weeks on the mountain, I learned a lot about leadership. Gary Talcott was so gentle and calm and was really in tune with how everyone was feeling and what they were thinking. In the end, he wanted to get on top as much—if not more—than anyone. I like that about Gary. He was gentle, but driven. Books on leadership talk a lot about "styles" and which is best. Leadership is about guys like Gary making the call to wait out the big storms and then having the guts to push into the wind when it counts.

I went back to Rainier in September, and I was at a hotel in Ashford after the climb. Gary heard I was in town and came by just to see me. He truly cared about us. I also learned a lot from Kent. He was hard to get used to at first—brash, opinionated, and nonstop. When he did back-to-back summits, he achieved legendary status among the RMI guides.

I had the post-expedition blues for a couple of months after I got home. After being on Denali, it was hard to get excited about anything. I just went through the motions every day for quite some time.

I think stepping off the airplane in Talkeetna after it was over was about the best. I remember struggling up Heartbreak Hill thinking that I was going to be noble and give up my seat on the plane so someone else could get off the glacier. But when Gary pointed to me and said I had the first plane out, I wasn't about to sacrifice that seat for anything.

NAME: Bill Hatcher

OCCUPATION: Photographer

FAMILY STATUS: Married

BORN: December 17, 1959

HOMETOWN: Dolores, Colorado

PREVIOUS CLIMBS: Alps, Paine Ranges (Chile), Fitzroy region (Argentina), Cilo Sat Mountains (Turkey), El Capitan, White Throne (Mexico), Trango Towers (Pakistan), Fatima Spires (Africa)

TO ME, THE DAYS SPENT AT 14,200 FEET went by quickly. Having been to 20,000 feet on the Nameless Tower in Pakistan, I knew that being tentbound in the basin on Denali was allowing us to gather our strength. I was relaxed, and every day I was prepared to go higher. If we had to turn around at 14,200 feet, at least I would have had all my fingers. I understand how savage Denali storms can be, and I trusted Gary Talcott's decisions completely.

Clay's illness and departure were so sudden. I knew that at altitude small things like dehydration, lack of sleep, or not being able to eat can affect your performance. Clay's illness got my attention and inclined me to check more closely on my tent buddies—Matt and Dick—to make sure they were eating and drinking enough. They did the same for me. Clay's departure also played on my biggest fear—that I would get sick and not be able to continue. I was on the mountain to photograph the climb, and I was worried I wouldn't be able to do my job.

Our group was a perfect example of how positive attitude is imperative to a group's performance. We suffered as a group, and we celebrated as a group. On the way up the mountain, I went from doubting the ability of my rope mates to trusting them fully. On the descent from high camp, I watched Matt, on the rope in front of me, execute a perfect ice-ax arrest when Dick lost his footing and fell. Matt took him tight on the rope and held Dick until he could get his footing.

When I was lying in my tent the morning of summit day and heard the wind blowing, I figured we would still go up for a look-see, at least up to Denali Pass. So I was ready for action, even if we ascended only 1,000 feet. I think everyone in our group felt that Brent was compromising our chances for the summit when he pulled Kent onto his summit climb. I suspected that Kent would have a hard time doing back-to-back summit days, but Kent is clearly much stronger than any of us realized.

On the summit day, I felt okay but I had a headache. The climb up to Denali Pass was easy, but for me the climb from Denali Pass to the Football Field was very difficult. I felt ragged and weak. When we reached the Football Field, the wind was blowing steadily, so we pulled the hated balaclavas over our faces. I was eating dried salmon during the climb, so in the balaclava I was breathing recycled air that smelled like fish. Then there was all the equipment: harness, camera, down jacket. I felt encumbered like a scuba diver, outfitted with tanks and regulator, trying to walk on dry land.

We met many climbers above the Football Field and on the summit ridge coming down. It was the largest crowd I've seen on any big mountain. The climbers were all cordial and cheered all of us on to the summit. One climber said to me: "From the summit the views are 360 degrees and dizzying." Every climber I met on the summit ridge urged me to "be safe."

My camera batteries had died from the cold by the time I reached the summit, and I tried to warm them as the others arrived. Eventually they started working again, and I was able to take pictures of smiling, excited climbers. I especially enjoyed the special signs the climbers had brought to the summit. Dick proposed to his fiancée, Nat greeted his wife and son, and Dave hailed his friends, family, and workmates back home.

When I look back on the climb, the summit was definitely the prize, but my fondest memories were not on the summit but during the time we spent getting there. I remember the moments in the cook tent, talking and drinking tea. I remember catching the deep blue light in the crevasses as we walked over them, watching the midnight alpenglow on Mount Foraker from our camp below Motorcycle Hill, the wind blowing the snow across the Football Field during our 8:30 p.m. descent, watching a startled Dave struggle out of a crevasse, and touching granite rock on the West Buttress after so many days of crunching nothing but ice and snow.

Weather is a valid reason for not getting to the summit, especially on such a cold mountain as Denali, but there are a dozen other reasons some don't reach the summit. I trained harder for Denali than for any mountain I have been on, I tested all of my gear on my local 14,000-foot peaks in Colorado before taking them up Denali, and I quizzed everyone about what I should expect. I just wanted to be prepared and reduce the possibility of poor health or broken gear hindering my efforts on the expedition.

There are many lessons I learned from my time on the mountain. Some were technical and derived from the extensive time we spent walking among crevasses and dealing with constant cold. But the most important lesson I learned is that a group of strangers can set aside their differences, tame their egos, and focus on reaching the summit of one of the most difficult mountains in North America as a team.

As we were about to fly onto the glacier, our pilot said we were going up to the mountain as friends, but that we'd hate each other by the time we came back down. He couldn't have been more wrong.

REFLECTIONS OF A
RETIRED MOUNTAINEER

GARY LETS US SLEEP IN on Summit Day +1, and we don't begin stirring until nearly noon. Kent, evidently up for hours, greets us with a grin and a pot of boiling water. The Johnston family's camp is empty; they're on the way up, along with several dozen other climbers who are making their way toward Denali Pass. As it turns out, Dave and his family will indeed make it to the top, enabling 11-year-old Galen to return to elementary school in the fall with a remarkable report on how he spent his summer vacation.

My focus on the summit, once so intense that it masked my feelings of fear and apprehension, has been supplanted by a growing edginess to flee this brutal mountain. We've accomplished our primary mission, but a difficult 10,000-foot descent lies between us and our return to a world of comfort and east. Base camp seems so very far away; even farther the beer taps and pay phones of Talkeetna, and farther still the lush green hills of east Tennessee.

Up to this point, though I've often thought about home, I haven't allowed myself to succumb fully to the pangs of longing that would have heightened my suffering. But I yield to them now, as do my climbing buddies. We give voice to vivid fantasies—most of them involving food items conspicuously absent on the mountain—that have tormented us for the past three weeks. The mental image of a hamburger and a basket of greasy fries triggers a cascade of drool.

Before breaking camp, I consider asking to borrow Nat's cell phone to call the girls and let them know I'm okay and heading home. It's something I swore I wouldn't do. Mooching things—whether gear items or telecommunications devices—runs counter to the precept of self-reliance that I've tried to honor since the trip began.

Nat's been coddling the phone—sleeping with it at night and sheltering it from the cold inside his parka during the day. By rationing the phone's use and calling his wife, Karen, and son, Clark, only once or twice, Nat has managed to extend the unit's battery life through conditions that clearly defy the "suggestions for optimum performance" in the user guide. Even the motor drive on Bill's high-end camera, pushed well beyond its tolerances, has fallen victim to the cold; it has begun emitting mournful groans and chirps.

Nat has made his final call home, and now the phone lies idle on his sleeping bag.

"Nat, any chance I could borrow that for a second?"

"Sure. Go for it."

I walk to the edge of camp and peer down at the Kahiltna Glacier and our exit ramp from the mountain. It's midafternoon in Tennessee, and I hope to catch the girls at home. Instead I get the answering machine, and irony washes over me: I'm standing in snow at 17,200 feet in one of the more hostile and remote parcels of wilderness in the United States, holding one high-tech device against my ear and listening to another tell me there's no one home to take my call.

Between gasps for breath, I wait for the beep, and as I do my heart brims. There's so much I want to share with my daughters about my pilgrimage up this mountain—the things I've seen, the hard-won lessons I've learned, the depth of the struggle, the joy of standing on the summit, the way thoughts of them have buoyed me through the bleakest hours—but I realize that no answering machine tape could ever accommodate all that I have to say. Instead, I tell the girls simply that I've reached the summit, that I will be home in a few days, and that I love them.

My ex-wife, Susan, tells me later on that she called the girls to the phone one at a time and played the message for them. On hearing my voice, both of them let loose nearly a month's worth of pent-up worry about Dad and cried. When I return home, they show their artwork depicting various stages of the climb. The drawings portray a larger-than-life man standing on the apex of a diminutive conical knob, and they still grace the refrigerator door in my cabin. To my daughters, still young enough to cling to the childhood illusion that their parents are capable of accomplishing anything, the summit of Denali was a foregone conclusion.

ON THE DESCENT FROM HIGH CAMP, I negotiate the exposed ridge of the West Buttress with quaking knees, profoundly aware of the perils that three days before seemed of so little consequence in relation to the summit. Even as my body poises on the narrow ledges above the Peters Glacier, my head has already checked into the Roadhouse in Talkeetna. It's a distraction that could prove deadly.

Three hours later, with most of the objective risk—particularly the West Buttress and the fixed lines—behind us, we stop for the night at 14,200 feet, and I discern in the ascending climbers the same fretful preoccupation with storms and food and fuel stores that gripped us during the nine stormbound days we spent here. They probe us with questions, but I suspect that our answers will be of little use to them. Each day, Denali—with its constantly shifting winds and weather—becomes a new mountain. That means these climbers will scale a peak distinctly different from the one we summited yesterday.

The next morning, we arise at 5 a.m., break camp in -10°F temperatures, and depart an hour before the sun emerges from behind the eastern peaks. Along the way, we stop to chat with a few ascending climbers who have heard over their radios about Kent's back-to-back summit days—

a feat that has already earned him the nickname "Do-It-Again" Wagner.

Later in the afternoon, having picked up all the gear we cached on the way up, we approach the landing strip at 7,200 feet, where we are greeted by the drone of arriving and departing planes. The lower altitude has us sweating and "chewing on air," as Bill Hatcher puts it.

The warmer temperatures and blazing sun have transfigured the lower Kahiltna Glacier. What was a wide, uniform river of snow three weeks earlier has now cleaved and fractured, forcing us to execute end runs around the margins of opening crevasses.

We sink up to our shins in soupy slush and stop to put on our snow shoes. Soaked in sweat, my socks bind and roll beneath the soles of my feet, and I can feel blisters rising. Had this happened higher on the mountain, a commitment to self-maintenance would have forced me to stop and tend my wounds. Now, however, the shifting weather is a bigger concern than my stinging feet.

A wall of dense clouds has blocked the sun and bisected the sky— one side deep blue, the other side wispy gray. The approaching storm may delay our evacuation from the mountain, Gary tells us, yet he continues to stop hourly for rest breaks. Though I've managed to keep Mr. Hyde in check for the past 21 days, Dr. Jekyll senses that he's about to put in his first appearance.

If clouds continue to encroach, reduced visibility will ground the pilots; One-Shot Pass is dicey enough in perfect conditions. But Gary seems largely unfazed. He reclines on his pack, his snowshoes crossed in front of him, as if he were lounging at the beach. Eventually he removes his two-way radio and calls Hudson Air to let them know we're approaching the runway.

Gary's nonchalance riles me at the time, but it hits me later—once the amenities of civilization have moderated my mood—that an expedition is a way of life for him and the other guides who return again and again to high mountains such as Denali. They thrive here, on the ice, and return with reluctance to a world that lacks the simple focus, the constant challenge, and the deep fulfillment they find amid the jarring cold and steeply pitched slopes. The final few hours of a climb are always difficult for him, Kent confides. When these long expeditions come to an end, he often feels like crying.

If Gary appears to be in no hurry to depart, it may have something to do with his determination to enjoy the last few hours on the glacier, basking in the success of guiding a team of unlikely mountaineers to the top of North America.

Brad and I, true to our type-A tendencies, protest the delay by standing throughout the break, hoping our shouldered packs convey to Gary our eagerness to get a move on. Dick, by contrast, has stripped off his shirt and is taking a snow bath, humming a carefree tune. Sedated by fatigue and grateful for the chance to rest their weary legs, the others stare blankly ahead.

After 15 minutes, Gary rises slowly to his feet. Soon we're cranking down the mountain, racing the clouds. I'm racked by exhaustion yet driven to keep moving, and when I feel the rope bind behind me, I can't be sure if it's my sled bogging down in the soft snow or Ken dragging on the line; I throw my shoulder into my pack harness and yank the sled as hard as I can, heedless that I might be pulling Ken off his feet. My domineering tendencies, no longer latent, have blossomed in full: I spend the last few hours of the expedition crazed by a longing for home.

It's a lapse I will long regret; instead, I could—*should*—have been savoring my last glimpse of the magnificent Alaska Range.

As always, Gary knows exactly what he's doing. We top Heartbreak Hill, and the tent city marking base camp heaves into view. A single plane is parked on the glacier, with "Hudson Air" painted on the side. Randy, our pilot, is sprawled in a lounger, waiting for us.

"You guys ready to go home?" he asks.

Nat, Ken, and I pile into the first plane, and within five minutes of clipping off the rope, removing our snowshoes, and knocking ice off our boots and packs, we're wedged into the Cessna and bouncing down the runway. Forty-five minutes later, we're standing on the sun-baked landing strip in Talkeetna as a woman wearing shorts approaches us with a fistful of cold beers. Absent any substantial transition from glacier to pavement, the scene is so surreal that I have to resist the urge to run from her.

CLIMBING MOUNTAINS may be a time-consuming undertaking, but descending them is remarkably rapid—too rapid, some might argue, in that it deprives you of adequate time to process your return to a world that has changed not one iota in the time you've been gone. All too suddenly you're back in some bar, slugging down cold ones, and struggling to find the words to describe the places you have been and the sights you have witnessed.

In the eight hours after our return to civilization, I inaugurate a feeding frenzy that will last several weeks, until I've restored the 17 pounds I lost on Denali and packed on an additional 10. Before leaving the hangar in Talkeetna, for example, I consume an entire bag of beef jerky and the several ounces of 12-year-old scotch (now aged an additional month) remaining in the flask my friend J. J. Rochelle gave me before I left. Its inscription—"David Brill, Mt. McKinley, 2001"—no longer seems quite so presumptuous.

Reeking and still clad in the clothes we've worn for 22 days, we enter a restaurant for dinner and commandeer a table in the center of the main dining room. The restaurant's other patrons—mostly well-scrubbed tourists—look upon us with expressions of rancor, even fear.

We are sailors newly arrived in port after months at sea, swaggering into the quayside grog shop intent on debauchery. We are mud-covered cowboys bursting through a saloon's swinging doors at the end of a long cattle drive, determined to wash the trail dust from our parched gullets with endless snorts of rotgut. Deprived for way too long of outlets for our hedonism, we arrive possessed of a single-minded commitment to a pair of clearly defined goals: Our burning thirst must be slaked, our gnawing appetites must be fed.

Maintaining that the table we've selected won't hold us all, the waitress ushers us to a room in the back of the restaurant. The move is clearly designed to avoid chasing off the rest of her customers.

As we rise to follow her, a white-haired woman turns to her husband and mutters, "Thank God they're leaving!"

I consume two T-bone steak dinners and more beers than I can count before we move on to the Fairview, where the bacchanal continues to gather steam. At 2 a.m., I bid Do-It-Again Wagner—predictably, the last man standing—a garbled goodnight. Then I stumble out into the hazy twilight and down the dirt road toward my room at the Roadhouse, weaving my way among mangy dogs that dart from my path.

Once I settle into bed, even in my altered state, I notice how stiflingly hot—how eerily quiet—the hotel room seems. I long for the bluster of mountain winds buffeting nylon tent walls.

MY FITFUL EFFORTS TO SLEEP mark the first of many adjustments I'll be forced to make over the coming weeks as I weather the reentry process. In the context of a lifetime, my days on Denali represent an inconsequential span of time. Yet the immersion they made possible in a world so foreign and hostile—so fraught with peril and risk, so richly imbued with power and beauty—has transformed me. The long periods of confinement in a crowded tent, the howling winds and blowing snow, the subzero temperatures, the constant struggle to breathe, the toil of making and breaking camp, the obsessive worry that weather would deprive us of our summit shot—all these have imparted a fresh perspective that pervades nearly every facet of my life.

Some of the changes are physical. I will bear the mountain's imprint on my dissipated body for several weeks. In Talkeetna, after a long, hot shower, I study my form in the mirror but find only the victim of some dreaded degenerative disease. My paunch has disappeared, but so has much of my muscle tone. The tips of my fingers and toes remain numb for nearly a month—the aftereffect of nerve endings damaged by the cold. My outsize clothes apparently belong to someone else.

The old friend who picks me up at the Knoxville airport will greet me with a candid assessment: "You look like shit."

Other changes, if more subtle, are also more enduring. Denali exposed me to physical and emotional challenges more extreme than any I'd faced before. It forced me to tap reserves of strength and endurance I never realized I possessed. Compared with kicking steps to the top of Denali, even the most pitched battles at sea level seem remarkably uncomplicated.

Two days after our return to Talkeetna, I say farewell to eight men I've come to love and deeply respect. No matter how much time and space separate us, the bond we share will endure. We've been talking about our next adventure—a climbing trip to South America, Europe, or the Himalaya—but I sense it will never happen. Despite our promise to stay in touch, I realize that opportunities like this one to fully disengage from jobs and families are both rare and fleeting. Within days of our return home, we will be entangled once more in the extraordinary demands of our ordinary lives.

I'M ON A PLANE BOUND FOR TENNESSEE. As soon as we're airborne, the pilot directs our attention to the snow-cloaked hulk of Denali, looming off to our left. While late-middle-aged tourists in Rockports mutter and point, I settle back in my seat and close my eyes. The view out the window, I realize, can't begin to compare with the image of that remarkable mountain fixed forever in my memory.

In the realm of high-elevation mountaineering, an ascent of Denali along the relatively gentle West Buttress Route is an unremarkable feat. Indeed, thousands of climbers have reached the summit, including elderly men and preteen children.

But Denali was my Everest. It pushed me farther and led me higher than I ever imagined I could go. The expedition marked a departure from the "quiet desperation" Thoreau wrote about. On Denali, I forced my shoulder into the margins that had once circumscribed my life, knocked them wide open, and reminded myself that, when the petty concerns at sea level begin to grind me down, there are spectacular arenas in this world where the real drama of life and death gets played out every day. And that I've been there, and that I survived.

In the weeks after the climb, I often thought back to the interview I'd done years earlier with Dick Bass, who at age 55 became the first man to climb the highest peak—Denali included—on all seven continents. Though Bass, like me, had endured divorce in the years leading up to his Everest climb, the perspective from 29,035 feet had realigned his thinking. Upon his return, he said, problems that had beset him back home suddenly dwindled to molehills.

"That mountain gave me peace," he told me. "Not a superficial sense of well-being, but the peace that comes from going through the fiery furnace, by God, hanging in there, and coming out alive."

I know just what he meant.

I now regard myself as a retired mountaineer with only one notable peak to my credit, but my Denali experience grows in significance even as it recedes in time. I joyfully returned to Dee and to my daughters, who seem to have forgiven their father's month-long disappearance to risk his life on something they can't yet grasp.

Challen and Logan often ask me about the expedition. All I can tell them is that Denali was a brutish mountain but more grand and beautiful a place than any I've ever seen. I also promise them I'll never go back. Some day, when they're old enough to understand, I'll explain to them that I traveled to Alaska on an ill-defined quest, and that somewhere on that ice-locked summit I found just what I was looking for.

Bibliography

The following books are particularly strong on Denali, climbing technique, mountaineering in Alaska, and mountain medicine.

Bass, Dick, and Frank Wells with Rick Ridgeway, *Seven Summits*. New York: Warner Books, 1986. This account of the Bass-Wells effort to become the first men to reach the highest peak on each continent contains an excellent chapter on the climbers' experiences on Denali.

Coombs, Colby, *Denali's West Buttress: A Climber's Guide to Mount McKinley's Classic Route*. Seattle: The Mountaineers, 1997. The definitive guide to the West Buttress Route on Denali, followed by more than 80 percent of climbers on the mountain. Contains Brad Washburn's aerial photos illustrating the route and its major features. Also includes a history of Denali National Park and Preserve, a history of mountain guiding and rescues, information for women climbers, sections on frostbite and altitude-related illness, and tips on accident prevention and emergency evacuation.

Davidson, Art, *Minus 148 : First Winter Ascent of Mt. McKinley*. Seattle: The Mountaineers, 1999. An engaging narrative of the first winter ascent of Denali, in 1967. Describes the death of a team member in a crevasse fall and a seven-day emergency bivouac at 18,000 feet, during which the windchill drove the temperature to 148 degrees below zero—reputedly the coldest conditions every endured by humans on a mountain.

Dunn, Robert, *The Shameless Diary of an Explorer: A Story of Failure on Mt. McKinley*. New York: Modern Library, 2001. First published in 1907, Dunn's book presents a frank, often funny account of the ill-fated 1903 expedition led by Frederick Cook, whose claim of being the first to summit Denali was later discredited. Good descriptions of the tools and techniques available to early climbers, as well as the grueling overland trek to the base of the mountain and the interpersonal friction it sparked.

Elliot, Nan, and Tom Walker, *Alaska*. National Geographic Society, 2001 (National Geographic Guides to America's Outdoors). If you don't have time to climb Denali, this richly illustrated guide directs you to myriad other nature sites throughout the state. Contains suggestions for where to hike, camp, kayak, fish, and spot bears and bald eagles.

Graydon, Don, and Kurt Hanson, eds. *Mountaineering: The Freedom of the Hills*, 6th edition. Seattle: The Mountaineers, 1997. A comprehensive primer on climbing technique and gear, high-altitude medicine, health and safety concerns, expedition climbing, and the mountain environment.

Hackett, Peter H., *Mountain Sickness: Prevention, Recognition, and Treatment*, 2nd edition. American Alpine Club, 1980. Hackett studied altitude-related illness in the Himalaya as well as on Denali. His research led to several major breakthroughs in understanding and treating the ailment.

Heath, Donald, and David Reid Williams, *High-Altitude Medicine and Pathology*, 4th edition. Oxford: Oxford University Press, 1995. A somewhat technical but comprehensive guide to altitude-related illness and methods for avoiding and treating it.

McPhee, John A. *Coming into the Country.* (New York: Farrar, Straus and Giroux, 1985). After touring Alaska and hanging out with prospectors, bush pilots, and settlers, McPhee captures the complexity of the state and its people. Required reading for those heading up north.

Joe McGinniss, *Going to Extremes* (New York: Plume, 1989). McGinnis portrays the essential Alaska, with all its quirks and eccentricities, its sprawling natural beauty, its penchant for excess and waste.

Moore, Terris, *Mt. McKinley: The Pioneer Climbs.* Seattle: The Mountaineers (for the University of Alaska), 1981. A fine history of Denali's early climbing days, with original photos and excerpts from expedition accounts.

National Park Service, *Mountaineering: Denali National Park and Preserve.* A valuable resource on Denali rules and regulations as well as tips for expedition planning, safe climbing, and emergency response. Available from Talkeetna Ranger Station (P.O. Box 588/Talkeetna, AK 99676/907-733-2231) or nps.gov/dena/home/mountaineering/booklet/mtbook.html.

Secor, R. J., *Denali Climbing Guide.* Mechanicsburg, PA: Stackpole Books, 1998. A lavishly illustrated guide to climbing routes on Denali, with detailed information on preparation, amenities in Talkeetna, weather, climbing and wilderness ethics, equipment, guide services, and air taxis.

Sherwonit, Bill, ed., *Denali: A Literary Anthology.* The Mountaineers, 2000. Presents first-person narratives, reflective essays, and Native Alaskan lore and legends inspired by Denali. Espcially interesting are the book's excerpts from the journals and published articles of Denali's early explorers.

Sherwonit, Bill, *To the Top of Denali: Climbing on North America's Highest Peak.* Alaska Northwest Books, 1990. Chronicles climbing milestones in Denali history, including major disasters and first ascents. Also addresses environmental concerns, guided climbing, self-sufficiency, and rescues.

Ward, Michael P., James S. Milledge, and John B. West, *High-Altitude Medicine and Physiology*. Philadelphia: University of Pennsylvania Press, 1989. Like *High-Altitude Medicine and Pathology*, this book is highly technical, but it contains comprehensive information on altitude's effects on the body's systems and an interesting history of altitude-related illness and the medical experiments that have been conducted to better understand its mechanism.

Washburn, Bradford, and David Roberts, *Mount McKinley: The Conquest of Denali*. New York: Abradale Press, 2000. Washburn, who has climbed Denali three times, pioneered the West Buttress Route, which now bears his name and is followed by most of the climbers on the mountain. Over the years, Washburn has extensively mapped and photographed the mountain from the air. The book features many of Washburn's dramatic photographs and a detailed history of climbing and exploration on Denali.

Waterman, Jonathan, *In the Shadow of Denali: Life and Death on Alaska's Mt. McKinley*. New York: Lyons Press, 1998. Waterman is a skilled mountaineer and writer who has logged extensive experience on Denali. The book's collection of essays—part history, part personal narrative—captures the tragedy, triumph, and humor that are central to expedition life on Denali.

Wickwire, Jim, and Dorothy Bullitt, *Addicted to Danger: A Memoir about Affirming Life in the Face of Death*. New York: Pocket Books, 1998. Wickwire's passion for climbing has led him to the tops of Denali (via the mountain's most difficult routes), K-2, and other daunting peaks worldwide. His description of the death of his friend Chris Kerrebrock in a crevasse fall on Denali's Peters Glacier bears gripping testament to the high price some climbers pay for a lifetime of adventure.

Glossary of Mountaineering Terms

ACCLIMATIZATION: The process of adapting to thinner air as one climbs a mountain. Slow ascent is the key to adequate acclimatization. Above 10,000 feeta, a good rate of ascent is about 1,000 feet per day.

ACETAZOLAMIDE (DIAMOX): A diuretic used to prevent and treat acute mountain sickness. Acetazolamide turns the blood slightly alkaline, which stimulates respiration, the body's effort to restore chemical balance.

ACONCAGUA: A 22,834-foot-high mountain in Argentina; highest peak in the Western Hemisphere.

ACUTE MOUNTAIN SICKNESS (AMS): An often transitory but sometimes debilitating physical response to the thinner air found at altitude. Symptoms include headache, fatigue, nausea, water retention, shortness of breath, loss of coordination, insomnia, and loss of appetite.

ALASKA RANGE: A 600-mile arc of mountains dividing south-central Alaska from the interior plateau. The highest point in the Alaska Range is 20,320-foot Denali (Mount McKinley).

ALTIMETER: A device that determines altitude by measuring barometric pressure. High-tech watches often feature altimeters.

ANCHOR: A device set in snow to secure a climber, tent, or other object.

ANNAPURNA: A 26,334-foot peak in the Himalaya first climbed in 1950 by a team led by Maurice Herzog. This first ascent of a peak more than 8,000 meters high is chronicled in Herzog's book *Annapurna*.

ASCENDER: A mechanical safety device, attached to a climbing rope (and usually to the climber's seat harness), that slides freely as the climber ascends but grabs the rope when downward pressure is applied.

AVALANCHE: A large volume of snow and ice that slides swiftly down a mountain slope. Avalanches pose a considerable risk to climbers, particularly those ascending a steep slope after a heavy snowfall.

AVALANCHE BEACON: An electronic device that emits a signal, helping rescuers locate the position of a climber buried by an avalanche.

BALACLAVA: A wool or synthetic hood with holes for the eyes, nose, and mouth.that covers the climber's head and protects him from the cold.

BAROMETRIC PRESSURE: The pressure of the ambient atmosphere, which decreases as altitude increases. Approaching storm events can also trigger a drop in barometric pressure.

BASE CAMP: The point from which an expedition begins its climb.

BELAY: To secure a climbing rope by attaching it to a fixed object, such as a rock or metal picket driven into the snow, or by attaching the rope to an anchored climber.

BERGSCHRUND: A large crevasse located at the upper edge of a glacier. It typically forms when a moving glacier pulls away from the ice cap covering the upper mountain.

BIBS: Protective pants with a chest flap and shoulder straps. Most are made of waterproof, breathable fabric and feature a trapdoor seat.

BIVOUAC: A temporary, often emergency encampment that provides little or no shelter. Climbers caught in a storm may be forced to bivouac rather than continue in the face of dangerous conditions.

BLUE BAG: A small plastic bag provided by the National Park Service on Mount Rainier for collecting human waste.

CACHE: A supply of food, fuel, or extra gear that is buried in the snow by an expedition for retrieval later on.

CARABINER: An oval device, made from lightweight metal with a spring-loaded gate, used to secure gear or to attach a climber's harness to a climbing rope.

CHEYNE-STOKES BREATHING (PERIODIC BREATHING): Irregular breathing at high altitude that occurs mainly during sleep, when the body's respiration rate falls. Cheyne-Stokes breathing is marked by cyclic periods of decreased respiration, or apnea, which alternate with periods of rapid breathing, or hyperventilation.

CORNICE: A lip of snow or ice on the leeward side of a mountain that overhangs a slope and poses an icefall risk to climbers.

COULOIR: An angled gully that can provide a preferred route of ascent because it is generally less steep than the cliffs that bracket it.

CRAMPONS: Metal spikes that attach to the soles of climbing boots, allowing mountaineers to ascend steep, icy slopes. Most crampons feature 12 points, including two that protrude from the front and allow climbers to ascend by "front-pointing" up a near-vertical slope.

CREVASSE: A crack in the surface of a glacier created when the glacier breaks apart in its movement down a mountain. Crevasses may be many yards wide and hundreds of feet deep. Because they are often hidden beneath the snow, crevasses are difficult to detect—and avoid.

DEADMAN ANCHOR: A device such as a snowshoe, picket, or ice ax buried in the snow to provide an anchor for belaying a climber or securing a tent.

DEATH ZONE: The region above 17,000 feet where oxygen deprivation causes the body to gradually decline. Climbers can endure only limited time periods in the death zone before their physical systems begin to fail.

DEHYDRATION: Loss of fluids through respiration, perspiration, and urination. Adequate hydration is essential in the mountain environment and may help prevent some forms of acute mountain sickness.

DENALI NATIONAL PARK AND PRESERVE: A park established in 1917 as

Mount McKinley National Park that now encompasses 6 million acres, an area larger than Massachusetts.

DOUBLE BOOTS: Mountaineering boots that feature an outer shell, usually plastic, and an insulated inner boot; together they prevent the feet from frostbite.

DOUBLE FALL LINE: A slope that pitches downward in two directions (vertically and laterally), exposing a climber to an increased risk of falling.

FALL LINE: The direction a climber would fall if he lost his footing on a slope.

FIXED LINES: Ropes permanently anchored to the mountain, usually on extremely steep pitches. Climbers often attach themselves to the rope using mechanical ascenders, which slide freely as the climber ascends but grab the rope should she take a fall.

FRONT-POINTING: A technique for climbing steep ice slopes by digging the front points, or spikes, of a crampon into the near-vertical surface.

FROSTBITE: Freezing of a body part caused by extreme cold. Frostbite is common on Denali, where 10 percent of climbers experience the condition. Victims of frostbite that affects only the surface tissue generally make a full recovery; deep-tissue frostbite often results in amputation.

FROST NIP: Damage to surface tissue caused by direct exposure to cold; less severe than frostbite.

GAITERS: Fabric sleeves that cover the lower legs and extend past the boot collar to prevent snow, ice, rock, or dirt from entering the boot.

GAMOV BAG: A portable, footpump-activated pressure chamber used to treat victims of severe altitude sickness who are unable to descend to a lower altitude.

GLACIER: A large body of ice moving slowly down a mountain slope or through a valley formed between ridges.

GLACIER GLASSES: Dark sunglasses equipped with side-shields to protect the eyes from direct sunlight, as well as light reflected from the surface of the snow. Glacier glasses should filter out 95 to 100 percent of ultraviolet light.

GLISSADE: A controlled slide down a mountain using the spike of an ice ax to steer and control the rate of descent. Climbers can glissade in a standing, crouching, or seated position.

GORE-TEX: A waterproof, breathable fabric used in making mountaineering clothing that protects climbers from rain and wind while allowing perspiration to escape.

HACE (HIGH-ALTITUDE CEREBRAL EDEMA): A potentially lethal form of altitude sickness in which the cranium fills with fluid.

HAPE (HIGH-ALTITUDE PULMONARY EDEMA): A potentially lethal form of altitude sickness in which the lungs fill with fluid.

HARNESS: A device, usually made from nylon webbing, that secures around a climber's waist and/or upper body and is then attached to the climbing rope.

HEADWALL: A steep ramp of ice or snow, sometimes thousands of feet in height, that connections the lower section of a mountain to the ridge above.

HIGH CAMP: The encampment highest on the mountain from which climbers launch their assault on the summit.

HYPOTHERMIA: A potentially deadly decrease in the core body temperature caused by exposure to cold and/or wind. Inadequate insulation and damp clothing pressed against the skin, which results in evaporative cooling, can hasten the condition.

HYPOXIA: A deficiency of oxygen reaching the body's systems. The reduced amount of available oxygen at altitude can result in hypoxia.

ICE AX (ALSO KNOWN AS ICE TOOL): A multipurpose tool usually cast from lightweight metal that features a spike, adz, and pick. The spike is used to secure tents in the snow or to stabilize a climber during an ascent. The adz serves to chop steps or to create a sleeping surface on hard ice. The pick is driven into the snow to stop an uncontrolled slide.

KAHILTNA GLACIER: One of the dominant glaciers in the Alaska Range and the primary path for climbers following the West Buttress Route to the summit of Denali.

KERNMANTLE ROPE: Strong climbing rope that consists of braided nylon filaments encased in a nylon sheath.

LENTICULAR CLOUD: A UFO-shaped cloud that forms above a mountain peak; it indicates strong winds, ergo dangerous climbing conditions.

MIXED CLIMBING: A climbing surface that presents a combination of rock, ice, snow, or dirt.

NORTH PEAK OF DENALI: At 19,470 feet, the north peak is 850 feet below the South, or true, summit of the mountain at 20,320 feet.

NYLON WEBBING: Flat, woven nylon, usually one-inch thick, that is used to create climbing harnesses or to tether sleds to a climber's pack.

OVERBOOTS: Made from neoprene or synthetic batting sandwiched between nylon, overboots are worn over mountaineering boots to provide additional insulation from the cold.

OVERMITTS: Nylon shells that fit over fleece or wool mittens and provide protection from wind, cold, and rain.

PICKET: A three-foot-long aluminum spike that's driven into the snow to provide an anchor. The climbing rope is attached by a carabiner to a webbing loop attached to the top of the picket.

POLYPROPYLENE: A synthetic fabric, usually worn as a base layer, that wicks perspiration away from the skin and helps retain warmth and prevent hypothermia, particularly if worn under an insulating layer such as down or fleece and wind shell.

POST-HOLING: The experience of climbing in soft, deep snow where the boots sink below the snow surface. Post-holing can make climbing difficult and enervating. Snowshoes worn over the boots can help a climber "float" on the surface of the snow.

PRESSURE BREATHING: The process of forcing air through pursed lips to increase pressure in the lungs and offset the effects of thin air at altitude.

PRUSIK SLING: A 5- to 7-millimeter cord tied in a loop and attached to a climbing rope using friction (most often prusik) knots; these slide freely up the rope, but grip when weight is applied. Two prusik slings—one attaches to the seat harness, the second forming a loop for the boot—can be rigged to enable a climber to escape a crevasse. The climber first straightens his leg in the boot loop, then slides the (slack) prusik attached to his seat harness up the rope. He then allows the prusik attached to the seat harness to bear his weight, and slides the now-slack boot loop up. The process is repeated until the climber reaches the lip of the crevasse.

RAPPEL: To descend from a cliff by sliding down a rope that is attached to the seat harness with a device that controls the rate of descent.

RESCUE PULLEY: A small, lightweight pulley that accommodates the climbing rope and can be rigged with other pulleys to extricate a climber after a crevasse fall.

REST STEP: A technique for placing weight on the lower, fully extended leg while allowing the bent upper leg to rest between steps. This takes the weight off the muscles and places it on the skeletal system.

RIME ICE: An accumulation of granular ice feathers on the windward side of exposed objects that builds horizontally into the wind.

RUNNING BELAY: An anchoring technique used on exposed pitches that uses one or more pickets driven into the snow. The climbing rope runs through carabiners attached to the tops of the pickets, and as each climber advances, she must clip on and off the rope to pass around the anchor.

SEAT HARNESS: A device made of nylon webbing that loops around the waist and thighs and provides an attachment point for a climbing rope.

SELF-ARREST: A climbing technique for stopping an uncontrolled slide on a mountain slope. The surest way to self-arrest is to maneuver onto one's stomach, then dig ice-ax pick and crampons into the snow.

SERAC: A pinnacle, ridge, or upthrust block of ice among crevasses.

SHOVEL SHEAR TEST: A method for assessing avalanche risk by digging out a column of snow and inspecting it for poorly consolidated snow layers that are prone to breaking free and causing a slide.

SLAB AVALANCHE: An avalanche that is caused when an entire layer, or slab, of snow and ice breaks away from the surface of a slope and begins to slide. A poorly consolidated layer of ice sandwiched between more stable layers of snow can trigger a slide.

SNOW BLINDNESS: Damage to the cornea caused by exposure to direct sunlight and ultraviolet (uv) rays reflecting off the surface of the snow, resulting in temporary blindness. The condition is extremely painful and can immobilize a climber until the condition improves.

SNOW BRIDGE: A layer of snow that covers and conceals the top of a crevasse. Some snow bridges are stable enough to bear a climber's weight; others are so fragile they break beneath him, resulting in a crevasse fall.

SNOW CAVE: A space excavated in a snow slope that shelters climbers from high winds and extreme cold. Some caves are elaborate structures that feature tables, sleeping platforms, and chairs, all hewn from snow. Climbers bereft of shelter and who are forced to bivouac on a descent often dig snow caves as a last-ditch effort to survive extreme conditions.

SNOW SAW: A serrated 18-inch blade used for cutting snow blocks, which are then used to create protective walls around a tent or to craft an igloo.

SNOWSHOES: Oblong frames crisscrossed with leather or man-made filaments and worn beneath the boots. Snowshoes distribute a climber's weight and allow him to "float" on the surface of the snow.

SOLO CLIMBING: Climbing a mountain alone. Solo climbing is inherently risky. If a solo climber becomes injured or caught in a dangerous situation, there is often no one to come to her aid.

SOUTH PEAK OF DENALI: The true summit of Denali, at 20,320 feet.

SUBJECTIVE HAZARD: A danger created by a climber from poor judgment, lack of skill, inadequate preparation, or physical or psychological problems.

SUMMIT PARKA: A stout down or synthetic-fill jacket that insulates the body from the wind and cold on a mountain's summit.

TALKEETNA: A town two hours north of Anchorage with a permanent population of 772 that serves as the staging area for most Denali expeditions. Most climbers are flown by air taxi from the Talkeetna airport to base camp at 7,200 feet.

TEAM ARREST: The technique effected by the members of a rope team to stop an uncontrolled slide down a mountain. In most cases, falling climbers attempt to anchor themselves by maneuvering onto their stomachs and driving in the picks of their ice axes and the spikes of their crampons.

TREELINE: The altitude at which vegetation ends on a mountain.

TURN-AROUND TIME: A pre-determined time by which an ascending team must turn and begin to descend if it has not reached the summit.

WAND: A three-foot long bamboo shaft that is used to mark routes on a mountain or the locations of buried caches. In snow storms, the wands help climbers find their way back to camp.

WASHBURN ROUTE (ALSO KNOWN AS THE WEST BUTTRESS ROUTE): The route to the Denali summit pioneered by Bradford Washburn in 1951. Today, more than 80 percent of the climbers on Denali trace the Washburn route, also known as the West Buttress Route, which follows the Kahiltna Glacier from base camp at 7,200 feet. The route allows climbers to avoid the difficult overland trek by arriving on the glacier via airplane.

WEST BUTTRESS: A dramatic ridge that culminates at 17,200 feet approaches the summit ridge of Denali from the west. The West Buttress is one of the dominant features along the route now followed by more than 80 percent of Denali climbers. Called the West Buttress Route, it is also known as the Washburn Route, named for Bradford Washburn, who pioneered the relatively safe and easy route to the top in 1951.

WHITE-OUT: Falling or blowing snow that reduces visibility to a few feet.

WINDCHILL INDEX: A temperature calculation that measures both ambient temperature and the wind speed. For instance, an air temperature of zero degrees combined with a 50-mile-per-hour wind would result in a windchill index of -31°F.

Index

Acknowledgments

In climbing Denali and later writing about it, I enjoyed the support and assistance of many people. With that in mind, I'd like to acknowledge and thank:

My editor, Allan Fallow, who guided my efforts in writing this book and knew just when to nurture and when to nudge. Allan, your energy for this project has never wavered, and over the past year you and I have scaled Denali together just as surely as if we had shared the same rope.

Keith Bellows, editor of *National Geographic Traveler* magazine, for his vision and willingness to wager on a neophyte mountaineer and his quest to scale North America's highest peak. Thanks also for 17 years of mentoring, superb editing, and choice assignments.

My agent, Giles Anderson, for guiding my career and helping me finance a remarkable summer vacation.

Jack Barkenbus, my boss at the University of Tennessee, for cutting me loose for a time to pursue my dreams.

Gary Talcott, Kent Wagner, Joe Horiskey, and the other RMI guides who lead ordinary men and women to extraordinary places.

My climbing mates—Dick Bowers, Nat Brace, Ken Coffee, Bill Hatcher, Clay Howard, Matt McDonough, and Brad Skidmore—for watching my back and ignoring the tobacco stains in the snow around our camps.

Dick Bass, entrepreneur and mountaineer. Some years ago, I had the privilege of interviewing Dick for a story, and during our days together he proved that raw drive, enthusiasm, and faith can power men up huge mountains.

Daryl Miller of the National Park Service, who proved more than patient in answering a mountain of questions about Denali and its history—and who instilled in the climbers on my team an abiding respect for the mountain and its power.

My father, for his unwavering support of my creative endeavors.